Gear Secrets
of the Guitar Legends

How to Sound Like Your Favorite Players

by Pete Prown & Lisa Sharken

Backbeat

Published by Backbeat Books
600 Harrison Street, San Francisco, CA 94107
www.backbeatbooks.com
email: books@musicplayer.com

An imprint of the Music Player Network
Publishers of *Guitar Player, Bass Player, Keyboard*, and other magazines
United Entertainment Media, Inc.
A CMP Information company

CMP
United Business Media

Distributed to the book trade in the US and Canada by
Publishers Group West, 1700 Fourth Street, Berkeley, CA 94710

Distributed to the music trade in the US and Canada by
Hal Leonard Publishing, P.O. Box 13819, Milwaukee, WI 53213

Text Design and Composition by Michael Cutter
Cover Design by David Hamamoto
Front Cover Photo © by Neil Zlozower
Sound Recordings (CD) © Pete Prown 2003

Library of Congress Cataloging-in-Publication Data

Prown, Pete.
    Gear secrets of the guitar legends : how to sound like your favorite
players / by Pete Prown and Lisa Sharken
        p. cm.
    Includes discographies.
    ISBN 0-87930-751-X (alk. paper)
    1. Guitar—Instruction and study. 2. Rock music—Instruction and
study. 3. Guitar—Equipment and supplies. I. Sharken, Lisa. II. Title.

MT580.P84 2003
787.87'193'166—dc21

                            2003045115

Printed in the United States of America
03 04 05 06 07   5 4 3 2 1

Contents

Foreword by Steve Vai

The guitar is such a dynamic and expressive instrument. You can play it incredibly tenderly and softly, or you can be brutal with it. You can get a tone out of an instrument just by touching it, and the way you touch it determines your tone. In addition, there are so many ways you can vary the sound, like cranking up your amp or playing through an effect.

One of the big misconceptions among guitar players is that tone is a reflection of the amplifier and the guitar you use. Actually, tone comes from your head and your fingers. I'll give you an example: I had been recording a guitar part in my studio, playing my guitar through my amp, miked the way I like it, and it sounded like *me*. Then Edward Van Halen came by, and when he picked up my guitar and started to play, it was *him*. Even though it was my rig, I heard his famous "brown tone."

It dawned on me that his sound had nothing to do with his amps or his guitars. You can buy the same kind of amp and guitar that he plays, but it's not going to matter. His sound is all in his *fingers*—and it's like that with every guitar player. It's the way you approach the notes, and that's a product of what you hear in your head. If you're able to identify the kind of sound you're imagining, you'll be able to craft your tone with the equipment that's available to you.

Different amps and guitars have different tonal colors, and the only way to really understand them is to try out everything you can, or listen to other players onstage or on record when you know what gear they're using. Remember that if you're trying to emulate a particular sound, you need to work within certain parameters. If you're playing a Gretsch hollowbody that has a Bigsby vibrato bar, you won't get a tone like Hendrix's in his version of "Star Spangled Banner." You've got to be realistic, and you have to know your instruments' characteristics. If you're plugging a Strat into a little Fender amp without a distortion pedal, you've got to approach what you're hearing in your head within those parameters. Just remember that no piece of gear sounds better than another—it's simply a matter of what you're looking for (especially these days, when any tone can be musically valid).

Beyond that, the way you interpret sounds is a reflection of your own talent, insight, and ability. What makes you unique as a player is the way you identify the sounds in your head and then make them real. Every note ever played on a guitar throughout history is like a snowflake: No two are the same, and that's one of the beauties of the instrument. This book is a good place to start your journey to finding your own special tone.

—*Steve Vai*

Grammy-winning guitar virtuoso Steve Vai first gained attention for his work in Frank Zappa's band. A pioneer in the use of 7-string guitar in rock, Vai has recorded a number of influential solo albums, including Flex-Able, Passion and Warfare, Alien Love Secrets, *and* The Elusive Light and Sound, Vol. 1, *a collection of his music for film, television, and theater. In 1995* Guitar Player *named Vai to its Gallery of the Greats.*

Introduction

For all guitarists, there is the eternal question: *How do I sound like . . .*

It's often difficult to translate the great sounds we hear on records and radio to our own guitars, effects, and amps. That is precisely why we created *Gear Secrets of the Guitar Legends*. For the first time, those magical tones and timbres have been deciphered into practical, applicable information for the aspiring guitarist.

To that end, we've compiled detailed gear profiles on over 35 top players, including rig diagrams, secret tone tips, amplifier settings, effects setups, and even interviews with the artists themselves. These profiles are comprehensive, but we say that with one big caveat: artists' gear setups are changing constantly. And when you're talking about a guitarist with a career of 10, 20, or even 30 years, then you're talking about *hundreds* of pieces of gear.

Since compiling every single component of a player's setup would be cumbersome, if not a little irrelevant, we decided on a more focused approach (really, who cares if Eric Clapton tried out a stompbox for five minutes during a 1974 tour rehearsal . . . and then never used it again?). Instead, we tried to zero in on the gear and settings used during each guitarist's heyday as well as what equipment is in his rig currently. We hope you agree that will be the most useful information. We've topped it all off with a full CD of recorded examples and performance notes discussing the tones you'll hear on the disc.

What should you expect to get out of *Gear Secrets of the Guitar Legends*? You'll learn more about the gear you can buy and the gear you already own. And you'll find answers to perennial gear questions. For example, why *does* a Strat sound one way when Jimi Hendrix plays it and completely different in Yngwie Malmsteen's hands? How does a 4x12 cabinet sound different from a 1x12 or a 2x12? Can I make a Strat sound like a Les Paul, and vice versa? The answers are in here.

So turn the page, crank up the volume, and begin your journey into guitar-gear mastery. We hope you enjoy learning about the setups of rock's finest guitarists as much as we enjoyed writing this book.

—Pete Prown & Lisa Sharken

Photo Credits

Lisa Sharken: pages 1, 7, 8, 50, 54, 59, 63, 67, 73, 76, 81, 87, 93, 99, 100, 102, 103, 106, 108, 109

Ross Pelton: pages 3, 42

Ken Settle: pages 5, 14, 19, 21, 29, 34, 38, 70, 84, 89, 96

© Michael Ochs Archives.com: pages 10, 25 (Scotty Moore and Carl Perkins)

Clayton Call: pages 17, 43

Rick Gould: pages 18, 56, 58, 62, 66, 111

© Jon Sievert/ Michael Ochs Archives.com: pages 22, 77

Courtesy of Janet Cedrone Alvarez: page 25 (Danny Cedrone)

Courtesy of MESA/Boogie: page 37

Joe Sia: page 46

Thomas Nordegg: page 53

Jay Blakesberg: page 104

Acknowledgments

I would like to thank a number of people who helped make this book possible. First, thanks to Lisa Sharken, a consummate gear expert and friendly colleague for many years. Another big thank you to our editor, Richard Johnston, who patiently guided this project from a basic concept to the book you're holding in your hands, and offered many insightful suggestions along the way. Richard, your input has been invaluable.

I'd also like to thank my frequent partners in crime, Rich Maloof and HP Newquist, for their support, constructive criticism, and endless good humor. I appreciate our continuing comradeship, not to mention the sound of your fine guitar chops. (Double kudos to Mr. Maloof for so expertly copyediting the text in this book.)

A warm thanks to my friends and colleagues at the Pennsylvania Horticultural Society.

Appreciation as always to my father, Jules Prown, along with my siblings, in-laws, nieces and nephews, and so on. Naturally, a huge thank you and love also goes to my wife, Shannon, for letting me pursue my many interests and hobbies without complaint (English translation: Thanks for putting up with me and my noisy guitar *lo* these many years).

Finally, I would like to dedicate this book to my children—Max, Sophie, Rowan, Fox, and Graeme—for making my life fun and joyful, as well as helping keep me a young guitarist at heart.

—Pete Prown

First, I'd like to acknowledge Pete Prown, who devised the excellent concept for this project. His encouragement and confidence made this intense work possible. A huge thank you for your continued friendship, and for offering me a creative outlet at *Guitar Shop* magazine.

A big thanks to everyone at Backbeat Books, especially to Richard Johnston for his guidance through this endeavor and to Amy Miller for her hard work as our production editor. A special thanks also goes to Rich Maloof for his editing.

Much appreciation to my grandparents and parents for providing my first guitars (the toys and the real ones) along with the years of music lessons and college. Thanks to my family and friends for their support and for understanding that I don't work in a 9-to-5 world.

An enormous thanks goes to all the great musicians, technicians, and gearheads who have shared their secrets and aided in the research for this book. Thank you for your inspiration and friendship, and for allowing me to pick your brains.

I would like to dedicate this book to my friend César Diaz, the legendary amp builder, technician, and guitarist who passed away in 2002. You guided me into the major leagues as a tech, and taught me how to safely disassemble a tube amp and spot the fakes when perusing vintage guitars. Thanks for always looking out for me. I miss you dearly and hope I've made you proud.

—Lisa Sharken

Angus Young of AC/DC

Born
March 31, 1955 in Glasgow, Scotland

Bands
AC/DC

Tone
Classic Gibson-thru-Plexi Marshall tone—not overly distorted, but with pronounced bass range

Signature Traits
Massive finger vibrato, edge-of-pick harmonics, sublime blues feel

Breakthrough Performance
"Highway to Hell" from *Highway to Hell* (1979)

History and Influences
Australian guitar hero Angus Young formed AC/DC in 1973 with his rhythm-guitarist brother Malcolm. They earned a reputation for simple, power-chord rock topped with the requisite macho, "party all night" brand of lyrics. The band began to earn an international reputation with 1979's *Highway to Hell* album, but suffered a setback when singer Bon Scott died of an alcohol overdose in 1980.

Scott was replaced by newcomer Brian Johnson in time for the recording of *Back in Black*, the seminal hard-rock album that made AC/DC a household name. Since then, the band has remained a top concert draw around the globe, commanding legions of fans for their no-brainer approach to heavy rock 'n' roll.

▶▶▶

Gear List

Guitars

1961 Gibson SG/Les Paul; '64 Gibson SG with engraved lyre vibrola (arm removed) in original cherry finish; '64 Gibson SG, with vibrola, in original cherry finish (used for the solo at the end of the show); Gibson Angus Young Signature SG

Pickups

Gibson Angus Young Signature humbuckers

Accessories

Ernie Ball strings (.010–.046), extra heavy picks (121mm)

Effects & Rack Gear

Samson UR-5 wireless system

Amps & Cabs

Four Marshall Model 1959 SLP 100-watt heads (all new reissues of original Super Lead Plexi. Each head powers two 4x12 cabinets. There are two stacks on each side of stage, behind Angus and Malcolm). One original Marshall JTM45 (runs into one 4x12 cabinet underneath the stage and into an isolation box)

Tone and Technique

Angus Young's tone is defined by simplicity. With just an old SG and a Marshall, this rocker has created one of the best guitar tones in the business: big, muscular, and full of bluesy dynamics. No muss, no fuss—just big, big *tone*.

Young's guitar tone derives much from vintage rock 'n' roll, blues, and blues-rock players such as Chuck Berry, Peter Green, B.B. King, and especially Eric Clapton. While he is normally pigeonholed as a heavy metal guitarist, his roots are clearly in the blues. Any guitarist who wants to sound like him would be wise to check out classic albums from Cream, John Mayall's Bluesbreakers, and the original Fleetwood Mac.

The key to imitating Angus is mastering string bends and developing a strong, steady finger vibrato technique, à la Clapton. Also work on the microtonal bends so prevalent in blues guitar solos. For example, when playing an *A* minor blues scale, bend the *C* note just a smidge—maybe a quarter-step—but not all the way to *C♯*. This kind of micro-bend on a minor 3rd is an effective way to increase the bluesy tone of your guitar work.

Edge-of-the-pick harmonics are another staple of Young's solos. (Billy Gibbons of ZZ Top favors this technique as well.) With a bit of overdrive on your amp, twist your pick just a little as you strike the string to create harmonic chimes, squeals, and chirps. The technique is particularly effective on the lower strings but can be recreated on higher notes with practice. And lest you think Angus plays only blues licks, he also makes use of classically styled hammer-on/pull-off patterns, as heard in the intro to "Thunderstruck."

Finally, don't be concerned with playing too many notes. Angus is from the "less is more" school of guitar and will use one note where another player might use 50. Simple bends, great vibrato, and a few well-placed blues phrases will help you approach Angus Young's sound and style. A solidbody electric with humbuckers and a vintage-styled tube head with a 4x12 cabinet will get you even closer to the mark. A classic combination, to be sure.

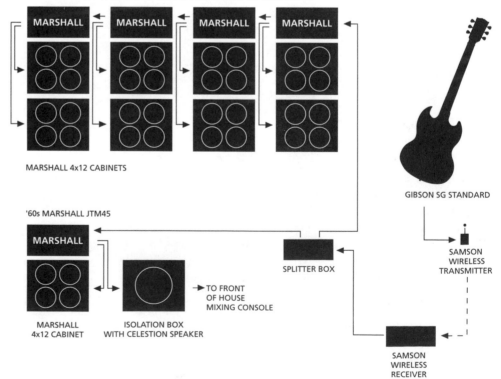

MARSHALL MODEL 1959 SUPER LEAD PLEXI REISSUE 100-WATT HEADS

MARSHALL MARSHALL MARSHALL MARSHALL

MARSHALL 4x12 CABINETS

GIBSON SG STANDARD

'60s MARSHALL JTM45

MARSHALL

MARSHALL 4x12 CABINET

ISOLATION BOX WITH CELESTION SPEAKER

TO FRONT OF HOUSE MIXING CONSOLE

SPLITTER BOX

SAMSON WIRELESS TRANSMITTER

SAMSON WIRELESS RECEIVER

Angus Young: In His Own Words

"Gibson SGs were the first real guitars I ever had, and I guess I've been using them since then. [My first] was a '68. I still have it and play it, too. What I like about SGs is that, with the double cutaway, you don't have to reach around, so it's easier to play up on the neck. I like its light weight and of course, I like the sound of it, too. I tried a Les Paul once, but I'm a little guy and the SG just felt more balanced for me. It's always been the right guitar for me. I probably have about four guitars that I use—one that I use for most of the show and the others are really just for backup, for when you get a bad fret or something like that happens.

"For amps, I like the old Marshall Plexis because they sound great, but you can't find any parts for them when you need them. The old ones all sound a little different, too, but the Plexi reissues sound good and they're more consistent. They're just more reliable to have out on the road.

"In the studio, I usually use older ones. My main amp in the studio is an old JTM45 that I also use live with an isolation box. I use that one and a 100-watt every now and again, but it just depends; sometimes you just might want a thicker lead sound and a 100-watt may be what makes it. The 100s have more bottom and are louder and cleaner, while 50s have a smoother sound and are easier to overdrive. I don't use any effects, either—just use the amp and no boost of any kind. I'm the only boost!

"Overall, I take what gear I know works for me. I just go with what's simplest and works best for me. I think this goes back to when I first started to play; back then, other people sort of wanted to knock down the walls with their amps, but my thing was to be able to play quiet, loud, and in the middle. The Marshall-and-SG combination worked for me, so I stuck with it. Basically, I'm just happy when I pick up a guitar."

Young's main tone tools: A '61 Gibson SG/Les Paul and four Marshall model 1959 SLP 100-watt heads.

Eric Clapton

Born
March 30, 1945, in Ripley, Surrey, England

Bands
The Roosters
Casey Jones & the Engineers
The Yardbirds
John Mayall's Bluesbreakers
Cream
Blind Faith
Delaney & Bonnie and Friends
Derek & the Dominos
Eric Clapton (solo career)
ARMS Benefit Concert tour (1983, with Jimmy Page and Jeff Beck)
Roger Waters (1984 tour)

Tone
Clapton is famous for his famous "woman tone" of the Cream era, as well as the thinner Stratocaster sound from his early solo career. More recently, he's tried to combine Strat tones with fatter Les Paul-like tones via a midrange booster in his namesake Fender solidbody

Signature Style
Blues-based, highly melodic solos with fabulous finger vibrato and emotive string bends

Breakthrough Performance
"Crossroads" from Cream's *Wheels of Fire* (1968)

History and Influences
From his beginnings with the Yardbirds to his acclaimed stint with John Mayall's Bluesbreakers to legendary work with Cream, Eric "Slowhand" Clapton was arguably the most revered rock guitarist of the 1960s. Clapton mastered the blues long before any other rock player save Mike Bloomfield, and has maintained his musical vision with boldness and clarity. His collective guitar work from 1964 to 1968 influenced *everybody*, including such heavyweights as Jimi Hendrix, Jeff Beck, and Jimmy Page.

While other white players had begun employing blues elements by the mid-'60s, few had conquered the subtleties of finger vibrato and full string bends as Clapton had. His first crucial steps to blues maturity are made evident by comparing the leads in the Yardbirds' 1964 single "Good Morning Little Schoolgirl" and its flipside, "Ain't Got You." On the former, Clapton's solo has the authority of a good blues break, but little passion or refined technique. On the latter, he rips a fiery solo that is full of convincing

▶▶▶

bends and hell-bent emotion. This is the sound of a guitarist actually improving before our ears.

Still, Clapton didn't really come into his own until leaving the Yardbirds in March 1965 to join John Mayall's Bluesbreakers a few months later. For the next year, the 20-year-old was playing hard electric blues on a daily basis, gigging all over England, and learning about the great bluesmen from Mayall's huge record collection.

When their sole album together, *Blues Breakers with Eric Clapton*, was issued in England in July of 1966, it was quite apparent how much the guitarist had progressed since his Yardbirds days. On muscular tracks like "Hideaway," "Key to Love," and "Steppin' Out," Clapton's lead work was bold and compelling, his confident string bends and flashy pentatonic licks traversing the blues and rock idioms with equal aplomb. This was the bedrock on which Eric Clapton has based all of his music since, even his forays into country and pop. And long before Jimmy Page made it a metal "must," the guitarist's predisposition towards sunburst Gibson Les Paul Standards and Marshall amps established this classic rig as rock's standard.

Yet, even before the "Clapton Is God" graffiti had dried on London's subway walls, Clapton had left the Bluesbreakers to form Cream. In the summer of 1966, along with bassist/vocalist Jack Bruce and drummer Ginger Baker, the guitarist took his new blues prowess to the next level, which was a full exploitation of the guitar's improvisational possibilities. Like the virtuoso "cutting sessions" at Minton's Playhouse in Harlem that ushered in the bebop jazz movement during World War II, Cream was pushing the instrumental limits of rock 'n' roll.

While the trio could muster up any number of fine pop compositions in the studio, it was in concert that they gave their most daring performances, treating audiences to the kind of extended jams that previously had been heard only in jazz clubs. Equipped with a Gibson Les Paul (or SG) and a pair of 100-watt Marshall stacks, Clapton played his energized blues solos at extreme volumes, improvising constantly and trying to keep up with his bop-bred bandmates, Bruce and Baker. Cream's first album, 1966's *Fresh Cream*, established the purity and weight of Clapton's blues-rock vision, while its follow-up, *Disraeli Gears*, showed the band on the cutting edge of psychedelia, mixing flower power and heavy-rock guitar riffs to earn their first hit single in America, the classic "Sunshine of Your Love."

Of all their recordings, *Wheels of Fire* tells the Cream story best, particularly since it devotes one record apiece to the band's live and studio personalities. From the studio side comes such definitive heavy rockers as "White Room" and Albert King's "Born Under a Bad Sign," each of which are saturated with impeccable breaks that range from the tastiest blues to the most ferocious rock 'n' roll. On another level, Clapton's heavy blues riff and dueling solos in "Politician" clearly prophesize the crunching guitar work of Led Zeppelin and other brash young metal acts who would follow shortly. (In fact, the guitarist has always been appalled that he's considered a "heavy metal forefather," but the proof is in these recordings.)

The definitive Slowhand track on *Wheels of Fire* is an electrified cover of Robert Johnson's "Crossroads" featuring two dramatic guitar solos. Call it rock or call it blues, but it is here that Eric Clapton put it all together—his blues roots, virtuoso rock technique, cocksure attitude, and killer guitar tones—and just played the hell out of his instrument. Had Clapton never

Gear List

Guitars
Fender Eric Clapton Signature Stratocaster (with 25dB mid-boost control); circa 1970 black Strat ("Blackie," made of parts from several different Strats); circa 1959 Gibson Les Paul Standard (Bluesbreakers era); Fender Telecaster, Jazzmaster, and Jaguar (Yardbirds); Gibson ES-335, early '60s Gibson SG/Les Paul (Clapton's Cream-era psychedelic SG); Gibson Firebird (Cream and Blind Faith); 1958 Gibson Explorer (mid-'70s tours); 1957 wine-red Les Paul (a refinished goldtop named "Lucy," used on the Beatles' "While My Guitar Gently Weeps"); 1939 Martin 000-42 acoustic; Martin Eric Clapton 000-42EC acoustic; Martin 000-28EC acoustic

Pickups
Stock Fender Strat pickups; Lace Sensor Strat pickups; Fender Vintage Noiseless Strat pickups; Gibson PAF humbuckers (on the Les Paul)

Accessories
Ernie Ball Regular Slinkys (.010-.046); Ernie Ball heavy picks

Effects & Rack Gear
Vox wah-wah, unknown fuzztone (Cream); Roger Mayer Voodoo Vibe, Dunlop CryBaby 535Q Multi-Wah, Bradshaw switching system, Ibanez Harmonics/Delay, dbx 160 compressor, Roland SDE-3000 delay, Tri Stereo Chorus (an early-'80s rack unit made by the Dyno-My-Piano company), BOSS CE-1 chorus, BOSS HM-2 Heavy Metal pedal, Roland GR-700 guitar synthesizer (mid-'80s solo)

Amps & Cabs
Vox AC30 (Yardbirds); 45-watt Marshall model 1962 2x12 combo with KT66 output tubes (Bluesbreakers era); Marshall Super Lead 100 100-watt heads and 4x12 cabs with 25-watt Celestion speakers (Cream); Fender Showman (Delaney & Bonnie tour); Fender tweed Champ (Derek & the Dominos); modified Music Man HD 130 Reverb heads ('70s solo); blonde Fender Twin (1983 ARMS tour); Marshall JCM800 50-watt heads (mid-'80s solo); Soldano SLO/100-watt heads and 4x12 cabs ('90s solo); various Fender tweed amps (recent solo work)

Amp Settings: Presence on 3; Bass and Mid on 5; Treble on 8; Volume on 8.5

recorded a note after "Crossroads," he would still likely be regarded as the guitar legend he is today.

Fortunately, he recorded plenty more. Two years after Cream's dissolution, Clapton cut *Layla and Other Assorted Love Songs* in a Miami studio with another powerhouse band, Derek & the Dominos. After completing a few tracks of *Layla*, Clapton invited Allman Brothers slide guitarist Duane Allman to join the sessions; unexpectedly, Allman ended up as a vital member of the band and played on the rest of the album. From potent blues cuts like "Key to the Highway" and "Have You Ever Loved a Woman" to the rockers "Anyday" and "Why Does Love Have to Be So Sad?" to their wrenching version of Jimi Hendrix's "Little Wing," the twin guitars of Clapton and Allman powered the Dominos' earthy sound. It also marked the only occasion Clapton ever seriously shared the spotlight with another guitarist—a sign of his deep respect for Allman's 6-string talents.

Following this great summit, Clapton slid into a heroin hell for several years, followed by nearly another decade of alcoholism—all of which left his guitar playing in a wretched state. It was within this same period that he morphed from guitar god to pop icon, with several Top 40 hits to his credit such as "I Shot the Sheriff," "Lay Down Sally," and the super-sappy ballad, "Wonderful Tonight." In 1985, he pulled out of his 6-string slump with the raucous single "Forever Man" and has since put out several sturdy pop and blues albums with their share of fine solos. Today, Clapton finds a steady balance between his pop and blues sides.

Still, the meaningful blues artistry Clapton injected into the Bluesbreakers, Cream, and Derek & the Dominos is irrevocably at the core of his legacy. He brilliantly reunited white rock guitar with its black blues heritage and, perhaps unintentionally, gave rock guitar a shot in the arm that would last for 25 years. For this he remains a towering icon of modern guitar. One could argue that Jimi Hendrix has a higher cachet (due to a combination of his musical genius and pop culture's affinity for dead rockers), but Clapton's achievements as a rock guitarist simply can not be denied. Say what you want about his recent commercial recordings, Clapton is unquestionably a living legend.

Tone and Technique

Clapton's so-called "woman tone" from the Cream era is created using the neck pickup of a solidbody with humbuckers. Roll the tone control all the way off and the volume knob

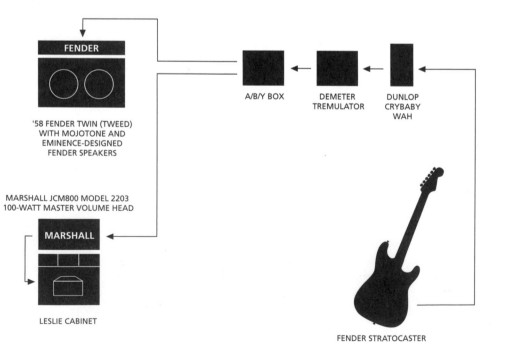

FENDER

'58 FENDER TWIN (TWEED)
WITH MOJOTONE AND
EMINENCE-DESIGNED
FENDER SPEAKERS

MARSHALL JCM800 MODEL 2203
100-WATT MASTER VOLUME HEAD

MARSHALL

LESLIE CABINET

A/B/Y BOX   DEMETER   DUNLOP
             TREMULATOR CRYBABY
                         WAH

FENDER STRATOCASTER

all the way up. (An alternate method of creating "woman tone" is to set a wah-wah pedal in the back position, towards its fatter, muted tone range.) To help increase the effect, the bottom-heavy thump of a 4x12 cabinet can't be beat. Prime examples of this sound can be heard on Cream's "Strange Brew" and "I Feel Free."

The other definitive Clapton tone is created with a Stratocaster through a vintage Fender tube amp, as heard in Derek & the Dominos and his early solo work. This sound is very "Strat-y" and employs far less distortion than his Cream tone. It was during the first half of his solo career that Clapton was trying to escape the guitar-hero reputation, and this cleaner, non-heavy rock texture helped him achieve that—much to the dismay of fans who wanted him to be a guitar god.

In 1985, however, Clapton kicked on the overdrive once again for the track "Forever Man" from *Behind the Sun*. Here, the guitarist found his "woman tone" again and rocked like he hadn't in 15 years. The cut "Miss You," from the following year's *August*, was even more explosive, featuring ol' Slowhand tearing up his Strat solos with fierce overdrive and speedy blues licks.

If you want to sound like Clapton, there are a few approaches to take. Start by listening to the blues, especially B.B. King, Buddy Guy, Muddy Waters, Otis Rush, and Albert King. Then get familiar with Clapton's recordings with John Mayall's Bluesbreakers and Cream. This contains the essence of Eric's guitar work.

For technique, you must appreciate the importance of finger vibrato. Clapton's vibrato is very wide, steady, and seductive. It's not a jittery, off-pitch vibrato, like that of Tony Iommi or Kirk Hammett, or a huge, overstated vibrato like Yngwie Malmsteen's. It's just smooth and perfectly intonated.

The next step is to learn some classic blues licks, as Clapton himself did. Beyond local teachers, there are many good instructional books and videos to consult. Here are three basic concepts of blues guitar to get you started:

1. Learn all your major pentatonic, minor pentatonic, and blues scales. Consult a reputable source to learn about scales and their applications.

2. Learn how to bend the minor 3rd of a given key just a shade off pitch for that sexy "blue note" sound. For example, if you're playing a blues in *A*, hit a *C* note and bend it up just a little, but not all the way to *C#*. This is a great blues idea to use again and again.

Essential Listening

The Yardbirds
"Good Morning Little Schoolgirl"
"Ain't Got You"
"Got to Hurry"

John Mayall's Bluesbreakers
"Hideaway"
"All Your Love"
"Stormy Monday"

Cream
"Spoonful"
"Strange Brew"
"Sunshine of Your Love"
"White Room"
"Crossroads"
"Badge"

Derek & the Dominos
"Why Does Love Have to Be So Sad?"
"Layla"
"Got to Get Better in a Little While"
"Bell Bottom Blues"

Eric Clapton
"Let It Rain"
"Let It Grow"
"After Midnight"
"Cocaine"
"Forever Man"
"Miss You"
"Hoochie Coochie Man"

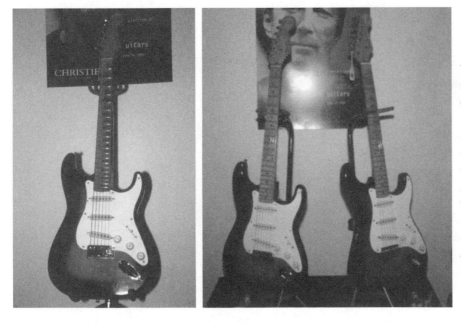

Three of Clapton's guitars on display at a 1999 New York charity auction (left to right): One of Clapton's favorite instruments, "Brownie." The 1956 Strat, serial #12073, was purchased on May 7, 1967, while he was with Cream. Clapton used this guitar extensively for stage and studio work. It appeared on the *Eric Clapton* and *Layla* album covers and was featured prominently on the tracks. Clapton's main slide guitars for stage and studio work: This 1956 Strat, serial #13385, was used throughout the '70s and featured on *Just One Night*, *Backless*, *Another Ticket*, and *Slowhand*. The 1954 hardtail (non-tremolo) Strat, serial #7431, was used from the mid '70s on, particularly for "Tulsa Time" in 1979–85.

3. Learn how to combine major and minor blues scales within a solo. Great blues players are often slipping between the two scales when playing over dominant 7 chords. In a classic I–IV–V blues (such as *A7–D7-E7*), one approach is to play a major blues scale on the I chord, minor blues on the IV, major blues on the I again, and minor on the V to finish off. This altering of tonal colors really enhances the blues vibe.

For recreating Clapton's tone, you can use a Strat or a Les Paul (or similar models). The key is to solo either on the neck pickup or on the bridge pickup with the tone knob rolled off. Either way you'll get a bassy, warm tone as opposed to the trebly bite of the bridge pickup with the tone knob full up. Playing through a tube head with a 4x12 cabinet will only improve the sound you're after.

The bottom line, though, is to appreciate the understated elegance of Clapton's approach. He's not about playing a lot of notes or trying to blow you away with volume. Like all great blues players, he wants to move the listener with the few notes he chooses. In rock circles, he may be the quintessential "less is more" guitarist. Again, our advice for mastering Clapton is to listen to all the John Mayall, Cream, and Derek & the Dominos music you can lay your hands on, not to mention plenty of vintage Chicago blues. After that, it should all start falling into place.

Eric Clapton: In His Own Words

Clapton told *Guitar Player* magazine in 1985, "When I get up there onstage, I often go through a great deal of indecision, even while I'm playing. If I've got the black Stratocaster on and I'm in the middle of a blues, I'm kind of going, 'Aw, I wish I had the Les Paul.'

"Then again, if I were playing the Les Paul, the sound would be great, but I'd be going, 'Man, I wish I had the Stratocaster neck.' I'm always caught in the middle of those two guitars. I've always liked the Freddie King/B.B. King rich tone; at the same time, I like the manic Buddy Guy/Otis Rush Strat tone. You can get somewhere in the middle, and that's usually what I end up doing, trying to find a happy medium. But it's bloody anguish."

This 1974 Martin 000-28, serial #353275, was Clapton's main acoustic throughout the '70s for writing, recording, and performing. The sticker on the side (SHE'S In Love With A RODEO MAN) refers to a song by Don Williams—one of Clapton's favorite artists.

Thin Lizzy

Brian Robertson, ca. 1977

Gary Moore and Scott Gorham, ca. 1979

Born
Scott Gorham: March 17, 1951, in
Los Angeles, California

Gary Moore: April 4, 1952, in Belfast,
Ireland

Brian Robertson: February 12, 1956,
in Glasgow, Scotland

Bands
Thin Lizzy
Asia (Gorham)
21 Guns (Gorham)
Colosseum II (Moore)
Gary Moore (solo career)
Baker, Bruce & Moore
Wild Horses (Robertson)
Motörhead (Robertson)

Tone
Distorted humbuckers through
tube-amp stacks

Signature Sound
Melodic twin-guitar harmonies,
barnburning single-note solos

Breakthrough Performance
"Cowboy Song" from *Jailbreak* (1976)

History and Influences
One of the greatest hard rock bands of
the 1970s, Thin Lizzy personified the
Les Paul-thru-Marshall guitar sound of
that decade. Thanks to such legendary guitar heroes as Gary Moore, Scott Gorham, and
Brian Robertson (not to mention the charismatic vocals and songwriting of Phil Lynott),
Thin Lizzy's recordings are a hotbed of overdriven guitar tones. From their hit "The Boys
Are Back in Town" to great albums like *Live and Dangerous* and *Black Rose*, Lizzy was a humbucker lover's dream come true. Gorham and Robertson powered the band from 1974–78,
when Moore came in for a yearlong stint (he was also briefly in the band back in '74).
Later, Gorham worked in Lizzy with guitarists Snowy White and John Sykes, both of
whom followed in the ferocious humbucker tradition laid down before them.

Thin Lizzy broke up in 1983, but at the same time, Gary Moore was emerging as a solo
star in his own right and, like thousands of other players, followed Eddie Van Halen's lead

▶▶▶

Gear List

Guitars

Gibson Les Paul Deluxe (Gorham)
1959 Gibson Les Paul Standard,
Charvel Strat, Fender Stratocaster
(Moore)
Gibson Les Paul Custom and Standard
(Robertson)

Pickups

Stock Gibson PAF humbuckers
Gibson "mini humbuckers" (on
Gorham's Les Paul Deluxe)
Single-coils (on Moore's Strats and
Charvel)

Accessories

Ernie Ball strings, Fender or Herco
heavy picks (Moore)

Effects

MXR Phase 90 phase shifter (Gorham)
Colorsound Overdriver, Maestro
Echoplex (Moore)
Crybaby wah (Robertson)

Amps & Cabs

Marshall 100-watt stacks (Gorham,
Moore, Robertson)

by plugging Strats and modified Strat-style solidbodies (with a Floyd Rose tremolo) into a Marshall amp. During that era, he was one of the fastest "shred" guitarists around, able to mix skittering lead flurries with soulful blues bends.

In 1990, however, he reverted to his blues-rock roots and cut the hit album *Still Got the Blues*. Here he returned to the Les Paul/Marshall formula, but cooled it down with tastier compositions in the style of his '60s heroes, Eric Clapton of Cream and Peter Green of Fleetwood Mac. In fact, in 1970 Moore bought Peter Green's original 1959 Les Paul from him for a mere $200, and it's still Moore's main guitar to this day.

Tone and Technique

It was only on the rarest occasion that a Stratocaster was heard on a Lizzy record—otherwise, it was all chunky Les Paul tones and Marshall 100-watt amplifiers. Technically, Gorham, Moore, and Robertson all emanate from the ubiquitous Clapton/Hendrix/Beck school of '60s rock guitar. Each of them generally soloed in

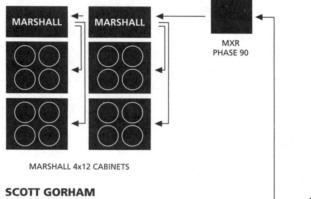

'70s MARSHALL SUPER LEAD 100-WATT HEADS

MXR
PHASE 90

MARSHALL 4x12 CABINETS

SCOTT GORHAM

GIBSON LES PAUL DELUXE
(or LES PAUL STANDARD)

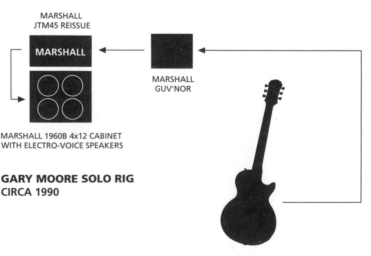

MARSHALL
JTM45 REISSUE

MARSHALL
GUV'NOR

MARSHALL 1960B 4x12 CABINET
WITH ELECTRO-VOICE SPEAKERS

GARY MOORE SOLO RIG
CIRCA 1990

1959 GIBSON LES PAUL STANDARD

GEAR SECRETS of the guitar legends

pentatonic- and blues-box patterns, adding tritones (the flatted 5th degree of the blues scale) and hyped-up string bends galore. And in fine hard-rock tradition, they ramped up the speed of their blues licks to make them more rhythmic than soulful, though at times each of these players could play a deeply emotive break.

Effects were few and far between for these rockers. Occasionally you can hear Robertson or Moore stomp on a wah-wah or Gorham flip on his phase shifter, but more often than not they preferred to run their guitars straight into their amps. In the 1980s, Moore temporarily got into the preamped "rack" sound of the day (with tons of chorus and digital delay), but returned to a purer guitar tone for his bluesy work in the '90s.

In a sense, all three of these guitarists are fairly traditional rock players, so copping their fat humbucker tones should not prove difficult. Just grab a solidbody electric with humbuckers (preferably a Les Paul or something of similar body mass, like a Paul Reed Smith or Ibanez Artist) and, more importantly, a 50- or 100-watt tube-amp head with a bottomy 4x12 cabinet. Make sure to turn it up real loud, and you're in business.

In Their Own Words

Gary Moore

"I used to go out with five Marshall heads and five cabinets and play these big auditoriums, but now we play smaller places because that's how I wanted to do it. So I've had to cut down on my onstage volume and just be careful not to go over the top and play too much.

"I favored using Les Pauls on *Still Got the Blues* and, as you know, they're not a real toppy guitar like a Strat is, so I had to really consider how to cut through. I didn't want to use Stratocasters because there're so many good blues-based guitarists in America who use them, like Stevie Ray Vaughan, Robert Cray, and Jeff Healey. I wanted to sound a bit different.

"When it comes to tone and gear, I come from a more traditional British blues-rock vibe. My background goes back to the 1960s when I was listening to all the great British blues players who took the black music from America and sold it to white audiences. I'm talking about Peter Green, who was very much an inspi-

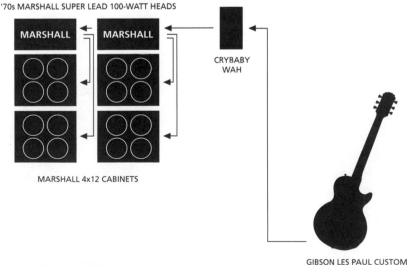

'70s MARSHALL SUPER LEAD 100-WATT HEADS

MARSHALL   MARSHALL

CRYBABY WAH

MARSHALL 4x12 CABINETS

BRIAN ROBERTSON

GIBSON LES PAUL CUSTOM
(or LES PAUL STANDARD)

ration to me, and, later on, Clapton and Hendrix. I was very strongly influenced by all these guys and they're all in my playing. I've tried to reinstate that sort of British tradition, with that rawness and Les Paul/Marshall sort of sound, but with a definite modern-rock aggression. I guess if I bring anything new to blues guitar, it's probably just a lot of volume!"

Scott Gorham

"Our [Thin Lizzy] gear was all Les Pauls and Marshalls—Brian Robertson played Customs and Standards, and I had a Deluxe with the mini-humbuckers. But I'm not really a big gear-hound. I like to try an effect out and if it works, fine, but I'm not one of those guys who really dives into the gear side. I prefer to just play.

"As far as players, Brian and I were a real guitar team in every sense of the word. He would really study my style and I'd study his, even to the point where we'd be checking each other's vibratos out. We'd try to get our vibratos in perfect sync during the harmonies because we knew if we didn't get it right, it would sound like a big jumbled mess and there'd be no discipline. We wanted to get it sounding as correct as possible, but not so far that it would sound really stiff.

"If there was ever one thing that I tried to copy from a guitar player, it was Clapton's finger vibrato. He did it at such an even pace and so sweetly. For me, vibrato really gives guitar players their emotion, and I try to make the notes like a voice when you bend and then vibrato it towards the end."

Dave Matthews

Born
January 9, 1967, in Johannesburg, South Africa

Bands
Dave Matthews Band

Tone
Clean, compressed acoustic-electric tone, mixed occasionally with a little overdriven signal

Signature Sound
In-the-pocket funk grooves that underpin his melodic pop vocals

Breakthrough Performance
"Ants Marching" from *Crash* (1996)

History and Influences

Perhaps the coolest group of the past decade, the Dave Matthews Band appeals to everyone from modern rockers to over-the-hill yuppies and everyone in between. Why? Because DMB combines great songs with catchy melodies, punchy grooves, and some incredibly tight musicianship. Guitarist/frontman Dave Matthews is a one-man groove machine who kicks off each track with some stone-cold *fonky* rhythms on a Gibson Chet Atkins SST acoustic- electric, as well as his Martin signature model and various Taylor acoustics equipped with Fishman piezo transducers.

Growing up in South Africa, Matthews developed an uncanny list of musical influences, from classical composers like Vivaldi and Bach to reggae master Bob Marley. He also learned to love piano music, such as the playing of jazz legend Keith Jarrett. Fusing these disparate sources, Matthews has unintentionally redefined the guitar hero for the 21st century. Not merely an "unplugged" strummer, he has combined pop, funk, and acoustic guitar in a way never before heard in rock music. And while he's not an over-the-top soloist like a Hendrix or a Van Halen, he's still regarded as a serious player by the guitar cognoscenti, and deservedly so. The man *can* play guitar.

Tone and Technique

To get a feel for the Dave Matthews groove, you have to work on two things: your groove and your tone. For the groove side, listen to some great funk and R&B guitarists like Jimmy Nolen on old James Brown records; Al McKay on classic Earth, Wind & Fire discs; or most anything by the Red Hot Chili Peppers. The key to a good groove is to really lock in with the bass and drums—sloppiness and a poor sense of rhythm do not cut it here. Matthews has a terrific sense of time, and his guitar playing creates the only harmonic backdrop in his band; there's no other guitarist or keyboardist in the group playing chords besides him. *That's* impressive.

Guitars

Gibson Chet Atkins SST acoustic-electric; Taylor 914ce, 714, W65ce 12-string, custom Baritone; Martin Dave Matthews DM3MD Signature model, HD-28

Pickups

Fishman piezo transducer

Accessories

D'Addario medium-gauge bronze strings; Jim Dunlop .60mm picks; Korg DT-1 pro tuner; API Lunchbox self-powered rack module; Whirlwind Selector A/B/Y box, Whirlwind Splitter; Beyerdynamic TG-X 50 microphone (on Fender amp in isolation cabinet)

Effects & Rack Gear

White DSP 5024 multi-function digital signal processor (provides parametric filters, high pass/low pass filters, high/low shelving filters, digital delay, peak limiting, and crossover functions), Meyer Sound S-1 processor (for clipping protection), Eventide GTR 4000 Ultra-Harmonizer, Nady 950 and Xwire 950 wireless units, Meyer Sound CP-10 parametric EQ, Rocktron MIDI pedals

Amps

API 512 preamp, Crest 7001 power amp, Fender Hot Rod Deluxe combo (in an isolation cabinet located offstage), Meyer Sound USM-1 Stealth monitors

To get your guitar to sound like Matthews's, consider your gear. A thin-body acoustic-electric guitar will help get you on track, but be mindful about the pickups. If you're using a standard acoustic-electric guitar, chances are it has a pickup onboard; i.e., you use a standard guitar cable instead of a microphone. Of the different acoustic pickup systems out there, more often than not acoustic-electrics will have a piezo pickup, which senses the vibration of the strings and transforms it into the voltage that flows down a guitar cable and creates your tone. This is largely what Matthews uses—but it's not the highest-grade tone you can achieve. Far more natural-sounding acoustic results can be derived from using a microphone on a separate mic stand (especially for recording, where using at least two mics is commonplace), but for live work, a plug-in piezo is among the more convenient methods to amplify one's acoustic.

Other pickup variations include magnetic "soundhole" pickups and internal mini-mics, both of which can add different flavors to an acoustic's tone. Many acoustic players actually use two or more of these pickup methods to record their guitars, such as combining an internal piezo with an external or an onboard microphone. Then, using a "blender" preamp (such as models made by Fishman, PreSonus, and others), the guitarist can then blend the direct signal with the mic signal to create a realistic acoustic sound. All told, amplifying acoustic guitars is more complex than amplifying electrics, but a little experimentation with different pickup types will undoubtedly give you better results in the long run.

The choice of amplifier is also critical. While a Strat will sound good through a pair of beefy 12" speakers, acoustic guitars require "full-range" speakers—separate speakers for highs and lows—to produce those booming bass notes, shimmering highs, and just the right dash of mids.

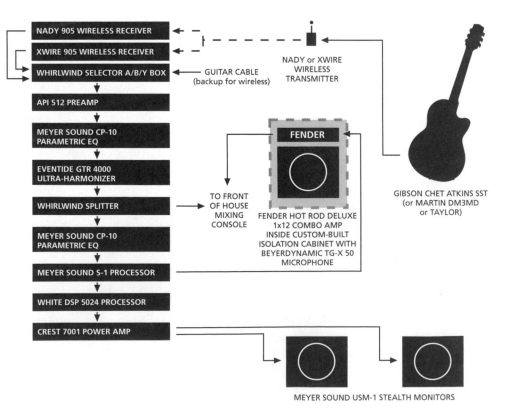

To that end, many manufacturers produce acoustic guitar amps specifically to cover the tricky sonics of amplifying acoustics. (Anyone who has ever plugged an acoustic guitar into a standard electric guitar amp can attest that it is *not* a match made in heaven. A helpful analogy: Think of electric amps as AM radio and acoustic amps as FM radio; AM radios have a cool, lo-fi tone, but for truer sound fidelity, FM is the way to go.) Acoustic amps also have EQs specially geared toward the tonal needs of the acoustic-electric guitar; likewise, they're typically loaded with appropriate speakers (again, usually including some sort of tweeter or horn to better reproduce the acoustic's high-end tones).

Today, there are more acoustic combo amps being built than ever before, all for the growing market of players who want good live sound via the all-in-one convenience of a combo amp. (Numerous rack amps and cabinets are also available.) Higher-end models also come with notch filters, which are great for solving feedback problems that inevitably occur when you crank an acoustic's volume way up. By twisting this knob, you can find the offending frequency and simply pull it out of the EQ spectrum.

Of course, there are alternatives to dropping cash on a whole new amp. If you have a PA, you may be able to forget about the separate acoustic amp altogether and plug straight into the mixer, which itself has an EQ system that's perfectly ready for acoustics. (It's important that you make sure the impedance of the PA mixer's inputs matches the impedance of your pickups. You may also want to use a tube preamp between your guitar and the mixer to warm things up.) Again, most professional acoustic recordings are made using microphones or a combination of microphone and direct signal—neither option being so convenient for live work. But you can record a decent acoustic tone by plugging into a preamp and then a mixer, which in turn sends the signal to the recording deck of your choice. Bass amps can also work OK, providing better low-end response than a typical electric guitar amp.

There are also effects to consider for the acoustic-electric guitarist, whether you're Dave Matthews or not. If there is one effect that just about all amplified acoustic players rely on, it's reverb. Although dry acoustic can be cool in the right place, a touch of reverb can make a mediocre guitar sound like a million bucks. Another popular effect is compression. Since acoustic guitars span such a wide frequency range and can also be highly dynamic—going from barely audible fingerpicked passages to loud, clanky strumming—using a compressor reins in some of the instrument's wilder sonic attributes. Also, compression can give your amplified acoustic more of a polished, professional sound, as long as you don't overdo it and give it too much of the "squashed" compressor sound that electric country pickers dig so much.

The third most heavily used acoustic effect is chorus. Just as for a clean electric tone, chorus can add a shimmering depth and sparkle to acoustic rhythm parts, whether it's soft strumming, fingerpicking, or melody lines. But just as on electrics, beware of using chorus for solos, since it sounds as if you're using the effect to cover up any creative and improvisational deficiencies. On rhythm, chorus, along with a smidge of reverb and compression, is something beautiful to behold. Just listen to a Dave Matthews guitar part to hear why.

Essential Listening

"Tripping Billies"
"Drive In, Drive Out"
"Ants Marching"
"Proudest Monkey"

Discography

Remember Two Things (RCA, 1993), *Recently* (RCA, 1994), *Under the Table and Dreaming* (RCA, 1994), *Crash* (RCA, 1996), *Live at Red Rocks 8.15.95* (RCA, 1997), *Before These Crowded Streets* (RCA, 1998), *Live at Luther College* (RCA, 1999), *Listener Supported* (RCA, 1999), *Everyday* (RCA, 2001), *Live in Chicago 12.19.98 at the United Center* (RCA, 2001), *Busted Stuff* (RCA, 2002), *Live at Folsom Field, Boulder, Colorado 7/11/01* (RCA, 2002)

Allan Holdsworth

Born
August 6, 1948, in Bradford, Yorkshire, England

Bands
Tempest
Soft Machine
Gong
The Tony Williams Lifetime
Jean-Luc Ponty
Bruford
UK
Allan Holdsworth (solo career)

Tone
Thick, rounded overdrive reminiscent of a violin or cello for solos; lush rhythm guitar tone drenched with layers of chorus and delay

Signature Sound
High-speed hammer-on runs using non-diatonic chord colors and amazingly wide intervals between notes

Breakthrough Performance
"In the Dead of Night" from *U.K.* (1978)

History and Influences
From his early records with Tempest, Gong, Tony Williams, and Soft Machine to the groundbreaking work with Bruford and UK, and further to his noted solo career, Allan Holdsworth remains an enigmatic and singular soloist who has always been years ahead of his time.

As a fusion guitarist, he was seemingly influenced by everyone *except* other guitar players, which accounts for his singular sound and style. Over his formative years, he soaked up ideas from unlikely sources ranging from jazz saxophonist John Coltrane to 20th-century classical composers such as Arnold Schoenberg and Igor Stravinsky, not to mention a number of violinists (in fact, Holdsworth is a very good violinist himself).

Holdsworth's influence on modern guitarists has been simply enormous: Eddie Van Halen, Scott Henderson, Bill Connors (Return to Forever), Alex Lifeson, Steve Vai, Joe Satriani, Dean DeLeo (Stone Temple Pilots), and a host of others count him as a major inspiration. The jazz-rocker also made major inroads into the world of guitar synthesizers, staking a unique voice for himself using this new kind of 6-string technology. In sum, Allan Holdsworth is without question one of the most important and influential guitarists of the last 25 years.

▶▶▶

Tone and Technique

Along with Eddie Van Halen, Holdsworth spearheaded the use of the legato hammer-on technique, which creates a flowing cascade of notes (as opposed to the clipped staccato sound of traditional alternate picking). He also introduced a manner of using a tremolo bar as a subtle tone tool, creating dramatic dips and swells. This often made his guitar sound as mellifluous as a tenor sax while still retaining a fierce electric-guitar persona.

Holdsworth's tone is just as dramatic as his playing, again recalling a sax or violin more than a standard guitar. In the 1970s, Holdsworth was among the first guitarists to put humbuckers into a Stratocaster, combining a humbucker's dual-coil power with the pitch-bending capabilities of a tremolo bar. His rhythm guitar tone is especially intriguing, as he uses extensive chorus and delay effects with a volume pedal to create beautiful chord swells; at times he sounds like a one-man symphony orchestra.

The first step to sounding like Allan Holdsworth requires more work on the technique side, mastering hammer-ons and pull-offs. This can take a little while, but the concept is simple enough: play three successive notes on a given string while only picking once. With a hammer-on, you pick the first note fretted by the index finger and then "hammer" the following two, usually with the middle, ring, or little fingers. Conversely, with a pull-off you pick the first note fretted by the pinky, release to sound a note with the ring or middle finger, and fret the last note with the index finger. This sounds complicated, but with practice it's quite doable. Of course, with his amazing reach, Holdsworth can perform hammer-ons that are seven or more frets apart. For most of us mortals, typical hammer-ons and pull-offs take place within four or five frets.

Gear List

Guitars

Carvin Allan Holdsworth Model, modified Fender Stratocaster, Charvel Strat-style, Steinberger and DeLap custom headless electrics, Gibson SG, SynthAxe MIDI controller

Pickups

Carvin Holdsworth Humbucker

Accessories

Jim Dunlop 1mm black nylon picks; LaBella or Ernie Ball strings (.008 set)

Effects & Rack Gear

Yamaha UD-Stomp modulation/delay processor, Lexicon PCM 41 digital delay, DeltaLab Effectron digital delay, Rocktron Intellifex multi-effects processor, homemade effects and load boxes (the latter for delivering line-level signals to power amps)

Amps

Custom amplifiers (made by Allan Holdsworth); MESA/Boogie Mark IV and Dual Rectifier amps; Yamaha DG-80 and DG-100 digital modeling amps

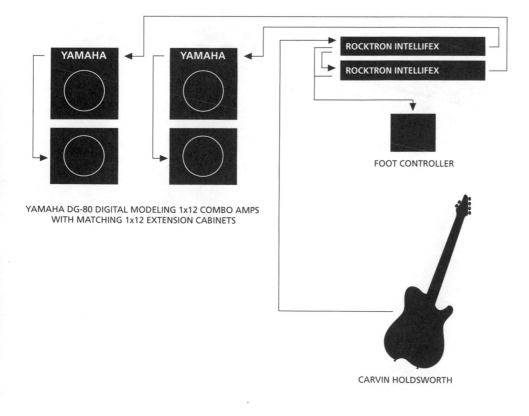

YAMAHA DG-80 DIGITAL MODELING 1x12 COMBO AMPS
WITH MATCHING 1x12 EXTENSION CABINETS

FOOT CONTROLLER

CARVIN HOLDSWORTH

Essential Listening

Bruford

"Hell's Bells"
"The Abingdon Chasp"
"One of a Kind"
"Five G"

UK

"In the Dead of Night"
"Nevermore"

Allan Holdsworth

"Three Sheets to the Wind"
"Tokyo Dream"

Discography

Bruford

Feels Good to Me (EC, 1977), *One of a Kind* (EC, 1979)

UK

U.K. (EC, 1978)

Allan Holdsworth

Velvet Darkness (CTI, 1976), *I.O.U.* (Enigma, 1982), *Road Games* (Warner, 1983), *Metal Fatigue* (Enigma, 1985), *Atavachron* (Enigma, 1986), *Sand* (Relativity, 1987), *Secrets* (Intima, 1989), *Wardenclyffe Tower* (Restless, 1992), *Hard Hat Area* (Restless, 1994), *None Too Soon* (Restless, 1996), *Sixteen Men of Tain* (Gnarly Geezer, 2000), *Igginbottom's Wrench* (Cleopatra, 2000)

Allan Holdsworth: In His Own Words

"In the studio, I don't use a clean amp—I just DI out through the mixer in my rack and go right into the tape machine, which I feel gives a truer tone. My main effect is a combination of eight delay lines that I use for chorus. To me, a good chorus is really just a bunch of single mono delay lines, but it takes a lot of them chained together to get that effect.

"Now I use the Yamaha UD-Stomp a lot, but at one point my rack had two Lexicon PCM 41s, two Yamaha 1500 delays, two Roland SDE-3000 delays, and two DeltaLab Effectrons—which was eight delays total. And it sounds better when you use units from different manufacturers, because each company has its own sound. When you blend them, you get the best tone. If you used eight delays from the same company, it wouldn't sound nearly as good. I don't use MIDI, either, because I like real-time control over it. Plus, I just set the units and pretty much leave them; if I do change anything, I like to do it myself, manually.

"As for amp settings, I set the gain at around 2 o'clock, treble and middle about 2 o'clock, the bass all the way off, presence at 10 o'clock, and the master wherever it sounds good, because I don't run the amplifier into a speaker cabinet—I run it into one of my own little load boxes. Then I take the line output from that and feed it into a power amp that drives the speakers. That way, I can play really soft and still get a sound that I like. I don't want to have to play loud to get a sound I like. Actually, at the volume I use, I could easily play electric guitar with an acoustic band."

The 2001 version of Holdsworth's ever-changing stage rig, with his Carvin signature guitar, Yamaha DG-80 amps, and various rack and floor processors.

Eric Johnson

Born
August 17, 1954, in Austin, Texas

Bands
The Electromagnets
Session musician (Christopher Cross, Carole King, Cat Stevens, Steve Morse Band)
Eric Johnson (solo career)
G3 tour (with Joe Satriani and Steve Vai)

Tone
Eric's famous "violin tone" for solos is heavy with bass, sustain, and echo effects

Signature Traits

Unlike most speedsters who wail using diatonic modes, Johnson is adept at speed-picking pentatonic "blues box" patterns, as well as melodic phrases using arpeggios based on the chord changes he's playing over

Breakthrough Performance

"Cliffs of Dover" from *Guitar Player* magazine "Soundpage" (1986)

History and Influences

For many years, Eric Johnson was just a rumor, something about "this amazing guitar player from Texas." Locals in Austin were aware of him, but the rest of the world had barely heard a peep. Then, in 1986, Johnson released his first solo album, *Tones*, and suddenly everyone understood what all the fuss was about. At the same time, he released a special live version of his signature track, "Cliffs of Dover," on a plastic flexi-disc inside the pages of *Guitar Player* magazine, which only cemented his reputation as a monster player.

Stylistically, Johnson synthesized influences from rock, bebop, country, pop, and classical music into one simmering fusion stew. His chops were stunning—unlike the soulless shredders of the '80s, Johnson could play fast but with taste, style, and pure finesse. In short, the coming of Eric Johnson was a 6-string revelation.

Four years later, he released his second disc, *Ah Via Musicom*, and after sitting on the shelves for a few months it suddenly exploded up the charts. Driving the album was a new studio version of "Cliffs of Dover," and other rockers like "Trademark" and "Righteous." Quickly Eric Johnson became a household word among guitarists and his raucous instrumentals became regular fare on FM radio. "Cliffs" also won him a Grammy for Best Rock Instrumental.

▶▶▶

Gear List

Guitars

1954 and 1958 Fender Stratocasters, 1965 Gibson ES-335, Gibson Flying V, Martin D-28 acoustic

Pickups

DiMarzio HS-2 stacked humbuckers (wired as single-coil pickups)

Accessories

Dunlop Jazz III picks

Effects & Rack Gear

Dallas-Arbiter Fuzz Face, Maestro Echoplex, BK Butler Tube Driver overdrive, MXR Digital Delay, T.C. Electronic Stereo Chorus

Amps & Cabs

Fender Vibrolux Reverb and Deluxe Reverb combos (rhythm channel), Marshall Super Lead Plexi 50- and 100-watt heads and 4x12 cabinet with Celestion speakers (lead channel), Dumble tube amp, Manzamp preamp, and Dumble Odyssey power amp

Amp settings: Tone controls set between 10 and 12 o'clock; volume at 8.5

The key to Johnson's guitar approach is a wide range of influences. From rockers like Jimi Hendrix, Eric Clapton, and Johnny Winter, Johnson appropriated a sense of soulful but aggressive psychedelia, while the music of B.B. King provided a direct shot of blues purity. Jazz legend Wes Montgomery added a touch of melody, and fusion players like John McLaughlin, Jeff Beck, and Pat Metheny injected the harmonic complexity that helped form his lead and rhythm style.

As for gear, Eric Johnson has the reputation for being a perfectionist, one who's able to distinguish alkaline and non-alkaline 9-volt batteries in a stompbox just by the sound. He's also been known to re-record entire albums because he's unsatisfied with the tone. This kind of dedication to musical craftsmanship has been a hallmark of Eric Johnson's career, both in the studio and onstage.

Tone and Technique

Eric Johnson's tone is complex but not impossible to emulate. First take a look at his basic tone tools: a Stratocaster, an overdrive unit, an echo, and a high-quality tube amp. On the Strat, Johnson prefers to solo using the neck pickup, which helps create that warm, thick "violin tone." (During his years with Cream, Eric Clapton had derived a similar sort of "woman tone," as he called it.) The other critical piece is the vintage-style tube amp with a 4x12 cabinet. What you'll want to avoid is a modern high-gain tube head, which would generate more saturated distortion than is needed. Johnson likes vintage tube amps that can be overdriven a little, and then pumps them up further by using an external preamp pedal (to duplicate that sound, you could use a classic Ibanez Tube Screamer or Fuzz Face).

The combination of a Strat set on its neck pickup, a tube head with 4x12 cabinet, and overdrive box will get you close to approximating the basics of Eric Johnson's lead-guitar tone. On top of that you'll want to add an echo/delay unit, preferably one that can emulate the tape echoes of the 1970s. This will add sonic girth and dimension to the bassy tones you're generating with the Strat and 4x12 cabinet.

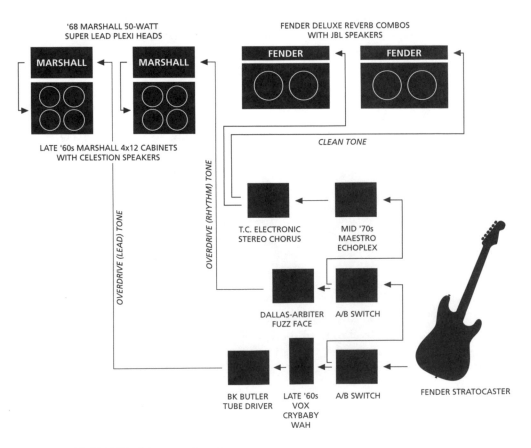

Johnson's clean tone, on the other hand, uses the same Strat/tube amp/echo combination, but in place of a preamp pedal he adds a chorus unit to sweeten the sound. For live work, he has an A/B setup, so he can jump between the overdriven lead side and the lush, chorused rhythm aspects of his guitar work. Many gigging guitarists have gotten great results using a similar type of rig.

Eric Johnson: In His Own Words

"My main guitar is a 1954 Fender Stratocaster that I call 'Virginia,' and it's loaded with DiMarzio HS-2 stacked humbuckers. The HS-2 is a real sweet-sounding pickup, and I like using them better as single-coils. I disconnect the humbucking part of the pickup and just use it as a single-coil, but the mere fact that you have that extra coil in the proximity of the other cancels about 30% or 40% of the hum that you'd get from a stock Strat pickup. It has a little more gain and it's a little tighter on the bottom end than the stock Strat pickups. In the bridge position, it gives my Strat a thicker, 'violiny' tone. After I heard that sound, it spurred me to try different types of leads that used a little bit more of that kind of sound.

"I don't use tons of effects, but one I do like is the old Echoplex. I prefer the solid-state version with two knobs, made in the '70s and early '80s. I have a love/hate relationship with them because they're such a pain in the butt to use, but it's the only thing I've ever found that doesn't ruin your direct tone. I also dig Marshall Plexi amplifiers, although they can be temperamental and aren't always reliable on the road. I'm kind of an addict for '67s and '68s. But after '69, they changed the wiring—I really don't like the way post-'69 Marshalls sound. I don't know what they did, but they started doing some weird stuff to them. And the Dumble amp I use has a big, smooth sound, like an overgrown Twin with lots of voltage running through it.

"My clean tone is just a couple of old Fender Reverbs set about halfway with a T.C. Electronic Stereo Chorus and an Echoplex. Of course, the Strats I use contribute a lot to the sound. The new Stratocasters are probably made as well as the old ones, but the grade of metal they used in the old ones was better and the wood that was available was of a better quality than is generally around today. I use the neck pickup a lot to get my tone."

▼ Essential Listening

"Cliffs of Dover"
"Righteous"
"Trademark"
"Friends"

Discography

The Electromagnets (EGM, 1975, reissued by Rhino), *Tones* (Reprise, 1986), *Ah Via Musicom* (Capitol, 1990), *Venus Isle* (Capitol, 1996), *G3: Live in Concert* (Epic, 1997), *Seven Worlds* [reissue from 1978] (Ark 21, 1998), *Live and Beyond* (Favored Nations, 2000)

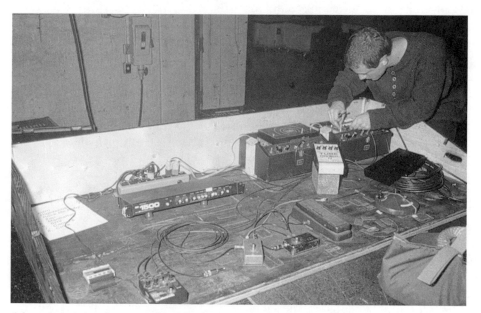

Johnson's tech tweaks a venerable Echoplex on Eric's spacious pedalboard.

Steve Morse

Born
July 28, 1954, in Hamilton, Ohio

Bands
The Dixie Dregs (a.k.a. The Dregs)
Steve Morse Band
Kansas
Deep Purple

Tone
Eclectic, from fat neck-pickup tone on upper notes to squealing, Tele-toned bridge-pickup sound on lower notes

Signature Traits
Bluesy flavor added to high-speed fusion guitar

Breakthrough Performance
"Take It Off the Top" from the Dixie Dregs' *What If* (1978)

History and Influences

Since his 1977 debut with the Dixie Dregs, Steve Morse has defined the term "virtuoso" among rock guitarists. But unlike other so-called virtuosos, Morse isn't simply adept at one innovative style—he's mastered everything from rock to fusion to funk to country to classical guitar. A large part of his electric work is indebted to the blues, too. Fans and music critics have raved about his staggering technique while still being moved by the deep soulfulness of his playing. Morse is also a talented composer, penning some of the most intriguing instrumentals in recent memory. Whether he's being praised for his work with the Dregs, Deep Purple, the Steve Morse Band or Kansas, it's clear by now that Steve Morse is a guitar hero who's accustomed to having superlatives tossed his way.

Morse's influences read like a "who's who" of classic rock and jazz-fusion guitar. At the top of the list are masters like Jeff Beck, John McLaughlin, Pat Metheny, and Steve Howe. The guitarist also soaked up the sounds of countless country, jazz, and classical players. And for his pronounced blues influence, he ironically cites not a traditional bluesman, but rocker Ted Nugent, who mixed post-Clapton blues licks with '70s-era metal riffing. Somehow, all of these sounds boiled down into the staggering style of Steve Morse, perhaps the most *eclectic* guitarist in the history of rock.

Tone and Technique

Morse's killer technique is at the heart of many players' admiration for him. Yet, while much has been written about his incredible fusion chops in the past decade, the deep-rooted blues textures that are so central to his playing are frequently overlooked. His solos, in particular, are frequently laden with growling bass-string bends and lickety-split chromatic runs that are set within a pentatonic box framework, tritones inclusive. In fact, Morse's blues sensibility is the one thing that has always set him apart from contemporaries like

Eddie Van Halen, Al Di Meola, and Allan Holdsworth, none of whom have ever used more than a smattering of straight blues in their own lead work. So when you're thinking about coming up with a sound and style similar to Morse's, don't forget about learning the blues.

Morse's lead style incorporates a very slow, pronounced finger vibrato. He often will bend a note and hold it for a second or two before gently starting the vibrato, much like an opera singer. He frequently twists his pick to get edge-of-the-pick chimes, squeals, and harmonics, notably when he's using the bridge pickup. To get a handle on his lead lines, use chromatic pentatonic runs. That is, experiment with playing the standard pentatonic blues-box patterns, but fill in all the notes of the box so that runs are chromatic. Lean on scale tones like the flatted 5th and flatted 3rd, which help Morse create fluid lead phrases that remain bluesy.

If you've ever witnessed Morse in concert, you know that the man is a total gear fanatic. No mere "plug 'n' play" 6-stringer, Morse is constantly manipulating his tone, volume, and effects during shows, all while playing some of the most monstrous guitar licks on the planet. Even during a solo, the guitarist's right hand endlessly tweaks his volume and tone pots, as well as his pickup selectors. His feet, meanwhile, are in command of an array of volume pedals and switches, which he uses to turn on effects, activate his guitar synthesizer, adjust monitor levels, and artfully blend one effect into another.

Since Morse is constantly adjusting his tone via his footpedals, tone knobs, and pickup selector, it takes a bit of choreography to nail his tone accurately. His favored sounds include a fat, humbuckers-on-neck-pickup tone (like Clapton's "woman tone" or Santana's lead tone), as well as an overdriven Tele-bridge–pickup sound. He also uses a variety of dry crunch tones for power chords or go-for-the-throat metal solos.

His clean work, meanwhile, varies from compressed Tele "twang" for country chicken-pickin' licks to deeply chorused, echoey tones for volume swells, à la Allan Holdsworth.

Suffice it to say, there are a lot of Morse sounds to investigate. However, here's one shortcut that can help. A classic Steve Morse maneuver is to use the neck pickup for lead lines above, say, the 9th fret and then switch to the bridge pickup for any of the low notes below that. This gives you the creamy, round notes of the bridge pickup for your high notes, and the screaming, edge-of-the-pick harmonics for any low notes you hit. You will find this combination all over Morse's recordings.

Steve Morse: In His Own Words

"My main electric is an Ernie Ball/Music Man guitar, which is pretty much a copy of my original Telecaster. It does have some material changes, though. The neck is held on by six screws instead of four, and it has four-and-two peg winders instead of six in a row, which makes for a shorter string pull and a shorter head-stock. There's a metal bridge instead of the Tele's nylon-piece bridge, so there's much better sustain and harmonics. And the wood is a little heavier and stronger. It also has the DiMarzio pickups that are on all my guitars.

"In the studio, I use the Ovation classical, and live, I use the Gibson Chet Atkins model constantly because it doesn't feed back. For steel-string, I'm using an old Fender 12-string acoustic and an electric-acoustic Ovation medium-bowl.

"I use a variety of amps, depending on the situation. I have a Marshall Jubilee with JBL speakers, Peavey 5150s, and an Ampeg V-4. Nothing does it like the Ampeg—it has a big ol' fat sound for soloing. In 'The Road Home' [from 1989's *High Tension Wires*], the guitar solo starts right away and that fat sound is the Ampeg, which has a three-position midrange control to get that big tone. I just sit in the control room with the headphones on and play my guitar, alternating between Celestion and JBL speakers in the studio.

▼ Gear List

Guitars
Ernie Ball/Music Man Steve Morse model, modified Fender Telecaster, Steinberger 12-string, Buscarino electric classical, Gibson Chet Atkins electric classical, Peavey acoustics, Ovation classical and steel-string, Fender steel-string acoustic, Fender 12-string acoustic

Pickups
DiMarzio (from neck to bridge): DP-205 Morse Signature (20.5k ohms resistance), DP-108 Vintage Single Coil (6.0k), Proprietary Custom Wound (5.5k) and DP-200 Morse Signature (9.6k); Shadow MIDI synthesizer pickup

Accessories
Ernie Ball strings

Effects & Rack Gear
T.C. Electronic Booster, Ernie Ball volume pedals, Lexicon PCM 41 delay, Lexicon PCM 80 delay, Prime Time delay, Eventide 3000 Harmonizer, DigiTech GSP 21 multi-effects processor, Ensoniq ESQ 80 synthesizer module

Amps & Cabs
Numerous tube heads (Ampeg V-4, Peavey 5150 and VTM-120, Marshall Jubilee and 25/55, Carvin Steve Vai Legacy, Trace Elliot); miscellaneous Marshall, Carvin, and Peavey 4x12 cabinets (Peaveys with Black Widow and Scorpion speakers); Crate and Peavey combo amps; MESA/Boogie TriAxis preamp; Peavey power amp

"My tone with the Dixie Dregs is more midrangey than the tone I use with Deep Purple. When we got ready for Purple's *Abandon* album [1998], we tried different amps and sounds. I used 5150s, and that works better in conjunction with the tone of the organ because the organ has a lot of midrange in it, too. It leaves a little bit of a hole and we can balance the guitar and organ on different sides in the mix. They both have similar kinds of distortion, but they are different enough so that they work together now. But with the rig that I use with the Dregs and on my solo gigs, which is a Marshall Jubilee head, my sound is a little more focused with harder midrange. So the main thing I did with Purple was to change the amp.

"For the delays I have the Eventide Harmonizer, which I use as a delay, old Lexicon 41s, and I have DigiTech GSP 21 models where I can write my own presets and then change it to all wet and no dry. I also use Ernie Ball volume pedals to send the sound to a little passive mixer and that goes into the second amp, which is a Peavey VTM-120 tube amp. It doesn't have channel switching, so I couldn't use it as my main amp, but I use it as a tube slave and just plug into the effects return. That returns to three 4x12 cabinets with Black Widow speakers which give it a little more *oomph* but aren't as pretty sounding as the Scorpion speakers. The Black Widows also weigh a lot, but with Deep Purple, I finally have a guitar roadie, so it's the ultimate luxury. Most of the time, if I broke a string at a gig, I just stopped playing and changed the string really quick. Now I just kind of turn around and a fresh guitar magically appears. It's pretty decadent."

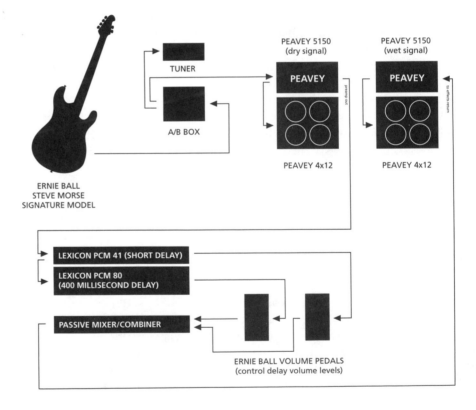

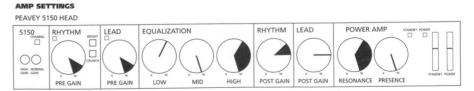

Early Rockers: Scotty Moore, Carl Perkins, Danny Cedrone

Scotty Moore (on right) with Elvis

Carl Perkins

Danny Cedrone

Born

Scotty Moore: January 8, 1935, in Tupelo, Mississippi

Carl Perkins: April 9,1932, in Ridgely, Tennessee

Danny Cedrone: June 20, 1920, in Jamesville, New York

Bands

Elvis Presley (Moore)
Carl Perkins (solo career)
Johnny Cash (Perkins)
Bill Haley & His Comets (Cedrone)

Tone

Fat and clean with a dash of reverb or slap echo

Signature Traits

Spankin' clean tones that brilliantly mix jazz, country, blues, and pop into something called *rock 'n' roll*

Breakthrough Performances

"That's Alright (Mama)" (Moore)
"Blue Suede Shoes" (Perkins)
"(We're Gonna) Rock Around the Clock" (Cedrone)

History and Influences

Although they might not be household names, Scotty Moore, Carl Perkins, and Danny Cedrone are crucial architects of early rock guitar. All three came from backgrounds where blues, jazz, boogie-woogie, pop, and country music was pervasive, and it was this kind of musical "melting pot" that gave rise to rock 'n' roll as well as its distinctly Southern offshoot, rockabilly.

While only Perkins was a known performer in his own right, Danny Cedrone is perhaps the leading

▶▶▶

Gear List

Guitars

Gibson ES-295, L-5, and Super 400C
(Moore)

Gibson Les Paul goldtop and ES-5
Switchmaster, Fender Telecaster
(Perkins)

1947 Gibson ES-300 (Cedrone)

Pickups

Stock

Accessories

Gretsch flatwound strings (Moore)

GHS light guage strings (.009 set)
(Perkins)

Effects

Slap echo

Amps

Ray Butts custom amplifiers (Moore
and Perkins)

Gretsch amp (Cedrone)

  Amp settings: Tone controls at 12
o'clock, treble at 1 (Moore)

Essential Listening

Scotty Moore

"That's Alright (Mama)"
"Let's Play House"
"Jailhouse Rock"

Carl Perkins

"Blue Suede Shoes"
"Honey Don't"
"Boppin' the Blues"
"Matchbox"

Danny Cedrone

"Rocket 88"
"Rock the Joint"
"(We're Gonna) Rock Around the Clock"
"Shake, Rattle & Roll"

contender among the three for the title "father of rock 'n' roll guitar." Based in Philadelphia, Cedrone began recording with Bill Haley in 1951, laying down "Rocket 88," a remake of the R&B hit from earlier that year by Ike Turner (this track is considered by some as the first rock 'n' roll single, although it's still very rooted in R&B). In 1952, he recorded "Rock the Joint" with Haley, important not only because it's a genuine piece of rock 'n' roll but also because Cedrone plays a solo identical to the one he would play two years later on "(We're Gonna) Rock Around the Clock." That initial recording is superior, too, allowing one to really savor Cedrone's fast single-string picking and wild bends.

In early 1954, Haley signed a deal with Decca Records, and on April 12th (about three months before Elvis Presley's epic Sun sessions), the band went to a studio called the Pythian Temple in Manhattan to record one of producer Milt Gabler's tunes, "Thirteen Women." Eventually that track was hammered out, and with studio time running out, Haley told Gabler that the Comets also could squeeze in another track, "(We're Gonna) Rock Around the Clock." The band cut two takes of the song which were eventually spliced into one master version. Although originally issued as the B-side to "Thirteen Women," the song took on a life of its own in the soundtrack to the movie *Blackboard Jungle* in 1955, a flick that helped usher in the rock era.

Tragically, it was Cedrone's last major recording session. On June 17, 1954, after a gig with his own group, the Esquire Boys, in Philadelphia, Cedrone returned home and was asked by his wife Millie to go get her a sandwich. When returning from the restaurant, Cedrone—a big man over six feet tall and weigh-

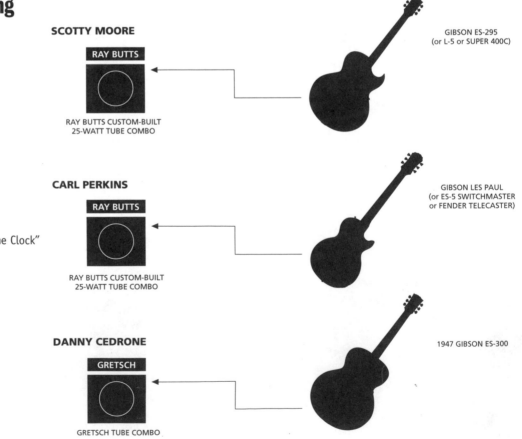

SCOTTY MOORE

RAY BUTTS

RAY BUTTS CUSTOM-BUILT
25-WATT TUBE COMBO

GIBSON ES-295
(or L-5 or SUPER 400C)

CARL PERKINS

RAY BUTTS

RAY BUTTS CUSTOM-BUILT
25-WATT TUBE COMBO

GIBSON LES PAUL
(or ES-5 SWITCHMASTER
or FENDER TELECASTER)

DANNY CEDRONE

GRETSCH

GRETSCH TUBE COMBO

1947 GIBSON ES-300

ing nearly 300 pounds—fell down a flight of stairs and broke his neck in two places. He died instantly. In one of the most profound tragedies in rock history, Cedrone would never know of the success of "Rock Around the Clock." To him, it was just another song cut for a local band led by Bill Haley.

Scotty Moore's story is just as memorable, as it's tied in with the greatest rocker of all time, Elvis Presley. Their early recordings together at Sun Studios in Memphis in July, 1954, are considered important blueprints for rock 'n' roll. During one session, Presley reputedly grabbed his guitar during a break and started singing a comedic version of Arthur Crudup's "That's All Right (Mama)." Moore and bassist Bill Black picked up their instruments and joined in. Soon Crudup's laidback blues tune was injected with wild R&B vocals, a snappy country groove, and Moore's feisty guitar licks. Producer Sam Phillips quickly told the three musicians to do it again, only this time with the tape rolling. Within a few minutes, rock history was made, launching both Elvis's career and the fledging sound of rockabilly, rock 'n' roll's Southern cousin.

On Elvis's early recordings from the Sun sessions and on later hits for RCA Records like "Jailhouse Rock" and "Hound Dog," Scotty Moore proved to be an excellent sideman. Moore blended multi-string licks and fingerstyle techniques from country guitar (heavily inspired by Chet Atkins and Merle Travis) with the string bends and soulful blues styles of T-Bone Walker and B.B. King, among others. He had also listened to post–Charlie Christian bebop guitarists Barney Kessel and Tal Farlow, and popster Les Paul. Again, this kind of melting-pot guitar work strongly contributed to the rock formula. Moore would go on to play guitar with Elvis until 1969.

Like Cedrone's, Carl Perkins's story is a mixture of talent and tragedy. Perkins followed in Elvis's wake at Sun Records after the King left to join RCA and find superstardom. In addition to being a fine singer and guitarist, Perkins was a strong songwriter and, in early 1956, he scored a huge hit with "Blue Suede Shoes." Besides having clever lyrics and a driving beat, "Blue Suede Shoes" also sported a red-hot guitar solo that remains a classic.

However, Perkins's success proved to be brief, as he was soon after involved in a serious car accident that required a very long recovery. By the time he was back on his feet, the public's attention had been diverted by the Elvis phenomenon and Perkins's glory days were largely over (in the 1960s he would tour as a sideman with Johnny Cash). Still, Carl Perkins was highly influential, especially on the Beatles, who covered his songs "Matchbox" and "Honey Don't."

Tone and Technique

To capture the sound of these early rock 'n' rollers, a few crucial tone tools need to be acquired. For guitars, you need to get either a vintage solidbody like a Telecaster or Les Paul (preferably with P-90 pickups), or a fat-body jazz archtop, which was a popular rock instrument right up to the early 1970s when solidbodies became the norm.

Next is a vintage-style tube amp, such as the models by Fender or Matchless without master volumes. All gain for an old-time rock tone should come by simply turning up the single volume knob on the amp and overdriving the tubes to create a little grit (this style of amp, which features a unique wiring scheme, is called Class A).

Now that you have a vintage-styled guitar and amp, the crowning piece to the puzzle is a bit of reverb and/or a little slap echo. Slap echo would be a setting of 50–125ms on your delay stompbox or digital processor, with no echo repeat (set the feedback or regeneration to 0). It's a very short delay that adds the chiming, metallic *thwack!* prevalent on many early Sun records.

Discography

Scotty Moore (all with Elvis Presley, on RCA)

The Sun Sessions (1954, reissued in 1976), *Elvis Presley* (1956), *Elvis* (1956), *Loving You* (1957), *Elvis' Christmas Album* (1957), *Elvis' Golden Records* (1958), *King Creole* (1958), *For LP Fans Only* (1959), *A Date with Elvis* (1959), *50,000,000 Elvis Fans Can't Be Wrong: Elvis' Golden Records, Vol. 2* (1960), *G.I. Blues* (1960), *Girls, Girls, Girls!* (1962), *Elvis' Golden Records, Vol. 3* (1963), *Elvis' Golden Records, Vol. 4* (1967), *Elvis—NBC TV Special* (1968), *Elvis, Scotty & Bill: The First Year* (Very Wonderful Golden Editions, 1979), *Elvis Aron Presley* (1980), *The Top Ten Hits* (1987)

Carl Perkins

Greatest Hits (Columbia, 1969), *On Top* (Columbia, 1969), *Boppin' the Blues* (Columbia, 1970), *Carl Perkins* (Harvard, 1970), *Original Golden Hits* (Sun), *Blue Suede Shoes* (Sun), *The Man Behind Johnny Cash* (Columbia, c.1970), *My Kind of Country* (Mercury), *The Rocking Guitar Man* (1975), *The Original Carl Perkins* (1976), *Sun Sound Special* (1978), *The Carl Perkins Dance Album* (1981), *The Sun Years* (Sun, 1982), *Born to Rock* (Universal, 1989), *706 Reunion* [with Scotty Moore] (Belle Meade, 1992)

Danny Cedrone

BILL HALEY & THE SADDLEMEN: "Rocket 88"/"Tearstains on My Heart" (Holiday, 1951), "I'm Crying" (Holiday, 1951), "Sundown Boogie" (Holiday, 1952), "Rock the Joint" (Essex, 1952), "Rockin' Chair on the Moon"/"Dance with a Dolly" (Essex, 1952)

BILL HALEY & HIS COMETS: "Real Rock Drive" (Transworld, 1953), "(We're Gonna) Rock Around the Clock"/"Thirteen Women" (Decca, 1954), "Shake, Rattle and Roll"/"A.B.C. Boogie" (Decca, 1954)

And that's all there is to it—a guitar, amp, cord, and a little echo, and you're ready for some authentic '50s rock guitar. And don't forget the hair grease, Daddy-O.

Scotty Moore: In His Own Words

"When I got out of the service in 1952, I got a Fender Esquire but just couldn't play it—my fingers couldn't get a hold of it. Then I saw that gold ES-295 and thought, 'Boy, that looks sharp,' so I bought it. I used that one on all the Sun stuff with Elvis. I bought it at a Memphis music store called O.K. Houck for about $250. It has those P-90 pickups. Later on, I traded it in on a Gibson L-5 after the platework on it started to tarnish. That was just prior to the point when we went to RCA. Eventually, I got myself a deal with Gibson and got a Super 400. Elvis was playing a Martin D-18 dreadnought, and later a D-28.

"In the studio, we were lucky if a place had one or two mics: one for Elvis and one for the bass. Gosh, if they had three or four, we were thrilled. At Sun, though, everything was miked up and running into a mixer. Of course, it was mono and you'd use leakage to your advantage by moving the mic or amp around. And for beating feedback, I learned to damp the strings and move to a better spot. I also used a piece of foam stuffed behind the bridge to help stop some of the overtones—still do.

"At the time, I had a custom-made amp by Ray Butts that had a built-in tape loop to get the slapback echo effects that Sam [Phillips, Sun owner/producer] used on the whole record. This was pretty rare for the time—and expensive, too: it cost about $495, which back then was a lot of money. In fact, Ray couldn't sell it to me on time, so I had to have Fame Music buy it and put it on installments for me. The first tune I used it for was 'Mystery Train.' I've still got it, too. It doesn't have reverb, just the echo.

"After we left Sun, I didn't use the echo much, but I used that amp for a lot of stage work. It's only a 25-watt amp, and when we started we had small crowds. But when they grew, we couldn't hear it anymore. So Ray built me two 50-watt boosters. Each one had four 8" JBL speakers and I could turn those things wide open, placing them on each end of the stage. My little amp then became sort of like a preamp. At 125 watts total, it was probably the first high-power stage setup. And we *still* couldn't hear it because of all the girls screaming!"

James Hetfield & Kirk Hammett of Metallica

James Hetfield

Kirk Hammett

Born
James Hetfield: August 3, 1963, in Downey, California

Kirk Hammett: November 18, 1962, in San Francisco, California

Bands
Exodus (Hammett)
Obsession, Phantom Lord, Leather Charm (Hetfield)
Metallica

Tone
Dark, crunchy, chunky, and heavily overdriven with scooped mids

Signature Traits
Hetfield hammers out the tight, intricate rhythm guitar patterns, while Hammett serves up the solos. Hetfield's rhythm work is aggressive but precise. Hammett's solos often incorporate staccato picking, edgy legato runs, Hendrix-inspired blues riffs, and wah-wah work.

Breakthrough Performance
"Hit the Lights" from *Metal Massacre, Vol. 1* (1982)

History and Influences
Metallica emerged in the early '80s, an age when Spandex, hair bands, and glam metal were at their peak. The group was born in 1981 in Los Angeles when guitarist James Hetfield met drummer Lars Ulrich through an ad in a local music paper. Hetfield had grown up listening to '70s hard rock bands like Led Zeppelin, Black Sabbath, Thin Lizzy, and Aerosmith. Danish-born Ulrich turned him on to the heavier sounds of groups referred to as the New

▶▶▶

Gear List
Kirk Hammett

Guitars

ESP Kirk Hammett KH-2, KH-3, M-II models; Gibson Flying Vs, Explorers, Les Paul Custom and various Les Paul models, Super 400, ES-295; Jackson Randy Rhoads, Roswell Rhoads, Soloist; various Fender Stratocasters; Fernandes Strat-style; Parker Fly Deluxe; Danelectro U2

Pickups

EMG-81 (neck and bridge)

Accessories

Dunlop Tortex .88mm picks, Dean Markley strings (.010–.046), brass slides, Floyd Rose tremolo bridge

Effects & Rack Gear

Juice Goose Ground Loop Control 320, custom-built rackmount EMB Adjustable Remote Wah-Wah, Crybaby wah, Vox wah, Ernie Ball volume pedal, Ibanez Tube Screamer, Eventide H3000 SE Harmonizer, BOSS SE-50 Stereo Effects Processor, T.C. Electronic M2000 multi-effects, Rocktron/ Bradshaw RSB-18 Rack Switching System and pedalboard; Roland VG-8 Virtual Guitar Modeling System, Sony wireless system, Aphex Parametric EQ, Custom Audio Electronics 4x4 Switcher, MESA/Boogie High Gain Amp Switcher

Amps & Cabs

MESA/Boogie TriAxis preamp, Dual Rectifier and Mark IV heads, Strategy 400 Stereo Power Amps, Marshall JMP-1 preamp; ADA MP-1 preamp; Custom Audio Electronics preamp; MESA/Boogie 4x12 cabinets; Marshall 2x12 cabinets; Matchless Chieftain; Little Lanilei practice amp

Wave of British Heavy Metal (NWOBHM), which included Judas Priest, Iron Maiden, Diamond Head, Venom, Saxon, and Motörhead. The two started jamming on cover songs but strived to play their own music and create a similarly aggressive sound—which was a direct contrast with the metal bands on the L.A. scene. To complete the group, bassist Ron McGovney and lead guitarist Dave Mustaine were later added.

Metallica's first recording, "Hit the Lights" (which featured Hetfield on vocals, rhythm guitar, and bass, Mustaine on lead guitar, and Lloyd Grant adding the second guitar solo), was released in 1982 on a heavy-metal compilation by Metal Blade Records called *Metal Massacre, Vol. 1* (a 1991 reissue of the album includes a different version of the track, with McGovney on bass and without Grant's solo). The track was by far the best on the album and helped to spark interest in the group.

The group's second demo tape, *No Life 'Til Leather*, was heavily circulated by tape traders throughout the U.S. and Europe, broadening interest in the band. Although the demo versions of future Metallica classics were slightly different from the later album versions, many rockers had never heard music so heavy, fast, and furious with complex breaks and several varying themes within a song. This was the beginning of a new branch of metal that was first called speed metal, then "thrash metal" when the rage and intensity hit the next level.

By March 1983, McGovney had been replaced by bassist Cliff Burton of the San Francisco group Trauma. In the deal to recruit Burton, the group agreed to relocate to San Francisco. With a strong buzz building, Metallica secured a deal with Megaforce Records and headed to New York to cut tracks. Shortly following the group's arrival in New York, and before the recording had begun, Mustaine was kicked out and sent back to the West Coast. He was immediately replaced by San Francisco native Kirk Hammett, a friend of Burton's. At the time, Hammett was a member of Bay Area metal group Exodus and a student of Joe Satriani.

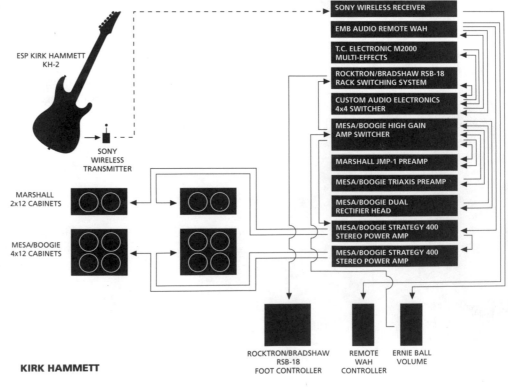

KIRK HAMMETT

With Burton's influence on the writing, the material was becoming heavier and more complex. *Ride the Lightning,* released the following year, featured the classics "For Whom the Bell Tolls," "Creeping Death," and the ballad "Fade to Black." In 1986, Metallica released *Master of Puppets,* which many consider to be the band's finest work—and perhaps the single most important disc to shape the sound and style of thrash metal. The opening two annihilating tracks, "Battery" and "Master of Puppets," show the group was getting into more complex rhythm patterns, and the instrumental, "Orion," demonstrates a variety of diverse themes and intricate melodies.

Just as Metallica's career was really taking off, it received a devastating blow. On September 27, 1986, while on tour in Sweden promoting the *Master of Puppets* release, the group's bus was involved in an accident. Bassist Cliff Burton was killed. Eventually, Flotsam & Jetsam bassist Jason Newsted was enlisted and the group carried on. For its first outing with Newsted, Metallica recorded a collection of cover tunes by Budgie, Diamond Head, the Misfits, Holocaust, and Killing Joke. The disc, released in 1987 as *The $5.98 E.P./Garage Days Re-Revisited,* was quickly snatched up by fans and praised by critics.

After taking time to initiate Newsted, the band rebounded with the powerful *…And Justice for All.* Despite the album's notably poor sound quality (the bass was lost in the mix), the disc featured several crushing tracks like "Blackened," "Shortest Straw," and "One," which was nominated for a Grammy in 1989. Ironically, the group performed the song live on the show, but lost the award for Best Metal Performance to Jethro Tull.

With the help of producer Bob Rock, the group revised its sound and style in 1991, shifting gears toward the mainstream. The resulting self-titled disc (known widely as "The Black Album" for its Spinal Tap–like all-black cover) included shorter, radio-friendly songs that had few extended instrumental breaks and featured

Gear List
James Hetfield

Guitars
ESP James Hetfield JH-1, JH-2, JH-3 models, custom-built Explorer-style models, 6/12 Explorer-style double-neck; Gibson Explorer and Flying V, various new and vintage Les Paul models, SG; Fender '52 Reissue Tele with Parsons-White B-Bender; Gretsch White Falcon; Jerry Jones 6-string bass; National Resolectric, Martin D-28, Fender Shenandoah 12-string

Pickups
EMG-60 neck and EMG-81 bridge

Accessories
Dunlop Tortex .88mm picks, Ernie Ball strings (.010–.046)

Effects & Rack Gear
EBow, BOSS SE-50 Stereo Effects Processor, Juice Goose Rack Power 300, Bradshaw RSB-12 Rack Switching System and pedalboard, Sony wireless system, Aphex Parametric EQ, Custom Audio Electronics 4x4 Switcher, MESA/Boogie High Gain Amp Switcher

Amps & Cabs
MESA/Boogie Dual and Triple Rectifier Solo heads, Mark IV head, TriAxis pre-amps, Strategy 400 Stereo Power Amps, MESA/Boogie 4x12 cabinets; Marshall 4x12 cabinets loaded with Celestion Vintage 30 speakers; Roland JC-120, Blues Cube; Magnavox 2x12 combo

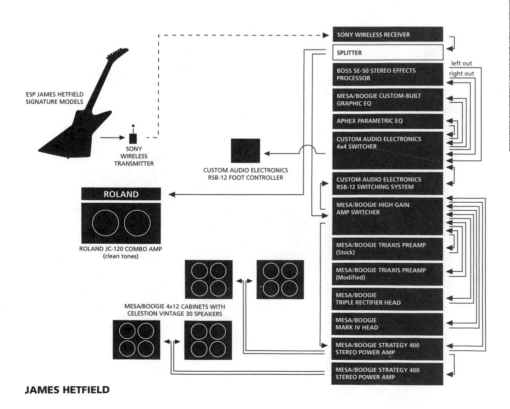

JAMES HETFIELD

Essential Listening

"Hit the Lights"
"Battery"
"One"
"Sad but True"
"Nothing Else Matters"

Discography

No Life 'Til Leather (demo, 1981), "Hit The Lights" [from *Metal Massacre, Vol. 1*] (Metal Blade, 1982), *Kill 'Em All* (Elektra, 1983), *Ride the Lightning* (Elektra, 1984), *Creeping Death 12"/Garage Days Revisited* ["Am I Evil"/"Blitzkrieg"] (Elektra, 1984), *Whiplash* [EP] (Megaforce, 1985), *Master of Puppets* (Elektra, 1986), *The $5.98 E.P./Garage Days Re-Revisited* (Elektra, 1987), *...And Justice for All* (Elektra, 1988), *Metallica* (Elektra, 1991), *Live Shit: Binge and Purge* (Elektra, 1993), *Load* (Elektra, 1996), *Reload* (Elektra, 1997), "For Whom the Bell Tolls" [with DJ Spooky, *Spawn* soundtrack] (Sony, 1997), *Garage Inc.* (Elektra, 1998), *S&M* [live] (Elektra, 1999), "I Disappear" [*Mission Impossible 2* soundtrack] (Hollywood, 2000), *St. Anger* (Elektra, 2003)

more actual singing in place of Hetfield's trademark growl. Furthermore, Hammett and Hetfield were loosening up and breaking their own rules. They let go of the pulverizing scooped tone and experimented with a wider spectrum of tonal textures, bringing in an array of decidedly un-metal vintage instruments and amplifiers (many from Rock's collection), as well as mixing in some country and Southern rock elements.

Metallica returned in 1996 with a radical image change, sporting short haircuts and a more polished, less thrashy sound. Still sporting rock-infused production, the new album, *Load,* quickly reached #1. The recipe proved commercially successful, and was repeated the following year with *Reload,* which put Metallica right back at the top of the charts. In 1998, the group released *Garage Inc.,* a double disc of rare material, B-sides, and newly released covers.

Shifting gears once again in 1999, Metallica took a new approach by collaborating with conductor Michael Kaman, who arranged a selection of Metallica songs for the band and a full orchestra. The material was performed live with the San Francisco Symphony and recorded for *S&M* (Symphony and Metallica).

Metallica spent much of 2000 involved in a controversial copyright infringement lawsuit with the file-sharing service Napster. Still, the group scored a noteworthy hit on radio and MTV with the muscular single "I Disappear" from the *Mission Impossible 2* movie soundtrack. In January 2001, Newsted exited, moving on to pursue his own solo ventures with his own studio and record label.

Tone and Technique

As one of the first bands of the thrash genre, and the first to break into the mainstream, Metallica set the standards that future generations of metal bands would follow. The Metallica sound and style evolved as a natural progression of previous generations of hard rock, building on the dark, heavy tone of early '70s bands like Black Sabbath and Led Zeppelin, mixed with the edgy, aggressive sound and dueling guitars of late '70s/early '80s NWOBHM groups like Judas Priest, Iron Maiden, and Diamond Head, scrambled with the punk attitude of groups like Motörhead and the Misfits. Metallica built on this framework to develop music even harder, faster, and heavier.

An integral part of the Metallica rhythm guitar style is a precise downstroke. To achieve the distinct chugging rhythm that drives the music, Hetfield and Hammett use steady downstrokes played close to the bridge, with the side of the palm resting on the bridge and slightly muting the strings. This muting or "damping" technique is what creates the percussive rhythm. Working with a metronome or drum machine will help immensely to perfect your timing. Strive for a steady, even attack to keep the rhythm flowing consistently. Start slowly, and gradually build up your stamina to master the rapid-fire rhythms. Practice patterns incorporating the mandatory E, A, and F♯ power chords, first just using straight downstrokes, then throwing in the occasional upstrokes to sculpt rhythmic patterns. Precision and consistency are essential. Practicing with a distortion pedal will give you the right tone, which can help to make the work seem less tedious.

Hetfield and Hammett have always held clearly separate roles in Metallica as rhythm guitarist and lead guitarist. Hetfield is also responsible for a great deal of the songwriting, so when the band is in the studio to track, Hetfield handles all of the primary guitar work, then Hammett comes in to lay down the solos. In the earlier days, the thick sounds were built on multiple tracks that doubled parts using the same rig. However, when the group started working with producer Bob Rock, the formula changed and both Hetfield and Hammett began to incorporate numerous instruments, amps, and stompboxes on overdubs. Now bigger sounds are built by layering tracks using a variety of equipment to attain broader, multi-textured tones. However, when it comes to playing live, both still rely on their principal rigs.

To cop Hetfield's bludgeoning rhythm tone, grab your most powerful humbucker-loaded solidbody, preferably one without a tremolo. Hetfield's guitars are equipped with EMG-81 (bridge) and EMG-60 (neck) pickups, and he favors a MESA/Boogie Dual Rectifier head. Of course, other high-gain amps and guitars with different pickups can be used, too, but it's always good to have a guideline to know how the sound originated.

For the tight rhythm crunch, plug into the dirty channel of a high-gain tube amp and set the EQ for a scooped tone, with the mids pulled out. If your amp has an onboard graphic EQ, like the Boogie does, create a V-shaped curve with the mid frequencies at the bottom of the V. You can also use a graphic EQ pedal to achieve the same results. Set the amp's tone controls with bass on 10, middle 0–2, treble 8–10, gain 8–10, and master volume 3–4. Hetfield takes a basic guitar-and-amp approach, shaping his tone by using the EQ and allowing Hammett to handle the wilder effects.

Hammett's basic rhythm tone is very similar to Hetfield's, but inserts more midrange (set amp's mids around 4–5) to add girth to single-note riffs. He incorporates a selection of effects, including a wah pedal, which is often used for sweeping filtered effects, a harmonizer, and an overdrive pedal for boosted volume and added sustain on leads. Hammett generally uses an Ibanez Tube Screamer, but a similar overdrive box like a Boss Super Overdrive or Danelectro Daddy-O will also work well.

James Hetfield & Kirk Hammett: In Their Own Words

"It's dry as a bone!" Hetfield told *Guitar Player* magazine regarding Metallica's self-titled 1991 album. "Our second album, *Ride the Lightning,* always sounded thicker than the others—it had reverb, which we became afraid of using later on. We wanted the attack of the *Garage Days* EP, which was recorded live, but with the thickness of *Lightning.* And when I listen to *Justice,* I think, 'Fuck, man—this is really long and drawn out.'

"I used to double all the vocals line by line, vowel by vowel, so perfect," Hetfield recalls. "This time, we just did single passes. You can hear more personality, and I didn't have to play it safe knowing I'd have to double it. Same with the guitar stuff: There are layers and overdubs, but it's textured stuff, different sounds—not the Explorer through the MESA/Boogie doubling the same part 10 times. That made it thick but mushed things up. It's rawer this way.

"Our original sound was very raw," Hammett adds. "I wouldn't say we're tamed or watered down, but we've progressed into other forms. We've had so much aggression to start with that even though some has leaked out over the years, there's still a lot there."

Carlos Santana

Born
July 20, 1947, in Autlan, Mexico

Bands
Santana
Carlos Santana (solo career)

Tone
Super-fat neck pickup tone spiced up with trebly wah-wah breaks

Signature Traits
"The cry," a term coined for his emotional, sometimes long-sustained string bends

Breakthrough Performance
"Soul Sacrifice" from *Woodstock* (1970)

History and Influences

Few would question Eric Clapton's assertion that Santana is "Soul Man #1" when it comes to rock guitar. For 30 years now, Carlos has earned his keep by squeezing out the most soulful notes on the planet night after night. Inspired by players like B.B. King, Wes Montgomery, Peter Green, Gabor Szabo, and Jimi Hendrix (as well as non-guitarists like John Coltrane and Miles Davis), Santana's eclectic style encompasses everything from his patented Latin rock to blues, jazz, pop, R&B, and fusion.

Santana burst onto the scene at Woodstock in 1969 and scored some of the first platinum albums in rock history with *Santana* (1969) and *Abraxas* (1970). On the strength of early hits like "Oye Como Va" (penned by Tito Puente) and a cover of Fleetwood Mac's "Black Magic Woman," Santana became a popular concert draw in the 1970s. In 1971, 17-year-old guitar whiz Neal Schon (later of Journey) was added to the fold and, in 1973, Carlos recorded the popular *Love Devotion Surrender* with fusion star John McLaughlin. In 1977, Santana issued the classic part-studio/part-live set *Moonflower*, which perfectly captured the guitarist's glorious tone and remains a high point in the band's catalog.

During the 1980s and '90s, Santana continued to tour, but his record sales were not what they had been during his post-Woodstock heyday. In 1999, however, he teamed up with producer/record mogul Clive Davis to cut *Supernatural*, an all-star CD featuring artists like Lauryn Hill, Eric Clapton, and Dave Matthews. This album turned into a monster hit, thanks especially to the catchy single "Smooth" featuring Matchbox 20 singer Rob Thomas. Thirty years after Woodstock, Santana was again the biggest band of the land and surely one of the most sensational comeback stories in rock history.

Tone and Technique

Although he's grabbed a Strat from time to time, Carlos Santana has always gravitated towards humbucker-loaded guitars: first Gibson's SG, Les Paul, and L5-S models; Yamaha SG-2000 axes later in the '70s; and Paul Reed Smith electrics since 1982. Today, he plays on one of several PRS Carlos Santana models, all based on the original guitar built for him by the guitarmaker.

Carlos's current favorite PRS is dubbed "Number 1." This gold-stained guitar is a replica of the original PRS that Paul built for him *lo* these many years ago, but it differs from the production Santana in a few ways. It has no tone control and a single volume control, while mini toggle switches control the neck and bridge pickups. The peghead and wooden truss rod cover boast custom mother-of-pearl inlays (the bird motif is common to all PRS Customs).

Identical copies of this guitar were built for Carlos, including a turquoise model with a PRS tremolo and separate volume and tone controls. Each guitar has mini toggle switches to activate the pickups or turn them off. For the occasional acoustic parts he plays onstage, Carlos also uses an Alvarez-Yairi Electric Classic nylon-string.

His amp journey started with ancient Fender Twins and Gallien-Krueger amps. But then Carlos hooked up with yet another "Smith"—this one amp guru Randy Smith—and the result has been a 20-plus-year association with MESA/Boogie amplifiers. With Boogies on the backline and a PRS in his hands, Carlos has codified a sound that has become synonymous with soulful rock guitar.

The essence of Santana's tone can be recreated with the combination of humbucking pickups and a tube amplifier. If you already have a good solidbody electric—preferably with a maple body and maple top (like a PRS or Les Paul)—you need to find a good amp, preferably a tube model. Carlos gravitates towards a warm, creamy amp sound that really accentuates the neck-humbucker pickup setting he often uses. MESA/Boogie amps are renowned for their multi-stage preamps that create a "saturated" type of gain, that is, super rich and full of sustain

Gear List

Guitars
Paul Reed Smith 24.5"-scale Carlos Santana models; Alvarez-Yairi Electric Classic nylon-string; 1982 PRS Santana prototype; Yamaha SG-2000; Gibson Les Paul, SG Special, Explorer, L5-S; '57 Fender Strat

Pickups
PRS Dragon humbucker (bridge), Santana model humbucker (neck)

Accessories
D'Addario nickel strings (.010–.042), GHS La Classique super-high tension strings

Effects & Rack Gear
Mu-Tron wah-wah, Ibanez Tube Screamer overdrive

Amps & Cabs
Mid-'70s Dumble OD-100WR Overdrive Reverb; MESA/Boogie combo loaded with single 12" Altec speaker, Mark I; MESA/Boogie Mark IV, Heartbreaker heads, SimulClass 2:90 power amp, MESA/Boogie 1x12 (with Altec 12" speaker), 4x12 cabinets and Revolver rotating speakers; '70s Marshall 100-watt head and 4x12 cab; '65 blackface Fender Twin

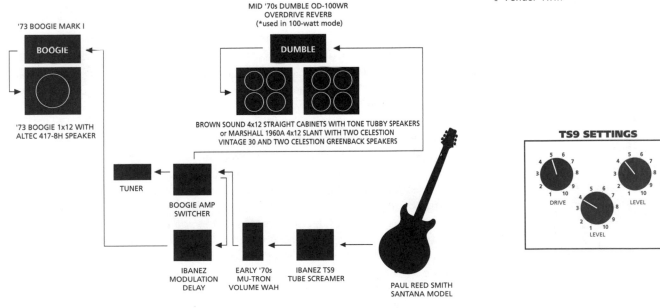

'73 BOOGIE MARK I

BOOGIE

'73 BOOGIE 1x12 WITH ALTEC 417-8H SPEAKER

MID '70s DUMBLE OD-100WR OVERDRIVE REVERB (*used in 100-watt mode)

DUMBLE

BROWN SOUND 4x12 STRAIGHT CABINETS WITH TONE TUBBY SPEAKERS or MARSHALL 1960A 4x12 SLANT WITH TWO CELESTION VINTAGE 30 AND TWO CELESTION GREENBACK SPEAKERS

TUNER

BOOGIE AMP SWITCHER

IBANEZ MODULATION DELAY

EARLY '70s MU-TRON VOLUME WAH

IBANEZ TS9 TUBE SCREAMER

PAUL REED SMITH SANTANA MODEL

TS9 SETTINGS

DRIVE   LEVEL

LEVEL

and harmonics. This might sound like the formula for a heavy-metal guitarist's tone, but within the context of Santana's music the result is light and elegant. Today, there are many amp manufacturers that create high-gain amps of this type—Rivera, Soldano, Marshall, and so on.

Santana's original Boogies were 1x12 combos, but today he employs several 4x12 stacks onstage for maximum impact. Experiment to see what sounds best to you, but the formula for the most bottom end is simple: the bigger the cabinet, the better the tone.

Live Rig

Carlos's live setup is elegantly simple. His MESA/Boogie amp rack contains two Mark I heads and a Mark IV head. The top Mark I is for the quintessential Santana lead tone—think "Europa" or "Samba Pa Ti." The one underneath is its backup. The Mark IV on the bottom is used for special guests who come onstage to jam or, occasionally, for clean guitar parts.

On the right is the "Heartbreaker rack." On top is an Alesis QuadraVerb II. Carlos uses a program called Ambient Chorus, to which he adds 510ms delay to beef up the "Marshall sound" he uses for power chords. This Marshall-type sound—a big, fat rock tone with plenty of bottom end—is delivered by a Heartbreaker head. If Santana is going through the Mark I and decides to pump it up, he can turn on the Heartbreaker head, combining the two for an even fatter tone.

A second Heartbreaker underneath is used for clean tones. Each of the Heartbreakers drives a 4x12. There's a slave signal from the clean Heartbreaker that also goes into the Boogie SimulClass 2:90 power amp located under the QuadraVerb. This power amp goes out to power the two Revolvers, which are MESA/Boogie's answer to a Leslie rotating speaker cabinet. These are always on for clean parts.

His cabinets include a Boogie with 1x12 Altec speaker (main lead tone from the Mark I head), a Boogie 4x12 (powered by top Heartbreaker head for "Marshall sound"), a Revolver rotating-speaker cabinet, another Boogie 4x12 (bottom Heartbreaker for clean), and a Fender Twin to run an old Echoplex for spacey effects, often used at the end of "Exodus." It also serves as a last-resort backup amp, or if he simply decides he wants to play with a little Twin sound.

On his pedalboard, Carlos has an amp switcher which can turn any amp on or off, both independently and in combination. Next is the QuadraVerb bypass pedal (marked "Echo Bypass"), followed by an Ibanez Modulation Delay pedal labeled "Boogie Echo" (this is in Boogie Mark I's signal path). On the far right of the board is a Mu-Tron wah-wah from the early 1970s.

Carlos Santana: In His Own Words

In August, 1999—exactly 30 years after Woodstock—Carlos talked to *Guitar Player* magazine about the recording of the smash CD *Supernatural*:

"I used Marshalls, Boogies, and Twins for the album. I went through my six Marshalls and got rid of the amps that weren't consistent. Some you plug in and it's glorious; some you have to babysit and change diapers and change tubes. I found the ones that are happening in the studio or a coliseum or anywhere, and I kept those. We mark them, 'These speakers go with this head.' That way, you're not shooting in the dark. You know exactly what you're going for when you're recording.

"I bring my amps and microphones to every studio, because I found out that when you position certain microphones in a certain way, the room doesn't matter after a while. I have one microphone placed at the amplifier and another one positioned farther back so you can hear the ghost sound. You can't get that with knobs. They just give you an emulation.

"I'm also very honored to have worked with [guitar tech] René Martinez, who worked with Stevie Ray Vaughan. René can play the hell out of the Segovia [nylon-string] guitar. I should be *his* roadie! He told me everything that Stevie Ray went through to get his tone on tape: amps all over the place—in the kitchen, bathroom, halls, and everything. Everybody has to find out what works for them.

"As for guitars, I still use the PRS, although with Eric [Clapton, on the track "The Calling"] we both played Strats because I wanted to keep it even. It's such a pretty tone. Because of René, I finally played through a[n Ibanez] Tube Screamer. In the past I always said, 'I'll never use those things because I want to sound like me.' I would just mark the floor in the places where my guitar sustains. When I'm onstage, there are marks for this song, marks for that song.

"Anyway, at first I told René that I didn't want to play a Strat, because to make it sustain I'd have to play so loud that I didn't know if I could have babies! So he goes, 'You don't have to play that loud. Try this Tube Screamer.' So we plug it in and—*bam*—it sustains right through a Twin or a Marshall. You can still talk, but you're sustaining furiously. I said, 'Oh, I shouldn't have been so bullheaded. I'm so stubborn.' And he says, 'You didn't know. Stevie used pedals to sustain.' I went, 'No kidding? I thought he was just loud.'

"It has been a real education working with René. In fact, the entire process of making this album is new to me. Even though I've been recording since '67, all of a sudden I'm thrown into a whole new way of doing things. I really like it—it's fresh and very challenging."

Dubbed priceless by collectors, this vintage amp is one of the most important amplifiers in the world. At Carlos Santana's behest some 20 years ago, Boogie founder Randall Smith took a small Fender Vibro-Champ practice amp, stripped its insides, and installed the souped-up circuitry from a larger 60-watt Fender Bassman 4x10. He then added an extra "master volume" circuit that would drive the tube preamp section into natural distortion. The usual volume knob controls the level of sound coming out of the amp. Middle and Presence knobs sculpt the tone. The sound is then squeezed through a single 12" JBL speaker. This greatly helped shape the unique tone that Santana is known for, and became the blueprint for future MESA/Boogie amplifiers.

Eddie Van Halen

Born
January 26, 1955, in Nijmegen, Holland

Bands
Mammoth
Van Halen

Tone
Originator of the "brown" sound—the raw yet warm tone of an overdriven British-style tube amp cranked to the max

Signature Traits
Tapping, hammer-ons and pull-offs, tapped harmonics, tremolo divebombs, toggle flicking, scorching solos, rapid-fire three-note arpeggiated runs

Breakthrough Performance
"Eruption" from *Van Halen* (1978)

History and Influences

The sons of a Dutch bandleader, brothers Edward and Alex Van Halen relocated from the Netherlands to the United States in 1967, settling in Pasadena, California. As children, both studied classical piano, then were turned on to rock and roll by bands like the Beatles and the Dave Clark Five. In their teens, Alex took up guitar and Edward started to learn drums. The two would trade off, but later switched instruments permanently once older brother Alex had become more proficient on drums. Now focusing on guitar, Edward was listening to blues-oriented rock players like Eric Clapton, Jimmy Page, Jeff Beck, and Leslie West. Later, he was greatly inspired by the technical work of Allan Holdsworth.

In the early '70s, the Van Halen brothers formed a band they called Mammoth and began playing shows around Pasadena, rounding out the lineup with flamboyant frontman David Lee Roth and bassist Michael Anthony. In 1974, the group changed its name to Van Halen and soon became the area's leading live act, performing a combination of covers and original material. Three years later, the group cut a demo financed by Kiss's Gene Simmons that scored them a deal with Warner Bros. Records. Following the release of the group's debut album in 1978, Edward began receiving worldwide praise for his stunning technique. He was immediately touted as the most innovative rock guitar player to emerge since Jimi Hendrix.

Van Halen's popularity grew steadily with each album, as did admiration for Eddie's incredible technique. While demonstrating dizzying skills on most every track, EVH completely blew listeners away with the trademark two-handed tapping techniques heard in bold relief on solo spotlights like "Eruption" and "Spanish Fly."

With the release of *1984*, their sixth album, Van Halen was at its best both musically and commercially. However, Roth's antics and the commencement of his solo career created tension in the group, which ultimately led to his dismissal in 1985. Singer/guitarist Sammy Hagar, who sang for Montrose and had a solo career, debuted as Van Halen's frontman on *5150* the following year. With Hagar, the group had a more pop-like sound—to the dissatisfaction of many longtime fans—and achieved even greater commercial success. Van Halen released five more albums with Hagar before his departure amid group tensions in 1996.

Faced with another lineup change, the group flirted with a possible Roth reunion and recorded two new tracks with him for the greatest-hits collection *Best Of Volume I*. However, Roth was never officially asked to rejoin the lineup. Former Extreme frontman Gary Cherone was hired for *Van Halen III*, released in 1998. Aimless and unfocused, the disc saw disappointing sales, as did the supporting tour. Less than two years later, Cherone made his exit. Currently without a frontman or a record label, Van Halen is officially on hiatus.

Tone and Technique

Edward Van Halen is completely self-taught on guitar, which may help explain how he devised such an unorthodox approach. Although he did listen to other guitarists, like his hero Eric Clapton, he never sounded like any of them. Even his picking technique is somewhat unconventional. He typically grasps a pick one of two ways: between his thumb and middle finger or between his thumb, index, and middle fingers. When tapping harmonics, he tucks the pick in between the joints of his middle finger—a trick that he picked up from watching Hendrix on film.

Throughout his career, Van Halen has played a variety of guitars. His very first electric was a Teisco Del Rey and, in his early club days, he was playing various Gibson guitars, including Les Pauls (a modded 1952 goldtop and a '55 Junior) and a Flying V. He also had a '59 Stratocaster that was used briefly, before he started building his own instruments.

The guitar that became Van Halen's main axe was a homemade Strat copy assembled from parts he had purchased from Charvel (in some interviews he has also said these parts came from Boogie Body in Seattle). The body was made of ash and it had an old Gibson PAF humbucker in the bridge position that had been swiped from a '61 ES-335. The neck was maple—his favorite wood for necks—which he left unlacquered. Van Halen fretted the neck himself using larger Gibson wire, and he installed a set of Schaller tuners. The custom finish was applied with Schwinn bicycle paint, and he added the stripes using tape.

Other early guitars included an Ibanez Destroyer, heard on "You Really Got Me" and non-tremolo guitar parts from the first album. He later customized the Ibanez by cutting a V into the back of the body with a chainsaw, rewiring it, and repainting the finish with his signature stripes. Van Halen is shown posing with this guitar on the cover of *Women and Children First*.

As his main workhorse, the homemade Strat sometimes known as "Frankenstein" has gone through many transformations over the years with different finishes and parts. The guitar was originally black, then refinished white (as seen on the cover of *Van Halen*) and later red. The original bridge was replaced with a Floyd Rose tremolo bridge and locking nut, then updated again when Floyd added fine tuners. When the frets wore down, Van

▼ Gear List

Guitars

Various homemade guitars (including his original "Frankenstein" Strat-style solidbody); Kramer Baretta, Ripley, and Ferrington models; star-shaped Charvel with Danelectro neck, Charvel Strat-style; Boogie Strat-style; Ibanez Destroyer; Ernie Ball/Music Man EVH Signature; Peavey EVH Wolfgang and Wolfgang Special; Steinberger L-Series GL2T with TransTrem and EMG pickups; Fender Strato-casters; Gibson Les Pauls (1958 and 1959 Standards, Custom with tremolo, '55 Junior, '52 goldtop), 1958 Flying V, ES-335, EDS-1275 doublenecks; Petschulat mini Les Paul replica; Mighty Mite Megazone; assorted Danelectro guitars; Roger Giffin 12-string electric; Coral electric sitar, Musser acoustic, Ovation nylon-string

Pickups

Various humbuckers, including early Gibson PAF, Seymour Duncan, DiMarzio, EMG, Peavey EVH

Accessories

EVH D-Tuna (bridge attachment), Floyd Rose tremolos, Fernandes Sustainer, Custom Audio Electronics Amp Selector/Router and Foot Controller, George L's cables, Peavey light strings (.009–.042), medium picks

Effects & Rack Gear

Dunlop Crybaby wah pedal, MXR Phase 90 Phaser, MXR Flanger, MXR Dyna Comp, Eventide H3000 Harmonizer, Roland SDE-3000 Digital Delay, Lexicon PCM 70 Reverb, Palmer Speaker Simulator, Rockman Smart Gate noise gate, Univox EC-80 Echo box, Echoplex, DigiTech Whammy pedal, BOSS SD-1 Super Overdrive, BOSS OC-2 Octave

Amps & Cabs

Peavey 5150 and 5150 Mark II heads, Peavey 5150 straight 4x12 cabinets loaded with Celestion G12T 75-watt speakers, Marshall 100-watt Super Lead (various models from late '60s to present), Marshall 4x12 cabinets, Soldano SLO-100 Super Lead Overdrive, Laney heads, Music Man heads, H&H V800 power amps

Amp settings: On his old Marshalls, Van Halen had all tone and volume controls cranked to 10 and used a Variac to regulate the amp's power and bring the voltage down to approximately 89–90 volts. (*Author's note: This is not a recommended procedure.*)

Halen would swap necks and leave the fretwork for a more convenient time. In the early days, he did all of his own guitar repair, including fretwork. In addition to using Charvel replacement necks, some of the others he favored were made by Boogie Body.

In the early '80s, Van Halen hooked up with the Kramer guitar company, becoming the company's top endorser. He was frequently seen in guitar ads with Kramer's Baretta and Ferrington models, which he played onstage through the late '80s. By the mid-'80s, being the premier tremolo master of the day, Van Halen took a liking to Steinberger's transposable TransTrem and added several EMG-equipped L-Series GL2T models to his arsenal. Of course, they were painted up with his trademark stripes. The Steinberger can be heard on "Summer Nights" from *5150* and "Me Wise Magic" on *Best Of Volume I*.

In 1987 Van Halen teamed with Ernie Ball/Music Man to develop the first true EVH signature guitar. Made of basswood with a maple top, the Ernie Ball remained his main axe until 1995. After a falling out with the company, he secured a deal with Peavey and devel-

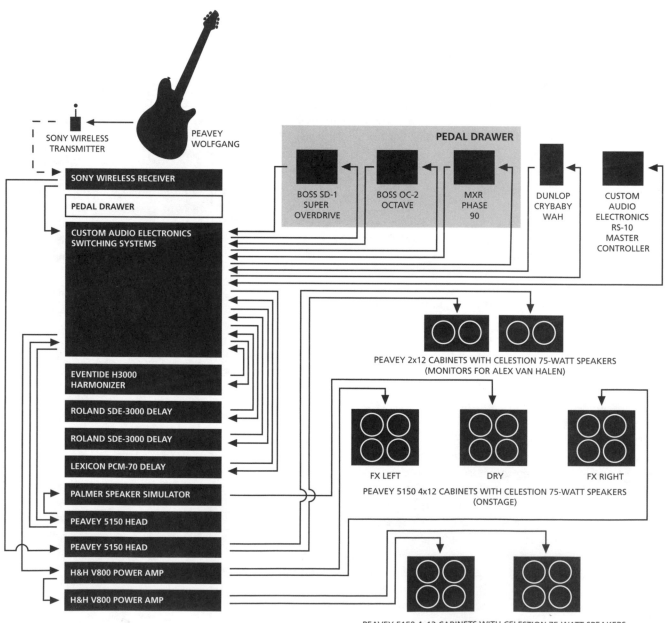

oped a new EVH guitar which he called the Wolfgang, named after his son. Van Halen had also helped to develop a device called the D-Tuna, a stock feature on the Wolfgang which fits onto the Floyd Rose tremolo bridge and drops the tuning of the sixth string from standard pitch to dropped-*D*.

Van Halen's legendary "brown sound" was derived from his favorite late-'60s Marshall Super Lead Plexi, a 100-watter he purchased as a teen. The legendary amp had been the house amplifier at the Pasadena Rose Palace. Over the years, he used many other early Super Leads, but this particular Marshall head was always his favorite. Though Van Halen often told interviewers that his amps had been souped up with various modifications, the truth was that he never did anything to them aside from driving them really hard and frequently changing tubes. He ran the amp's controls cranked to the max, often using a Variac to manipulate the power so that the tubes would run much hotter than usual—a practice that enhances the amp's warmth and saturation but shortens the life span of the power tubes to approximately 10 hours.

After some of the band's gear was temporarily lost in shipping while returning from a tour, Van Halen's original Plexi was eventually retired from road work for safekeeping. The amp was restored to stock and is now reserved only for use in the studio. Before his regular backline gear was returned, Van Halen temporarily used Laney, Music Man, and newer Marshall amps.

In the studio, Van Halen has experimented with a mixture of various tube amps for different textures. In addition to the amps mentioned above, he has used models by Bogner and Orange, as well as some newer Marshalls. Currently, for studio and live work, Van Halen prefers his signature Peavey 5150, a roadworthy amp which was introduced in 1993 and modeled on the tones of his favorite vintage and modern amps.

In the early days, Van Halen relied on a fairly raw amp tone with few effects added for color. Likewise, his late-'70s pedalboard was very basic. It was made of plywood and included an MXR Phase 90, MXR Flanger, and the two controls for his Echoplex, which were crudely attached to the board with some black duct tape. He also had a Univox EC-80 echo box (similar to an Echoplex), which is what he used in the early club days as well as in the studio on 1978's *Van Halen*. It's the Univox echo that was used to achieve the growling tone at the end of "Eruption." By the mid '80s, he had added a chorus unit to his rig and the chorus effect was becoming a more essential part of his sound.

Van Halen's rig continued to evolve in the '90s, updated for each tour. Some of his main rack units still include two Lexicon PCM 70 digital delays, two Eventide H3000 Harmonizers, and two Roland SDE-3000 digital delays. For the last Van Halen tour, EVH went back to basics and abandoned his wireless units in favor of George L's cables.

To cop the early Van Halen tone, use a solidbody guitar with a humbucking pickup in the bridge position and run it through a Marshall head with a 4x12 cabinet. In the early days, with his Plexi, EVH had all of the controls full up, but you may find the tone controls on modern amps to be more sensitive. Turn the amp's preamp control between 7 and 10, so that your tone is distorted but not completely saturated, and set master volume between 3 and 5 (or wherever needed). Set the bass around 7–9, mids on 8, treble 7–9, and presence around 6–8. If you need a bit more juice for riffs and solos, add in a BOSS SD-1 Super Overdrive or Ibanez Tube Screamer, set just a shade hotter than the amp's natural tone. A wahwah can also be used as a midrange booster to beef up the overdrive. For effects, add in a classic MXR Phase 90 and Flanger pedals, a delay or echo unit, and chorus pedal—or use a multi-effects processor that provides comparable sounds.

Essential Listening

"Eruption"
"You Really Got Me"
"Spanish Fly"
"Somebody Get Me a Doctor
"And The Cradle Will Rock..."
"Cathedral"
"Panama"
"Poundcake"

Discography

Van Halen (all Warner Bros. unless otherwise noted)
Van Halen (1978), *Van Halen II* (1979), *Women and Children First* (1980), *Fair Warning* (1981), *Diver Down* (1982), *1984* (1984), *5150* (1986), *Twister* [soundtrack] (Warner/Sunset, 1986), *OU812* (1988), *For Unlawful Carnal Knowledge* (1991), *Live: Right Here, Right Now* (1993), *Balance* (1995), *Best Of Volume I* (1996), *Van Halen III* (1998)

With Others
Nicolette Larson, *Nicolette* (Warner, 1978)
Dweezil Zappa, *Dweezil* (Barking Pumpkin, 1982)
Michael Jackson, *Thriller* (Epic, 1982)
Brian May & Friends, *Star Fleet Project* (EMI, 1983)
Sammy Hagar, *I Never Say Goodbye* (Geffen, 1987)
Steve Lukather, *Lukather* (Columbia, 1989)
Thomas Dolby, *Astronauts & Heretics* (Giant, 1992)
Rich Wyman, *Fatherless Child* (Apricot, 1996)
David Garfield & Friends, *A Tribute To Jeff* (Zebra, 1997)
Ennio Morricone, *The Legend of 1900* [soundtrack] (Sony Classical, 1999)
The Wild Life [soundtrack] (MCA, 1985)

Eddie Van Halen: In His Own Words

"I've never used an overdrive box. That's what made me use a Variac when I used to use the Marshall. For one, I'd lower the voltage to about 89 or 90 volts, instead of 110, because that seemed like the sweet spot to me. The Variac makes the amp overdrive, but at a lower volume. It's just like a light dimmer; you can crank the amp all the way up, but it won't blow up. It would make the amp a lot quieter and I'd get the exact same tone. The only way I can use a Marshall is with everything turned all the way up. But for a Marshall, when you turn everything all the way up, it's flat. So you're not adding anything, you're just taking it out, when you touch any of the controls. Those old Marshalls are all so different and you won't find two that sound the same. It's like a guitar; it depends on how much it's been spanked and used, what kind of tubes it's got in it, and what parts they happened to have that day to put in it when it was made.

"My old Marshall is a cranking little amp, but now the Peavey 5150 is the main amp I use. For recording, I use three 5150 heads through three cabinets and I have them all miked a little bit different. So when you go to mix you would have three sounds to combine: one setup clean, one's kind of medium, and one's full over-the-top. When you're mixing, you're bringing in and out the balance between the three. The Marshall has a time and a place. I'll probably end up using it again along with the 5150, but now the 5150 is the majority of the sound. Live, that's all that I use. They're so damn dependable, and I've never blown one. Tonally, the 5150 is a whole different ballgame compared to a Marshall. We added an extra preamp tube because I wanted more sustain but without a massive amount of distortion on top of it, and [Peavey amp designer] James Brown figured out a way to do it.

"With my guitars, the most important part is the setup. A guitar is a piece of wood and metal, and that's it. My guitars are set up with regular Peavey .009–.042 gauge strings. I lower the strings to the point of buzz and then back it off just a hair. Why make it hard to play? Tone comes from your fingers and how you play, not how high the strings are off the fingerboard. I'm not talking about having it so low that it's buzzing and fretting out, but having the action as low as possible. On the Wolfgang, the fingerboard radius is flat so you can have the action low and stretch a string *beyond,* and it won't fret out.

One of Van Halen's "Frankenstein" stage guitars and his effects rack from the 1995 *Balance* tour.

"But the main thing people have to understand is that even if you use the same gear as me, set up in exactly the same way, you're just not going to sound like me. As I've always said, how you sound is more about how you play than what you play. Years ago, we were opening for Ted Nugent at the Capitol Center in Largo, Maryland. I'm playing my original 'Frankie' and my 100-watt Marshall. I used a long speaker cable instead of a long guitar cable, and I had my amp right by my feet at the edge of the stage. I was going through my MXR Flanger, into my phaser, then into the Echoplex, and finally into the head. We were doing soundcheck, and Ted, who's a pretty funny guy, shows up. He comes up and goes, 'Hey, where's the little magic black box you got? How are you getting that sound?' I handed him my guitar, he played, and it sounds like Ted. If he expected to pick up my guitar and sound like me, I'm sorry. If anybody out there thinks that if they buy my guitar and my amp then they'll sound like me, you're wrong. It just doesn't work that way."

Danny Gatton

Born
September 4, 1945, in Washington, D.C.

Bands
The Offbeats
Roger Miller
Bobby Charles
Danny & the Fat Boys
Robert Gordon
Danny Gatton (solo career)

Tone
Classic Telecaster, with clanky bridge-pickup licks and fat, jazzy neck-pickup runs

Signature Traits
Cascading, super-rapid double-stops

Breakthrough Performance
"Harlem Nocturne" from *Cruisin' Deuces* (1993)

History and Influences
Among the best of the so-called "roots rock" guitarists was Washington, D. C.–based picker Danny Gatton. Able to jump from rockabilly to country to jazz to blues at the drop of a hat, Gatton gained a national reputation after on-again, off-again gigs with the likes of country leader Roger Miller and "swamp pop" singer/songwriter Bobby Charles, as well as the release of two impressive but hard-to-find solo albums, *American Music* (1976) and *Redneck Jazz* (1978). Gatton's reputation as a guitar maestro was spread even wider as a result of his recordings with '50s retro-rocker Robert Gordon, with whom he appeared on two albums, 1981's *Are You Gonna Be the One?* and Gordon's 1982 compilation set, *Too Fast to Live, Too Young to Die.*

Laying claim to his rockabilly, jazz, rock 'n' roll, blues, and country guitar influences, Gatton released his third solo in 1987, *Unfinished Business*. Here, Gatton fully realized his instrumental virtuosity. With a '53 Fender Telecaster in hand, he gave a command performance of complex chicken-pickin' techniques, pedal-steel guitar and Hammond organ imitations, slide guitar (played with a Heineken beer bottle), and more.

In 1991, having finally signed with major label Elektra, the virtuoso released *88 Elmira Street*. The album was brimming with the guitarist's brilliant chops, as heard on "Funky Mama" and "Elmira St. Boogie." 1993's *Cruisin' Deuces* was equally impressive, but sales were poor and he lost his record deal. Sadly, Gatton took his own life on October 4, 1994, at his farm in Maryland. Some have suggested that he was frustrated at his lack of commercial success, as well as the recent death of his friend and bandmate, singer Billy Windsor.

▶▶▶

Gear List

Guitars

1953 Fender Telecaster, Fender Danny Gatton Telecaster model prototype, Fender Custom doubleneck Telecaster, Fender Stratocaster, 1992 Fender Custom Shop Bass, 1954 Gibson ES-295, 1956 Gibson ES-350, 1955 Gibson L-5, 1961 Gibson Les Paul Custom, Vega *f*-hole archtop, Custom Randy Wood cutaway acoustic, Gibson J-200 acoustic

Pickups

Joe Barden Tele models

Accessories

Heineken beer bottle for a slide

Effects & Rack Gear

The Magic Dingus effects box (a pre-MIDI analog device mounted on his Tele that controlled echo volume and speed, amp reverb and vibrato, Leslie, phase shifters, and other effects, originally built by Danny and his father); Chandler digital delay; Echoplex

Amps

Late '50s tweed Fender Twins, Fender Super Reverb, Fender Bassman reissues, Fender Vibroverb reissues, early-'60s blackface Fender Vibrolux

Two years later, a famous bootleg of Gatton recorded with Robert Gordon's band was finally released to the public on CD. It was aptly titled *The Humbler*, because any guitarist who heard it was instantly humbled by Gatton's virtuosity. It's a Tele *tour de force* and more proof of his high caliber. *The Humbler* is a record every guitar lover should have in his or her collection.

Tone and Technique

Gatton's tone is simply that of a good Telecaster plugged into a good vintage-style tube amp. For a guitarist with so many sounds at his command, that may seem like an oversimplification, but it's accurate: Aside from reverb and occasionally a little echo, Gatton's distinct tone came from his fingers. What does that mean, exactly? This alludes to a certain truth that guitar players recognize as they get more experienced. While the right gear will help deliver your tone and talent, it's amazing how much of your sound comes from your fingers.

To emulate Gatton's tone, you'll definitely need that Tele and tube amp, but also consider the many ways he manipulated his gear and altered his playing techniques. He would frequently flip between the neck and bridge pickups for different Tele textures, and use the guitar's tone controls to create shadings. Gatton would flatpick one line and then whip out some claw-style chicken-pickin' on the next. He had a myriad of techniques he could use to affect tone.

In short, Danny Gatton's tone can't be replicated merely by equipment—it requires a certain touch, style, and feel for the music. To that end, listen to his records, and also listen to the players he grew up listening to, such as Charlie Christian, Les Paul, Chet Aktins, Scotty Moore (Elvis Presley's guitarist), and *lots* of vintage country players. If you have the gear and the ears to pick up some of his fabulous licks, you'll soon begin to capture that elusive Danny Gatton vibe. Twang on!

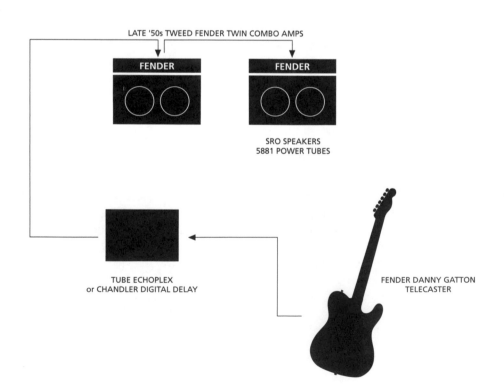

LATE '50s TWEED FENDER TWIN COMBO AMPS

FENDER   FENDER

SRO SPEAKERS
5881 POWER TUBES

TUBE ECHOPLEX
or CHANDLER DIGITAL DELAY

FENDER DANNY GATTON
TELECASTER

Danny Gatton: In His Own Words

Talking about his favorite '53 Telecaster, Danny told *Guitar Player* magazine in 1993:

"It never had any holes cut in it, never had a Charlie Christian pickup on it or anything. I never put a 22nd fret on that thing, either, though I used to do that to my other Teles. It just had Joe Barden pickups and a set of stainless steel knobs made by [guitar maker and former Gatton tech] Jay Monterose. My father made the stainless steel bridge plate that I used to mount the Magic Dingus effects box on. That plate makes a difference in the tone.

"I can't think of anything else I could do to a Telecaster to make it perform any better, unless you want a wangy [tremolo] bar. I'm having a doubleneck built that has a wangy bar on the top. It will have two Strat pickups and a Tele pickup. They're putting a 6-string bass on the bottom. Lord knows what pickups they'll use for that neck. I've always loved the sounds of a 6-string bass, and I've never had one before.

"My ES-350, on the other hand, has a bright sound like Wes Montgomery's old records. It's not that super muddy sound—it has some sparkle. I don't play with a dead tone, even when I play jazz. The muddier it is, the more you can get away with, but I always play with an edge so I can hear all the little things I do. Nothing's easier than turning on the distorto box and making a bunch of noise. A lot of people get away with murder with that stuff. I prefer to do it the old way—with a guitar, a cord, and an amp. If it comes out fine, good. If it doesn't, I'd better go home and woodshed some more."

Gatton guitar tech Jay Monterose contributed to the 1993 interview:

"Gatton prefers to use a pair of late '50s tweed Fender Twin amps. One of those amps is serial number 40. He's had that since the mid-'60s, and he's been playing it since then. The other Twin has four 5881 tubes and a pair of SRO speakers. He also owns a Super Reverb, two Bassman reissues, and three Vibroverb reissues that have been heavily modified."

On the subject of effects, Monterose further noted that Gatton only used a Chandler delay or Echoplex:

"He only uses it when we're doing the rockabilly stuff. Other than that, it's just reverb and tremolo on the amp. Danny gets all his organ effects by turning his tone pot down and turning the volume up. With the Barden pickups, he can get three distinct organ tones by selecting pickups."

Essential Listening

Danny Gatton
"Elmira St. Boogie"
"Puddin' and Pie"
"Harlem Nocturne"

Robert Gordon
"Lover Boy"
"Cruisin'"
"Love My Baby"

Discography

Danny Gatton
American Music (Ripsaw, 1976), *Redneck Jazz* (NRG, 1978), *Unfinished Business* (NRG, 1988), *88 Elmira Street* (Elektra, 1991), *New York Stories* (Blue Note, 1992), *Cruisin' Deuces* (Elektra, 1993)

Robert Gordon
Are You Gonna Be the One? (One Way Records, 1981), *Too Fast to Live, Too Young to Die* (One Way Records, 1982), *The Humbler* (NRG, 1996)

Tom Principato & Danny Gatton
Blazing Telecasters (K.O. CITY Studio, 1991)

Danny Gatton & Joey DeFrancesco
Relentless (Big Mo, 1994)

Jimi Hendrix

Hendrix rocks out with Vox wah, original Roger Mayer Octavia prototype, Dallas-Arbiter Fuzz Face, and Univox Uni-Vibe.

Born
November 27, 1942, in Seattle, Washington

Bands
James Brown
Wilson Pickett
Ike & Tina Turner
The Isley Brothers
Joey Dee
Jackie Wilson
Curtis Knight & the Squires
Little Richard
King Curtis
John Hammond, Jr.
Jimmy James & the Blue Flames
The Jimi Hendrix Experience
Gypsys, Suns & Rainbows
Band of Gypsys

Tone
Organic guitar/amp tones generated by a cranked non-master volume tube amp with basic analog effects occasionally added for color

Signature Sound
Over-the-top style, playing guitar behind his back, behind his head, and with his teeth; sometimes used the thumb on his fretting hand to catch bass notes in certain chord voicings

Breakthrough Performance
"Hey Joe" single (1967)

History and Influences
Hendrix got his first guitar, an acoustic from his father, by age 12. He soon upgraded to a cheap electric, and by age 15 had an Epiphone. He taught himself to play by watching other guitarists and listening to records. Early on, he was influenced by artists like Jimmy Reed, Chuck Berry, and Buddy Guy. As a teen, Hendrix played in local bands, working the area from Seattle, Washington, to Vancouver, B.C., and performing at local clubs and dances.

Between 1963 and 1964, Hendrix toured the South, working as a sideman with a vari-

▶▶▶

ety of groups, then moving north to New York. During that time, the artists he accompanied included Ike & Tina Turner, Little Richard, James Brown, and Curtis Knight & the Squires. In 1965, he formed his own group, Jimmy James & the Blue Flames. By the following year, the band was performing in Greenwich Village clubs (regularly at Cafe Wha?), and Hendrix—that is, Jimmy James—was making a name for himself among the local crowd, which included artists such as Bob Dylan. Word soon spread in the music world to big acts like the Beatles and the Animals.

It was former Animals' bassist Chas Chandler who approached Hendrix—then still known as Jimmy James—with an offer to manage his career. Chandler arranged for Hendrix to travel to England, where he put together a new band in hopes of earning a recording contract. It was also Chandler who suggested that Hendrix change the spelling of his first name to "Jimi" and reclaim his original surname. In London, Noel Redding and Mitch Mitchell were hired to play bass and drums, forming the Jimi Hendrix Experience. Track Records signed the group and swiftly released the singles "Hey Joe" and "Purple Haze" in 1967. Hendrix and the Experience became an instant success in England.

While Hendrix was considered the hottest act in the U.K., he was still an unknown back in the United States. On the recommendation of Paul McCartney, the Experience was booked to play at the Monterey Pop Festival. Hendrix performed on the last day of the festival, pulling out all the stops with a flashy performance that ended with a ceremonial burning of his Strat onstage. Today, the performance is recalled as a legendary moment in rock history.

The Experience's full-length releases—*Are You Experienced* (1967), *Axis: Bold as Love,* and *Electric Ladyland* (1968)—put them at the vanguard of psychedelic rock. By late 1968, the Experience was at the peak of its popularity, but its members were weary from endless touring and growing bored of playing the same tunes night after night. As a musician, Hendrix wanted to explore other musical interests, including jazz. The Experience played its final gig on June 29, 1969, at the Denver Pop Festival in Colorado.

Eager to take his music in a slightly different direction, Hendrix formed the short-lived Gypsys, Suns & Rainbows outfit with Mitchell, his former army buddy Billy Cox on bass, percussionists Jerry Velez and Juma Sultan, and Larry Lee on rhythm guitar. This was the lineup that performed with Hendrix during his legendary set at the Woodstock Festival on August 18, 1969. A few months later Hendrix returned to his three-piece format and put together Band of Gypsys with Cox on bass and Buddy Miles on drums. The lineup was together for just a handful of gigs, with debut performances at the Fillmore East in New York on New Year's of 1970, playing two back-to-back shows on the evenings of December 31, 1969, and January 1, 1970. These four performances were recorded and portions released as *Band of Gypsys.*

In spring and summer of 1970, Hendrix had been juggling a hectic schedule between recording and gigging, performing on weekends for what was billed as the "Cry of Love" tour. Following the opening party for his Electric Lady studios in Manhattan, Hendrix left for England to play a string of festival dates in Europe. He played his last gig on August 30, 1970, at England's Isle of Wight Festival. On September 18, 1970, Hendrix was pronounced dead on arrival at St. Mary Abbots Hospital in Kensington, England. The cause of death was recorded as an overdose of sleeping pills.

Tone and Technique

As many players are well aware, the heart of Hendrix's tone came not from his gear so much as from his fingers. The only way to get a true feel for his work is to spend time listening carefully to his recorded tracks over and over, paying special

▼ Gear List

Guitars
Fender Stratocasters from late 1960s to 1970; Gibson Flying V, Les Paul, and ES-330; Mosrite doubleneck; Acoustic (Acoustic Control Corporation) Black Widow; Rickenbacker 6- and 12-string models; Guild 12-string, Martin 6-string, and Gibson Dove acoustics; Hagstrom 8-string basses

Pickups
Stock pickups typically used in all guitars

Accessories
Ernie Ball strings (.010–.038 gauge), Fender Rock 'N Roll light-gauge strings (.010, .013, .015, .026, .032, .038), medium picks (usually Fender or Manny's Music store brand in tortoise shell color)

Effects
Vox wah pedal, Dallas-Arbiter Fuzz Face, Roger Mayer Octavia, Univox Uni-Vibe, Crybaby wah (pre-Experience), Maestro Fuzz (pre-Experience)

Amps & Cabs
Marshall Super Lead 100-watt heads, Marshall 4x12 cabinets loaded with 25-watt Celestion "greenback" speakers, Sunn Coliseum heads with Sunn 100-F cabinets (first loaded with one JBL D-130 speaker in the bottom and an L-E 100-S driver horn in the top; then two JBL D-130s; later, four 12" Eminence speakers), Fender Twin Reverb

Amp settings on Marshalls: presence, bass, middle, treble, volume all cranked to 10 [*Note: Marshall amps of this era did not include master volume control.*]

attention to his phrasing. Fortunately, there is a great deal of tablature and transcribed music available. But, again, to *really* sound like Hendrix you'll need to listen to his work and scrutinize his style.

Hendrix was a master at playing rhythm guitar as well as being an outstanding soloist. One of the most impressive aspects of his playing was the crafty way in which Hendrix was able to combine both rhythm and melody lines. While his lead riffs are certainly tremendous, it's the strong rhythm work that anchors each song and sets the scene to showcase his playing. Hendrix had developed his rhythm chops while working the R&B "chitlin" circuit in the early to mid-'60s, becoming a solid backup player. His ability to solo came instinctively, and he soon found a way to work them together. It's this combination of rhythm and melody that defined Hendrix as a player and enabled his power-trio style to work so well. Listen to his technique on tracks such as "Little Wing," "Castles Made of Sand" and "The Wind Cries Mary" for examples of this type of work.

In his early days of playing R&B, Hendrix was said to have used a Fender Twin Reverb as his main amp. His effects at that time included a Maestro Fuzz and a Vox wah pedal. Then, through his days onstage with the Experience and Band of Gypsys, Hendrix was typically playing Strats (favoring models with maple necks) and the occasional Flying V through 100-watt Marshall amplifier stacks. While with the Experience, he had briefly used Fender and Sunn setups in the U.S. (Hendrix had a momentary endorsement deal with Sunn, but always preferred his Marshalls), as well as venue-supplied WEM amplification at several U.K. gigs. But throughout his career, his favorite amps were Marshalls, and they became an essential part of his sound and the backdrop for his stage show.

His main stage rig was big and powerful, but very simple: three 100-watt stacks daisy-chained together. He cranked all of the amp's controls to 10, using the guitar's volume control for master volume, and used his stompboxes to add color and achieve texture variations. His pedals were always set up right on the stage, with no pedalboard to contain them. His most frequently used effects setup

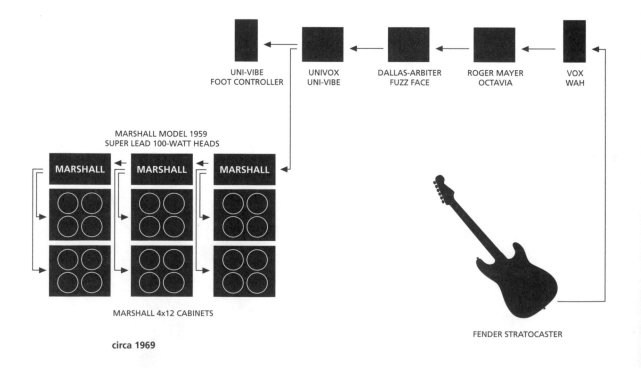

UNI-VIBE
FOOT CONTROLLER

UNIVOX
UNI-VIBE

DALLAS-ARBITER
FUZZ FACE

ROGER MAYER
OCTAVIA

VOX
WAH

MARSHALL MODEL 1959
SUPER LEAD 100-WATT HEADS

MARSHALL   MARSHALL   MARSHALL

MARSHALL 4x12 CABINETS

circa 1969

FENDER STRATOCASTER

included a Vox wah pedal (to help accentuate his "midrangey" Strat tone), Dallas-Arbiter Fuzz Face, custom-made Roger Mayer Octavia, and a Univox Uni-Vibe, all run inline and plugged straight into the front of the amp.

To achieve the dirty tones heard on tracks like "Foxy Lady" and "Fire," Hendrix combined the dirty fuzz tones of the Fuzz Face with the octave fuzz tones on the Octavia. One of the mistakes many players make today in attempting to emulate the Hendrix tone is to use modern-sounding distortion; in the late '60s, distortion boxes created a distinct fuzz tone which had far less clarity in the notes and more of a muted "buzz" sound than modern-type distortion boxes. There's a reason why these units were known as "fuzz boxes" and not distortion or overdrive pedals. So to duplicate that type of a tone, you'll need a box that generates a vintage-style fuzzy, buzzing effect. The Octavia creates a distinct-sounding effect with a certain sizzle and overtone, and it is highly recommended for use in recreating an authentic Hendrix tone. Additionally, you'll want to pick up a Uni-Vibe for the lush, chorusy modulation effects. Reissues of the original Fuzz Face, Octavia, and Uni-Vibe pedals are easy to find. There are also plenty of Hendrix-style effects available from a variety of boutique stompbox manufacturers, as well as some multi-effects processors that do a fine job of replicating those sounds. So, finding the right tools for these authentic tones shouldn't be too difficult.

Of course, there are other fine variables in creating an authentic Hendrix tone. For example, he used a right-handed guitar that was flipped over, then set up and restrung for playing lefty. By doing so, the bridge is upside down, with the bar on the wrong side. Plus, the strings are now different lengths, with what was the shortest string now being the longest and the longest now the shortest. Additionally, the pickups on an upside-down guitar will be working in reverse, with the poles aligning with different strings than originally intended. These details will create subtle differences. If you're right-handed and really want to get the full experience, try out Fender's Jimi Hendrix Strat, which was developed for those right-handed players who sought a more authentic Hendrix-style feel and tone.

Discography

Jimi Hendrix Experience

Are You Experienced (Reprise, 1967), *Axis: Bold as Love* (Reprise, 1968), *Smash Hits* (Reprise, 1968), *Electric Ladyland* (Reprise, 1968), *Monterey International Pop Festival* (Reprise, 1970), *Live at Winterland* (Ryko, 1987), *Radio One* (Ryko, 1989)

Band Of Gypsys

Band Of Gypsys (Capitol, 1970), *Band Of Gypsys 2* (Capitol, 1986)

Jimi Hendrix

Cry of Love (Reprise, 1971), *Rainbow Bridge* (Reprise, 1971), *Isle of Wight* (Polydor, 1971), *In the West* (Reprise, 1972), *Loose Ends* (Polydor, 1973), *Crash Landing* (Reprise, 1975), *Midnight Lightning* (Reprise, 1975), *The Essential Jimi Hendrix, Vol. 1* (Reprise, 1978), *The Essential Jimi Hendrix, Vol. 2* (Reprise, 1978), *Nine to the Universe* (Reprise, 1980), *The Jimi Hendrix Concerts* (Reprise, 1982), *Early Hendrix* (Baron), *Kiss the Sky* (Reprise, 1984), *Jimi Plays Monterey* (Reprise, 1986), *Johnny B. Goode: Original Video Soundtrack* (Capitol, 1986), *Isle of Wight '70* (Polydor, 1991), *Lifelines: The Jimi Hendrix Story* (Reprise, 1991), *Stages* (Reprise, 1991), *The Ultimate Experience* (MCA, 1993), *Blues* (MCA, 1994), *The Experience Collection* (MCA, 1994), *Jimi Hendrix: Woodstock* (MCA, 1994), *Voodoo Soup* (MCA, 1995), *Monday Morning: Jimi at Woodstock* (Polydor, 1995), *South Saturn Delta* (MCA, 1997), *First Rays of the New Rising Sun* (MCA, 1997), *Live at the Fillmore East* (MCA, 1999), *Live at Woodstock* (MCA, 1999), *Blue Angel: Live at the Isle of Wight* (MCA, 2002)

Jimi Hendrix and Lonnie Youngblood

Two Great Experiences Together (Maple, 1971), *Rare Hendrix* (Trip, 1972)

With Others

Curtis Knight with Jimi Hendrix, *Get That Feeling* (Capitol, 1967)
Stephen Stills, *Stephen Stills* (Atlantic, 1970)
Various Artists, *Woodstock* (Cotillion, 1970)
Love, *False Start* (Blue Thumb, 1970)
Various Artists, *Woodstock Two* (Cotillion, 1971)
Various Artists, *The First Great Rock Festivals of the Seventies* (Columbia, 1971)

Steve Vai

Born
June 6, 1960, in Carle Place, New York

Bands
Frank Zappa
Alcatrazz
David Lee Roth
Whitesnake
Steve Vai (solo career)
G3 tours

Tone
Fat, full-range tone of a humbucker-loaded guitar through an overdriven tube amp

Signature Sound
Provocative style with controlled feedback and daredevil tremolo tricks

Breakthrough Performance
"The Attitude Song" from *Flex-Able* (1984)

History and Influences
Steve Vai grew up in suburban Long Island, New York, and began taking guitar lessons while in high school. His teacher, Joe Satriani, was an older student at his school. Satriani proved to be an excellent teacher, ingraining a strong foundation which helped Vai to shed his inhibitions about the instrument. After graduation, Vai went on to study guitar at the Berklee College of Music in Boston, Massachusetts, where he learned to transcribe music and spent many hours woodshedding. It was during this period that Vai began to develop his own style and refine his technique. By then he was listening to players such as Frank Zappa, Jimmy Page, Jimi Hendrix, and Jeff Beck.

While at school, Vai transcribed several of Zappa's complicated works and sent Zappa copies of the transcriptions. Impressed with Vai's work and musical ability, Zappa offered Vai a gig with his band. Vai went on to record several albums with Zappa in the early '80s, including *Tinseltown Rebellion* (1981), *You Are What You Is* (1981), *Ship Arriving Too Late to Save a Drowning Witch* (1982), *Man from Utopia* (1983), *Them or Us* (1984), and *Thing-Fish* (1984). Vai then set out to create his own music, though he would continue to work with Zappa on projects through the years. Vai's first solo disc, *Flex-Able* (1984), demonstrated his stunning technique and Zappa-influenced creative style. One track from the album, "The Attitude Song," was included in *Guitar Player* magazine as a

Soundpage recording. It was many guitarists' introduction to Vai, and this sample track greatly helped to launch his solo career, establishing him as one of the most promising new players of the day.

In 1985, as power metal was on the rise, Vai replaced guitarist Yngwie Malmsteen in the metal outfit Alcatrazz, a band led by former Rainbow vocalist Graham Bonnett. Vai recorded one album with the group, *Disturbing the Peace,* which achieved only minimal success, so he set out in search of other ventures. The same year, Vai was commended for a cameo appearance in the film *Crossroads,* playing the devil's guitarist and shredding it up in an onscreen guitar duel with actor Ralph Macchio.

The following year, Vai landed a highly coveted gig with former Van Halen frontman David Lee Roth. Vai was thrust into the spotlight as the album's first single, "Yankee Rose," shot up the charts and the flashy accompanying video became a massive hit on MTV. The video provided an ideal platform to showcase Vai's technical ability and showmanship. Vai was lauded as a guitar virtuoso.

In 1988, Vai joined forces with the Ibanez guitar company and introduced the first Steve Vai model solidbody—the Jem 777. A variety of Jem guitars have since evolved from the original signature model, including the Universe 7-string. Following a short stint in Whitesnake, Vai began focusing all efforts on his solo career. His solo releases include the stellar *Passion and Warfare* (1990), which soared to #18 on the Billboard charts, a rare feat for a guitar-oriented release. In the past decade, the guitarist has released numerous solo efforts, launched his own record label (Favored Nations), and performed frequently with Joe Satriani as part of the G3 tours.

Tone and Technique

Although his approach is very contemporary, Vai's style is rooted in blues-based rock of the '60s and '70s, as a result of his taking cues from players like Jimi Hendrix and Jimmy Page and then mixing in the technical style and quirky elements of Frank Zappa. Vai spent many years honing his craft; likewise, copping his style and tone will take a great deal of diligent practice.

For starters, practice your rudiments to achieve uniform picking and optimum dexterity. Increase your knowledge of scales, and really learn your way around the fingerboard (that is, learn to play an *E* blues scale all over the neck, not just in one position, and then learn to do that with all the scales and chords). Also, work on playing smooth, legato lines and getting your picking as clean and accurate as possible. Using a metronome will definitely help your timing. As you work on improving your technique, try learning a few cool tricks from Vai's repertoire to help expand your own.

Vai has employed an assortment of different amplifiers (including Marshall, Soldano, Egnator, Bogner, VHT, and Carvin), rack effects, and stompboxes over the years. He regularly updates his equipment for each tour, building his stage rig around the music to be performed.

To emulate Vai's lead tone, grab an Ibanez Jem guitar and plug into an amp like the Carvin Legacy, which the guitarist co-designed. A solidbody guitar with a Floyd Rose (or Floyd-licensed) tremolo unit will suffice, as will a high-gain tube amp. Use a BOSS DS-1 or similar distortion/overdrive pedal for a bit more grease: Set the pedal's controls to add a tad more gain to enhance the amp's naturally overdriven tone and to provide a slight volume boost for leads. For wah effects, use a basic Crybaby or try a Bad Horsie wah-wah for tighter, more controlled wah playing. For pitch-shift and harmonizing effects, try out a DigiTech Whammy pedal or, if you can afford the high end, the Eventide H3000. Add a touch of digital delay for spaciousness. Many of the popular rackmount and floor-type multi-effects processors can also provide the entire range of appropriate effects.

Gear List

Guitars
Ibanez Jem 6-string and Universe 7-string, Carvin acoustic-electric, Taylor acoustic

Pickups
DiMarzio Evolution, The Breed, PAF Pro (neck and bridge)

Accessories
D'Addario strings (.009–.042), heavy picks, BOSS TU-12 tuner, Furman PL-8 Power & Light Conditioner, Custom Audio Electronics switching system, Fernandes Sustainer

Effects & Rack Gear
Dunlop Crybaby wah, Morley Steve Vai Bad Horsie wah, Morley volume pedal, BOSS DS-1 Distortion, DigiTech Whammy pedal, Eventide H3000 Harmonizer, Roland SDE-3000 Digital Delay, T.C. Electronic G-Force, Prescription Electronics Experience

Amps & Cabs
Carvin Legacy amplifiers and 4x12 cabinets

Steve Vai: In His Own Words

"The guitar that I use is really perfect for me—the Ibanez Jem. It just fits all the idiosyncrasies of my playing. I put a 7th string on it at one point and that led me to create a lot of other things. It was a whim of a decision to do something that I thought was different. It wasn't until afterwards that I learned the history behind it. I found out that the 7-string guitar was available many years before the Ibanez model came out. I didn't think it was really any great innovation, but I thought that it was a great idea and decided to do it anyway. It's pretty amazing how it's caught on. I don't think the 7-string became popular because of anything that I did. I had a hand in developing the Ibanez model, but I think it's become trendy because of the popularity of bands like Korn, Limp Bizkit, and Fear Factory. It's such an obvious evolution for the guitar and for that heavy sound. If you want to get heavy, get a 7-string, tune it down, and that's going to do it.

"As for my favorite personal guitars, I have about five of these white Jems that I got a while back, when I was going out on tour. They all looked pretty much the same, so in order to distinguish between them, I wrote 'Evo' on one of them because it had DiMarzio Evolution pickups in it [*Vai's older guitars had DiMarzio PAF Pros*]. That particular guitar has been the one that I keep going back to. There's something about the way it cuts, and it has the fattest bottom end. You can take one guitar right off the conveyor belt and then take the next one that comes out after it—the two guitars may both look identical, but they can sound a little bit different from each other. It's a matter of just going through them and finding which one works best for you. I've been using Evo for about eight years now. There's another white Jem that I use a lot and that one's called 'Flo' because

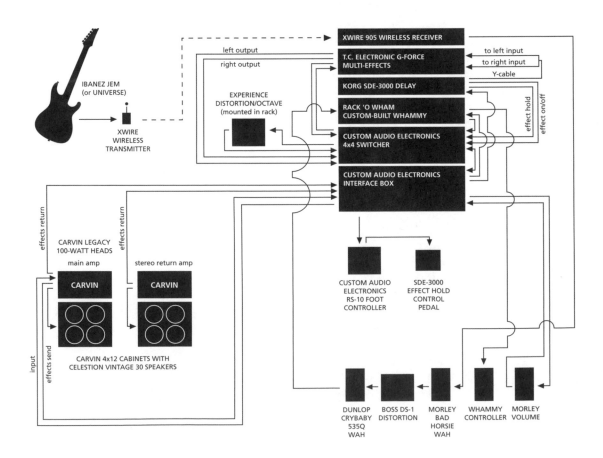

Vai's 2003 stage and studio rig.

of the floral inlay. That one is different because it has a Fernandes Sustainer built in. It allows you to play very clean and delicately, and the note will just ring on forever and ever. It's quite amazing.

"For effects, I'm always looking for something new to stomp on. I love effects like delay, as well as the morphing capabilities of some of the new gear that's come out. The pedals I usually go through are pretty basic. I still go through the BOSS DS-1 distortion pedal. When I was on my last tour I picked up a couple of guitar magazines and bought one of every new stompbox that had come out so I could compare what I was using with the new stuff that's out there. Some of the pedals were cool, but I'd just end up liking the same things I'd always used best. I'd discover this great new pedal and then after a day or so of messing around with it, I'd find it just wouldn't cut it as well as what I was already using.

"In my live setup, I use the Morley Bad Horsie wah, then go into the BOSS DS-1, then into a DigiTech Whammy pedal. I use the Whammy pedal quite extensively, but I don't set it to the typical octave setting. I set it to a fourth [interval] and when I hit the pedal down it's a fifth. I built a melody around those type of harmonies, but it was very difficult to get it to work out because you can't just randomly extend the pedal wherever you want. The intervals have got to work harmonically."

Discography

Frank Zappa (all on Barking Pumpkin Records)
Tinseltown Rebellion (1981), *Shut Up 'N Play Yer Guitar* (1981), *You Are What You Is* (1981), *Ship Arriving Too Late to Save a Drowning Witch* (1982), *The Man from Utopia* (1983), *Them or Us* (1984), *Thing-Fish* (1984), *Jazz from Hell* (1986), *You Can't Do That on Stage Anymore Sampler* (1988), *Frank Zappa: Guitar* (1988), *You Can't Do That on Stage Anymore, Vol. 1* (1988), *Guitar World According to Frank Zappa* (1988), *You Can't Do That on Stage Anymore, Vol. 3* (1989), *You Can't Do That on Stage Anymore, Vols. 4–6* (1992)

Steve Vai
Flex-Able (Epic, 1984), *Passion and Warfare* (Epic, 1990), *Sex & Religion* (Epic, 1993), *Alien Love Secrets* (Epic, 1995), *Fire Garden* (Epic, 1995), *G3: Live in Concert* [with Joe Satriani and Eric Johnson] (Epic, 1997), *Flex-Able Leftovers* (Epic, 1998), *The Ultra Zone* (Epic, 1999), *The 7th Song: Enchanting Guitar Melodies Archive* (Sony, 2000), *Alive in an Ultra World* (Epic, 2001), *The Secret Jewel Box* (Favored Nations, 2001), *The Elusive Light and Sound, Vol. 1* (Favored Nations, 2002)

David Lee Roth
Eat 'Em & Smile (Warner Bros., 1986), *Skyscraper* (Warner Bros., 1988)

With Others
Alcatrazz, *Disturbing the Peace* (Capitol, 1985)
Public Image Ltd., *Album* (Elektra, 1986)
Whitesnake, *Slip of the Tongue* (Geffen, 1989)
Joe Jackson, *Symphony No. 1* (Sony Classical, 1999)
Alice Cooper, *Hey Stoopid!* (Epic, 1991)

Aerosmith's Joe Perry & Brad Whitford

Joe Perry

Brad Whitford

Born

Joe Perry: September 10, 1950, in Lawrence, Massachusetts

Brad Whitford: February 23, 1952, in Winchester, Massachusetts

Bands

Aerosmith
The Joe Perry Project
Flash, Just Us, Plastic Glass, Jam Band (Perry)
Teapot Dome, Cymbals of Resistance, Justin Tyme, Earth Incorporated, Whitford/St. Holmes (Whitford)

Tone

Warm characteristics of classic tube amps to provide a solid foundation: Perry's is often textured and biting, Whitford's very smooth and evenly balanced

Signature Sound

A yin-yang guitar team: Perry gets the spotlight as the featured soloist, adding the wilder riffs and unusual textured effects on many of the group's songs, while Whitford's bluesy backing riffs and soulful tone provide the backbone

Breakthrough Performance

"Toys in the Attic" from *Toys in the Attic* (1975)

History and Influences

Aerosmith was formed in the summer of 1970 in Sunapee, New Hampshire, when Jam Band bassist Tom Hamilton and guitarist Joe Perry got together with vocalist Steven Tyler. Shortly after, Joey Kramer was recruited as their drummer. Guitarist Brad Whitford (who had attended Boston's prestigious Berklee College of Music) was later brought in to round out the lineup, replacing original guitarist Ray Tabano. The members moved into Boston, and by 1972 Aerosmith had gained a strong local following. That same year, they signed a management contract and landed a recording deal with Columbia Records. The group's self-titled debut was released in January 1973. Even with the single "Dream On," the album did little outside the Boston area. The band continued to tour and build up a following within the college and club circuits.

By the mid-'70s, the group had refined its sound, and Perry and Whitford had gelled as a guitar team. Aerosmith finally caught the attention of critics with its third disc, *Toys in the Attic*, which was released in April of 1975 and went platinum that summer. *Toys* was succeeded the following year by another platinum LP, *Rocks*, which many consider the band's finest effort.

In 1975, "Dream On" was re-released as a single and went gold—nearly three years after its original release. "Walk This Way" was also released that year, and became the band's second top-10 hit, making Aerosmith a major concert draw. Just at the peak of success, things turned sour due to internal conflicts and growing drug abuse within the group. In 1979, Perry left to form his own band and Brad Whitford followed suit two years later. On Valentine's Day, 1984, the original band members reunited and released the solid *Done with Mirrors* the following year. The follow-up, *Permanent Vacation*, was released in 1987 and achieved mass success at both radio and MTV with "Dude (Looks Like a Lady)," "Rag Doll," and the ballad "Angel." With *Pump*, released in 1989, the group had straightened up its act, kicking drugs and reclaiming its status with a string of major hits including "Love in an Elevator," "What It Takes," "Monkey on My Back" and "Janie's Got a Gun." Aerosmith has been elevated to supergroup status, and was inducted into the Rock and Roll Hall of Fame in 2001.

In 1997, the Gibson guitar company honored Joe Perry and his devotion to the Les Paul guitar with the Joe Perry Signature Les Paul, originally featuring a translucent blackburst flametop, white mother-of-pearl pickguard, black chrome hardware, and an active mid-boost tone-shaping circuit. Several updated versions of the guitar have since been introduced.

Tone and Technique

Over their three-decade-plus careers in music, Perry and Whitford have gone through mountains of gear, each having used massive assortments of guitars, amps, and effects both onstage and in the studio. Though both appreciate the qualities and tonal textures achieved from using various instruments and amps, the quintessential tone favored by both Perry and Whitford has always come from a beefy Les Paul played through a warm-sounding Marshall amp. Both also have deep affections for their Fender Strats, Fender Teles, and Gretsch models, and are known to use various tube amps such as Fenders, Vox AC30s, and Hiwatt models, as well as boutique clones of these instruments and amps. Still, it's the classic Les Paul-and-Marshall sound that serves as Aerosmith's benchmark tone.

To emulate the classic Aerosmith sound, think fundamentals. Grab your favorite humbucker-loaded Les Paul (or other heavy-

Gear List — Joe Perry

Guitars

Gibson Les Pauls (various models), Joe Perry Signature Model Les Paul, Les Paul Standard with Transperformance self-tuning system; Gibson SGs (various models), Firebird, Flying V, Explorer, ES-335, ES-355, and Chet Atkins SST electric-acoustic; Fender Stratocaster, Telecaster, Esquire, Telesonic, and Electric XII; Guild electric 12-string; various standard and custom-built electrics by Washburn, Schecter, James Trussart, Zemaitis, Travis Bean, Dan Armstrong, Jerry Jones, Danelectro, Silvertone, Gretsch, Hamer, and Fernandes; Chandler electrics and lap steels; Supro Ozark; Hofner electric; B.C. Rich Bich and Mockingbird; Gibson J-200, J-45, J-180, and J-160E acoustics; various acoustics by Martin, Guild, Alvarez, and Ovation

Pickups

Stock pickups; various Seymour Duncan, DiMarzio, Bill Lawrence, and Joe Barden models

Accessories

Monster cables; metal and glass slides; Whirlwind Selector A/B/Y boxes; BOSS LS-2 Line Selector; Lehlei switcher; various .009, .010, and .011 string sets; heavy picks

Effects & Rack Gear

Samson wireless; Roland VG-8 guitar synthesizer and multi-effects processor; Dunlop Crybaby wah pedal and DCR-ISR Crybaby rack wah; customized DigiTech Whammy WH-1; Klon Centaur overdrive; Line 6 DL4 Delay Modeler, MM4 Modulation Modeler, and FM4 Filter Modeler; BOSS DD-5 Digital Delay; MXR Digital Delay; custom-built talk box; Moog Etherwave Theremin; ProCo Rat

Amps & Cabs

Various new, vintage, and reissue Marshall 100-watt, 50-watt, JTM45, and Marshall Major heads, Marshall 4x12 cabinets and Lead 12 combo; Vox AC30; Fender Tonemaster heads and 4x12 cabinets, Fender Vibroverb, Twin Reverb, and Super Reverb combos; Wizard 100-watt heads and 4x12 cabinets; Music Man heads and cabinets; Hiwatt heads and cabinets; Gibson Goldtone GA-30RVS and GA-60RV combos, GA-30RVH head, and 2x12/2x10 and 4x12 cabinets

Gibson Goldtone GA-30RVS settings: Plugged into dirty channel, all controls cranked to 10

Wizard 100 and Fender Vibroverb settings: "The Wizard is set at about 70% across and the Vibroverb is set about the same. Sometimes, depending on where we are, I may have to dial in a little more or less top end on the Wizard. It seems like the outdoor concert sheds sound a little harsher, so we dial that out. Indoors, the tone is a little more true and, for some reason, it's not as loud onstage so my ears aren't taking nearly the beating as they do outdoors."

Gear List — Brad Whitford

Guitars
Gibson Les Pauls (various models), SGs (various models), Firebird, Flying V, Explorer, ES-335, and Chet Atkins SST acoustic-electric; Fender Stratocaster, Telecaster, Esquire, Telesonic, and Electric 12-string; Veillette baritone 6- and 12-string electrics; various standard and custom-built electrics by Tom Anderson, Terry McInturff, Jim Triggs, James Trussart, Gretsch, Schecter, Washburn, Fernandes, Danelectro, Silvertone, Supro; Gibson J-200 acoustic; various acoustics by Martin, Guild, Alvarez, and Ovation

Pickups
Stock pickups; various Seymour Duncan, DiMarzio, Bill Lawrence, and Joe Barden models

Accessories
Monster cables; metal and glass slides; Whirlwind Selector A/B/Y boxes; various .009, .010, and .011 string sets; medium picks

Effects & Rack Gear
Samson wireless; Roland VG-8 guitar synthesizer and multi-effects processor; Dunlop Crybaby wah; Klon Centaur overdrive; Line 6 DL4 Delay Modeler and MM4 Modulation Modeler; Z-Vex Wah Probe and Super Duper; Sweet Sound Ultra Vibe; Legendary Tones Time Machine Boost; Maxon Overdrive and Stereo Chorus; Danelectro Reel Echo; DLS Chorus~Vib; Ibanez TS9 Tube Screamer; BOSS DD-5 Digital Delay; Danelectro Cool Cat chorus; Korg ToneWorks Delay

Amps & Cabs
Various new, vintage, and reissue Marshall 100-watt, 50-watt, and JTM45 heads, Marshall 4x12 cabinets; Vox AC30; Fender Tonemaster heads and 4x12 cabinets, Fender Vibroverb, Twin Reverb, Super Reverb, and Super 6 combos; Wizard 100-watt heads and 4x12 cabinets; Music Man heads and cabinets; Hiwatt heads and cabinets; Bogner Ecstasy heads and 4x12 cabinets; Peavey 5150 heads and 4x12 cabinets

Bogner Ecstasy settings: Channel 1 controls: volume 3, treble 7, middle 8, bass 3, gain 1 on 10

Channel 2/3 controls: volume 2 on 4, treble 6, middle 9, bass 5, gain 2 on 9; volume 3 on 4, gain 3 on 9; presence 4, master volume 3

Vintage Marshall settings: "My '69 Marshall is turned all the way up—everything's on 10—and the two channels are jumped so I can get that low end out of the second channel. The same thing on the red one [a mid-'70s 100-watt JMP series model]. It's pretty loud, if you figure it's a 100-watter that's on 10. I keep the Plexi reissue idling just in case I need it."

bodied mahogany electric) and plug into a warm-sounding tube amp, preferably a vintage-style Marshall half-stack or combo. Another option would be a Vox AC30 or AC15 that's dialed for a dirty blues-rock tone. Think vintage. Think classic. Think timeless rock 'n' roll tone. That's Aerosmith.

With vintage-style, non-master volume amps, you'll probably need to turn everything up to 10. On a modern amp, with more sensitive tone controls, try setting the bass on 7, middle on 6, treble 5–8, presence on 6, gain 8–10, master volume 3–5. For added sustain and extra volume on riffs and solos, use an overdrive box like an Ibanez Tube Screamer, Boss Super Overdrive, or ProCo Rat (the latter favored by Perry). Set the pedal's controls just slightly hotter than the amp's natural overdriven tone, with the pedal's drive knob at 9 o'clock, tone at 6 and volume at 4–5. The overdrive pedal is mandatory, followed only by a wah pedal, which Perry relies on heavily. Listen back to the tracks on *Toys in the Attic* and *Rocks*. For the earlier Aerosmith tone, no reverb, delay, chorus, or flanging effects are really needed—just a Les Paul, tube amp, overdrive, wah, and you're good to go.

Joe Perry & Brad Whitford: In Their Own Words
"The first time I saw Jeff Beck, I think that's when I turned around and said, 'I *have* to have a Les Paul,'" Joe Perry remembers. "I saw [Jeff Beck Group] when they were touring on their first record. I actually sat in front of his amps when they were doing 'Plynth' and 'Shapes of Things.' It sure didn't sound like the Yardbirds. I had to have a Les Paul after that! It was really Beck, Page, Peter Green, along with Hendrix and Clapton who influenced me to play and influenced my choice in gear."

"In between '67 and '69," says Brad Whitford, "I saw Zeppelin and Hendrix play live, and those definitely made major changes in the way I felt about music—major, life-changing experiences. I bought a new Les Paul the day after I saw Led Zeppelin. It was before their second album was out and they were so on and so good that night. Nothing against Jimmy, because I love the man, but I don't think that I ever heard him play that well ever again. It was one of those nights that he was in tune with the cosmos and it was absolutely mind-blowing. He was playing all those great solos note for note, like 'Communication Breakdown,' and it was just devastating. I swear, I bought a Les Paul the next day. The next thing was

Perry's Gibson Goldtone wall of sound and his onstage foot controllers.

to get the amplifiers. He had two stacks of Marshalls and it was like no sound I had ever heard before.

"Guitars all have particular sounds, which I think does affect the way you approach things," Whitford continues. "Playing a Les Paul and playing a Strat is totally different, and it changes the whole way I hear and what I do. It's nice to be able to mess around with the different textures of different instruments and amplifiers. There's nothing like a good Strat into a Twin Reverb, and that makes me play a certain way. You can have a lot of fun with the classic, simple approach."

"Definitely," Perry adds. "When I hear a clean-sounding Strat or play my greenburst Washburn, that super-clean sound definitely has an effect on the style I play. By the same token, if I go the other way with my Les Paul/Wizard amp rig, it does a different thing. As far as the gear goes, see what works. You've got to go with what's best for the song, and it all depends on what sound you're after. For the sound I like, it's stripping it back to basics—the less stuff between me and my amps, the better. In the studio I use a 12-foot guitar cord and I stand next to the amp. When I've done clubs, I do the same thing. I'm very rarely using a wireless when I'm playing in a club because there's not that much room to move around anyway and you can take advantage of having that small circumstance to get a good guitar sound. You just have to see what sounds good to your ear.

"Another thing to remember when you're playing live is that smaller is better. You don't need a whole stack of Marshalls to sound good and you may not even need a very loud sound, especially in a small venue. What I mean is, it's not [about] volume. I've heard little combos sound louder through a mic and a PA than a big Marshall that's turned up. It may be loud, but the actual sound that's going out over the PA may not be that great. It's better to go with a smaller amp

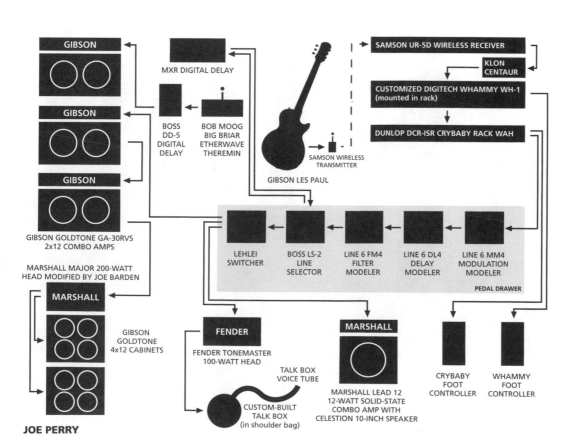

JOE PERRY

Discography

Aerosmith

Aerosmith (Columbia, 1973), *Get Your Wings* (Columbia, 1974*)*, *Toys in the Attic* (Columbia, 1975), *Rocks* (Columbia, 1976), *Draw the Line* (Columbia, 1977), *Live Bootleg* (Columbia, 1978), *Night in the Ruts* (Columbia, 1979), *Greatest Hits* (Columbia, 1980*)*, *Rock in a Hard Place* (Columbia, 1982), *Done with Mirrors* (Geffen, 1985), *Classics Live!* (Columbia, 1986), *Classics Live 2* (Columbia, 1987), *Permanent Vacation* (Geffen, 1987), *Gems* (Columbia, 1988), *Pump* (Geffen, 1989), *Pandora's Box* (Columbia, 1991), *Get a Grip* (Geffen, 1993), *Big Ones* (Geffen, 1994), *Box of Fire* (Columbia, 1994), *Nine Lives* (Columbia, 1997), *A Little South of Sanity* [live] (Columbia, 1998), "I Don't Want to Miss a Thing" from *Armageddon* [soundtrack] (Sony, 1998), *Just Push Play* (Columbia, 2001), "Theme from Spider-Man" from *Spider-Man* [soundtrack] (Sony, 2002)

The Joe Perry Project

Let the Music Do the Talking (Columbia, 1980), *I've Got the Rock 'N' Rolls Again* (Columbia, 1981), *Once a Rocker, Always a Rocker* (MCA, 1984)

Joe Perry session work

David Johansen, *David Johansen* (Razor & Tie, 1978)
Run-DMC, "Walk This Way" from *Raising Hell* (Def Jam, 1986)
Alice Cooper, "Trash" from *Trash* (Epic, 1986)
Mick Jagger, "Everybody Getting High" from *Goddess in the Doorway* (Virgin, 2001)
Eminem, "Sing for the Moment" from *The Eminem Show* (Interscope, 2002)

Brad Whitford

Whitford/St. Holmes (Columbia, 1981)
Rex Smith, *Camouflage* (1983, CBS)

and really get a good sound out of one or two speakers. You'll get a lot more *tone*.

"There's one last thing. If you're using amps that are heavily overdriven, it may sound really good when you're taking a solo and be really easy to play, but it's very easy for it to turn into mush out in the house, especially if you're working with keyboards and other guitar players. That's one of the things I've learned, and that's why my sound is so much cleaner, drier, and less overdriven. That overdrive may sound great when you're soloing, but when you start mixing it with other instruments that are playing in that same sound area, all in that midrange 2k to 5k range, you lose the definition if there's too much gain. That's true in the studio and it's true onstage. It just turns into mush. So if you're having trouble getting heard out there, a lot of it can be in the amount of overdrive you're using. Many of the modern amps have so much gain, and then people add fuzztones and it just comes out like a wall of noise. If you're having trouble getting some definition, just plug straight into a cleaner amp, like a Fender or an old Marshall, and if you need a little bit of juice for your solos, just tweak it a little bit with a fuzztone or some kind of boost."

Whitford's *Just Push Play* stompbox-loaded pedalboard.

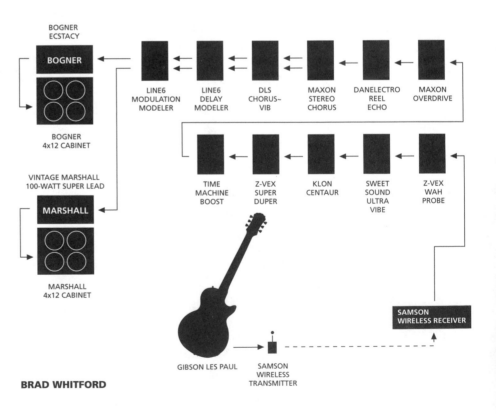

BRAD WHITFORD

Yngwie Malmsteen

Born
June 30, 1963, in Stockholm, Sweden

Bands
Steeler
Alcatrazz
Yngwie J. Malmsteen's Rising Force
Yngwie Malmsteen (solo career)

Tone
Thick, saturated gain—the classic crunch sound of a Marshall slammed in the front end by a preamp pedal

Signature Sound
Fastest metal runs on the planet

Breakthrough Performance
"Black Star" from *Rising Force* (1984)

History and Influences

Beginning with his thunderous arrival in 1983, Yngwie Malmsteen established a new order of heavy metal guitarist. Standing apart from the two-handed Van Halen clones of the day, Yngwie burned across the fretboard of his modified Fender Stratocasters with a dazzling blend of alternate-, sweep-, and legato-picking chops. Within two short years, the ambitious guitarist had established himself as a solo artist with his own group, Rising Force. His baroque-inspired brand of rock attracted thousands of metal fanatics and inspired countless imitators in the so-called "neo-classical" rock genre (also casually known as "Bach 'n' roll").

Yngwie's fascination with the guitar began when he saw Jimi Hendrix on Swedish television the day Hendrix died, September 18, 1970. The seven-year-old soon took up the guitar, and was further inspired by Deep Purple's *Fireball* album—notably, by the way Purple guitarist Ritchie Blackmore blended rock and classical ideas in his solos (such as mixing diminished or harmonic minor runs in with blues licks). Another player who would have a lasting effect on the young man's style was Scorpions legend Uli Roth. Like Blackmore, Roth was a groundbreaker who mixed superior technique with a taste for both Hendrix and classical themes, and Malmsteen became enamored of his playing after hearing the 1978 Scorpions live set, *Tokyo Tapes*. Yngwie also spent more than a little time listening to another great superpicker, jazz-rocker Al Di Meola.

▶▶▶

Gear List

Guitars

Vintage Fender Stratocasters (with scalloped fingerboards, high action, jumbo frets, brass nuts, and floating tremolos); Fender Yngwie Malmsteen Signature Stratocaster; white Flying V (with a scalloped fingerboard, Strat pickups, and tremolo); Les Paul gold-top (for recording rhythm tracks); Schecter Yngwie Malmsteen model; Rickenbacker bass; Fender Jazz fretless bass; Gibson Chet Atkins acoustic-electric (runs through a BOSS CS-3 Compressor/Limiter, and then into a DI box out to the PA); various Fender, Alvarez-Yairi, Ovation, and Carvin acoustic-electrics

Pickups

DiMarzio HS-3 Model (bridge position) and YJM (middle and neck) stacked humbuckers; stock Fender pickups

Accessories

Dunlop 1.5mm picks, Ernie Ball or Fender Super Bullet strings (.008–.046, .008-.048 tuned down a half-step)

Effects & Rack Gear

DOD YJM308 and Overdrive Preamp 250 pedals, Crybaby wah, Ibanez TS9 Tube Screamer, Korg SDD-2000 and DL-8000R delays, BOSS Chorus, BOSS BF-2 Flanger, BOSS OC-2 Octave, BOSS NS-2 Noise Suppressor, Rocktron Hush II, Roland PK-5 and Fatar bass pedals, Bradshaw switching system; Samson Synth 5 wireless, Roland DC-10 analog echo, Vox flanger, Johnson Amplification J-Station (for direct recording)

Amps & Cabs

Marshall 50-watt Mark II heads from the early 1970s (with Tesla EL-34 power tubes); Rhino YJM50 heads; Marshall 4x12 cabinets loaded with Celestion Vintage 30 speakers

Amp settings: Volume 10, bass 5-7, mids 2-5, treble 6-8, presence 4-6

After playing in two minor rock bands—Steeler and Alcatrazz—he released his first solo record, *Yngwie J. Malmsteen's Rising Force* at the end of 1984 (one witty pundit noted that the guitarist used his middle initial so people wouldn't confuse him with all the other Yngwie Malmsteens out there). For his debut, Yngwie's guitar work was pushed to the forefront of the mix—listen especially to his scintillating arpeggios and speed picking in the slow-grooved "Black Star." Another key track from the first album is "Far Beyond the Sun," a baroque stomper that kicks off with the guitarist's patented diminished-arpeggio sweeps and alternate-picking frenzies.

1985's *Marching Out* found Yngwie adding more vocal elements from Jeff Scott Soto, who had appeared on a few tracks from the first album. Check out the ferocious intensity of "I'll See the Light Tonight" for a sample of early Yngwie at his best. Of special note is the breakdown at 01:52, where Yngwie doubles a harpsichord line in a phrase right out of the book of Johann Sebastian Bach, one of the guitarist's heroes.

By 1986, it was clear that the guitarist had set his sights on mainstream commercial success with the release of *Trilogy*, his most tuneful and mass audience–oriented record to date. National tours opening for Emerson, Lake & Powell and other high-profile bands increased Yngwie's recognition factor, and *Trilogy* broke into the Top 50 on the U.S. record charts. Malmsteen continued in the same vein with the release of 1988's *Odyssey*. This disc contained such radio-friendly rockers as "Déjà Vu" and "Heaven Tonight," the latter bearing an MTV-worthy hook that wouldn't have been out of place on a Bon Jovi or Winger album. *Odyssey* peaked at number 40 on the Billboard charts, marking Yngwie's commercial summit as an American rock act.

Since then, Yngwie has regularly continued to release CDs and tour the world. His recent albums are often rehashings of his first few albums, indicating that the guitarist doesn't have much else to say, but his diehard fans still lap up the speedy guitar runs. While he's never been able to crack America's mainstream rock market, Yngwie remains hugely popular in Japan, South America, and Eastern Europe.

Tone and Technique

Love him or hate him, Yngwie has a tone to be reckoned with. From his early days with Steeler and Alcatrazz to his decade-plus solo career, Yngwie's fat Strat tone has become a mainstay among metal fans (basically a tone that mixes humbucker *oomph* with classic Stratocaster timbres). To get to the crux of his sound, look at his heroes: Ritchie Blackmore, Uli Roth, and Jimi Hendrix. The common bond among these three players is an affinity for Stratocasters and Marshalls. Hendrix pioneered the setup back in the '60s, but it was Blackmore and Roth who applied this sound to hard rock and heavy metal in Deep Purple and Scorpions, respectively (Robin Trower should also be given his due in this regard).

Yngwie takes the Strat/Marshall combination to the next level. Using vintage guitars and amps as the basis of his rig, he adds slight modifications to create a unique sound. On the Strats, he replaces the bridge pickup with a DiMarzio HS-3 "stacked" humbucker, which retains the single-coil shape. His neck and middle pickups are his signature DiMarzio YJM Model. Yngwie is also famous for the scalloped fingerboards on his Strats, a feature that's standard on Fender's Yngwie Malmsteen Signature Model Stratocasters ("scalloped" fingerboards sport concave depressions between each fret). All of his necks are also fitted with Jim Dunlop 6000 frets (1.47mm), and the guitarist uses Dunlop 1.5mm picks and Fender or Ernie Ball strings. Gauges are .008, .011, .014, .022w, .032w, .046w, except on his Flying V, where he uses a .048w since it's detuned to D (actually, it's C#, since all his guitars are detuned a half-step).

For live work, Yngwie uses Samson wireless systems on all guitars. From the receiver, the signal goes into a Bradshaw brain (built around 1984–85), which routes effects including Korg digital delays and a BOSS BF-2 Flanger. There's also a Rocktron Hush II, which he seldom uses. The outputs of the rack feed into two or more Marshall 50-watt Mark II heads, depending on the size of the venue. The amp's direct side (dry) drives two 4x12 bottoms at 8 ohms, while the wet side on stage right drives one 4x12 bottom at 16 ohms. Amplifier settings vary according to the small tonal differences among the amp heads and the acoustics of the nightclub or concert hall.

Despite all these tools for gigging, Yngwie's recording setup at home remains quite simple. As seen on a recent visit to his residential Florida studio, he just had his Strats, a good vintage Marshall head, and, for effects, an Ibanez TS9 Tube Screamer and BOSS Noise Suppressor. That's it. But perhaps the coolest part of his home studio rig is that his speaker cables are hardwired into the house. Yngwie can plug into his heads in the upstairs control room while four 4x12 Marshall cabinets sit on the other end of the house in converted maid's quarters, cranked to the bejeezus. Oh, yeah—he's also thinking about building a new garage for his twin Ferraris, so he can turn the current garage into a big soundroom for his drummer. Hope the neighbors won't mind.

Yngwie Malmsteen: In His Own Words

"In the last few years I've found myself very attached to the old vintage, white-cream Strats with maple fingerboards. The main ones I use are heavily modified '68–'72 Strats. They're very deeply scalloped and have Dunlop 6100 frets, which are the very biggest frets—you can drive a truck over them. They also have a DiMarzio HS-3 in the bridge and YJM pickups in the front and middle, and I've disconnected the tone controls. The

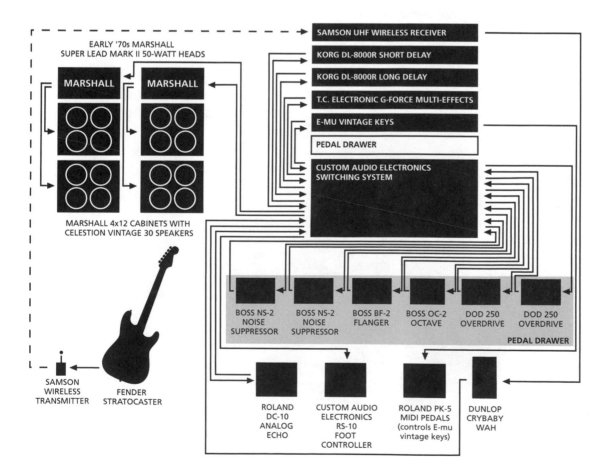

polepieces on the YJM are staggered like on a vintage pickup, but other than that it's the same as the original DiMarzio HS-3 I was using.

"I have about 200 guitars in the house right now. One of my favorites is a '71 Strat from the cover of the first album. I've had it forever, but it still plays well. Then there's a '61 Shoreline Gold Strat, a '66, a '55, '62 Lake Placid Blue, '61 Fiesta Red, and I also have one of the first Strats ever built. It's dated March 3, 1954, under the neck, but the body was refinished black at some point. But it's a Strat from the first month and the first year of production, and all the parts are original. I also have four custom doubleneck Strats that Fender made me. One of them is mono, but the others are stereo with 6- and 12-string setups. I also have an acoustic-electric Strat with nylon strings and piezo pickup. All the acoustic parts on my *Magnum Opus* album were done on that guitar.

"For amps, I use 50-watt Marshall Mark IIs that date from 1969 to 1973. I know a lot of guys that agree with me—like Michael Schenker and Gary Moore—they swear by the Mark IIs. All the Marshalls made during this period are hand-wired and actually they're all different. I know that because Jim Marshall and I got drunk one night and he told me that they just didn't give a fuck back then. When they ran out of one capacitor or transformer, they just threw in whatever was lying around. You know what their slogan used to be? 'Marshall, the sound of success . . . *no distortion!*' They didn't intend to make this thing sound like it does. But Marshalls are still the best. Every other amp company says, 'Ours sounds just like a Marshall,' but to me nothing beats an old Marshall stack. Here in the studio, I drive the front of it with a Tube Screamer and a BOSS NS-2 Noise Suppressor, and I get a really warm tone.

"For live work, I never have less than two amps. Out of the Bradshaw rack, there's one channel that's dry and the other one is delay, but only if I use that preset. If I don't use that preset, then both of them are on with the dry sound, on one side of the stage. When the delay is on, then the cabinets on both sides of the stage are on. I don't rely on monitors because I can't stand monitors. When I sing, I don't even have monitors. The Marshall is so directional, so if I'm on the side of the stage, I'm going to hear myself. The other reason they're that way is to get that effect of the stereo split, which is really cool. So the minimum is two amps, but sometimes when I play in Japan, I can use four, five, or six."

Malmsteen's live rig: A pair of vintage Marshall 50-watt stacks, assorted effects and coordinating foot controllers, mondo-modded Strats, and an Ovation nylon-string.

Steve Howe of Yes

Born
April 8, 1947, in Holloway,
North London, England

Bands
Tomorrow
Bodast
Yes
Asia
GTR
Steve Howe (solo career)

Tone
Eclectic—from round jazz
tones to sharp rock licks to
gentle country twang

Signature Traits
Incorporating jazz, country, and classical phrasing into rock 'n' roll licks

Breakthrough Performance
"Yours Is No Disgrace" from *The Yes Album* (1971)

History and Influences
Perhaps more than any other guitarist in '70s rock, Steve Howe has earned a place of honor simply by being different. While many other players spent the bulk of that era rehashing Hendrix and Clapton licks on their solidbody electrics *ad nauseam*, Howe approached rock from a decidedly eclectic background. He used a Gibson ES-175 hollowbody guitar—previously regarded as a jazz instrument—and he infused his playing with a multitude of non-rock influences from the worlds of rockabilly, jazz, country, and classical.

Among the diverse guitar players he credits as influences are rockers Danny Cedrone and Fran Beecher (both of Bill Haley's Comets), Buddy Holly, and Hank Marvin of the British instrumental band the Shadows. On the jazz side, he is indebted to Les Paul, Barney Kessel, Tal Farlow, Kenny Burrell, Django Reinhardt, and Charlie Christian. Also figuring in the mix are flamenco legend Carlos Montoya, classical masters Andrés Segovia and Julian Bream, and country pickers Jimmy Bryant and Chet Atkins.

On his Yes debut, 1971's *The Yes Album*, Howe made his mark on "Yours Is No Disgrace," an extended suite with several solos. What makes these breaks stand out are both the proficiency of his fast up-and-down picking and the clean guitar tone, which at the time was more often associated with jazz or country players. On another cut, "Clap," the guitarist again avoided the standard rock program with a few stunning minutes of ragtime fingerpicking on a steel-string acoustic, injecting another new concept into the rock-guitar vocabulary.

▶▶▶

Gear List

Guitars

1964 Gibson ES-175, ES-175D, ES-345 Stereo, ES-5 Switchmaster, ES-Artist, EDS-1275 doubleneck, and various Les Pauls; 1964 Gibson ES-175, ES-345 Stereo, Switchmaster, and various Les Pauls; Fender Stratocaster and Telecaster; Steinberger GM solidbody; Coral electric sitar; Rickenbacker 12-string; Sho-Bud and Fender steel guitars; 12-string Portuguese vachalia; Martin 00-18 acoustic; Sharpach SKD acoustic; Conde flamenco nylon-string; Kohno classical nylon-string; Dobro

Pickups

Stock

Accessories

Gibson strings (electric), Martin Bronze light-gauge strings (acoustic), numerous types of picks

Effects & Rack Gear

Electro-Harmonix Big Muff fuzz, Dunlop Crybaby wah pedal, Sho-Bud volume pedals, Maestro Echoplex, Korg A3 multi-effects, Roland SDE-2000 delay, Lexicon JamMan delay/looper, Lexicon Vortex multi-effects, Roland GP8 multi-effects, Korg DTR-1 tuner

Amp & Cabs

Fender Twin Reverb and Fender Dual Showman, each with two 15" JBL speakers, Fender Tremolux

"Würm," the finale to *The Yes Album*'s "Starship Trooper" suite, is a Bolero-paced chord sequence that builds into an explosive solo, this time revealing Howe's sinewy rock chops. But again, Howe didn't lean on stock blues-scale solos riddled with distortion, as one would hear in contemporary groups like Grand Funk or Mountain. Instead, the solo is filled with twisting phrases laced with rockabilly string bends and twangy country inflections that one would sooner expect to find on a Carl Perkins record than on something by a progressive rock band.

In 1972, Yes scored a major hit with "Roundabout," the single from the album *Fragile*, and its short guitar intro is what gained Steve Howe his greatest exposure. Commencing with a simple 12th-fret harmonic played on an acoustic guitar, this little lick was learned by countless young players who connected acoustic playing with electric, many in a way they'd never done before. The approach was further supported by Howe's solo acoustic piece on the album, "Mood for a Day," which is a lovely Spanish-flavored song that encouraged many rockers to take up classical guitar playing in addition to their rock 'n' roll studies.

While contemporary players may not understand the heights of his virtuosity in comparison to the technical excellence of such modern players as Yngwie Malmsteen or Steve Vai, in his early '70s heyday Steve Howe was perhaps the most skillful guitarist in rock 'n' roll—and its very first guitar virtuoso. Without his innovations, the technical standard of later guitar gods might have been far lower and far less imaginative.

Tone and Technique

To understand Steve Howe's complex guitar tone, read through the above list of his influences. It's eclectic, to be sure, but you can break it down into components. A large part of his sound is derived from playing jazz- and country-style licks in a rock context. He often uses archtop Gibson ES-175 and ES-5 Switchmaster guitars *without* distortion through a Fender amp or, at least, with less overdrive than your typical heavy rocker. Toggling between the fat, round sounds of the neck pickup and the brighter, trebly tones of the bridge pickup, Howe can generate an amazing range of sounds, from cool jazz to spankin' rockabilly twang.

Another secret weapon in the Howe arsenal is the Big Muff fuzz. The Big Muff–thru–Fender Twin sound creates a thick, jagged tone that can punch through concrete. It's not that warm, Marshall tube-amp tone. This is an analog stompbox sound that's edgy and fierce, something further complemented by Howe's modal (as opposed to pentatonic and blues) approach to lead phrasing.

Finally, you have to figure in his tasteful use of tape echo. Steve Howe often drops in a dash of deep echo (200ms or more) on certain notes within a solo, but not necessarily the whole break. This adds strong accents to these notes and makes them stand out from the rest of the lead. He also uses a lot of echo during his steel guitar solos. (Another of Howe's innovations was the use of steel guitar in a rock context—its classic slide sound is more often a part of country music.)

To get a handle on Howe's playing, listen to a variety of jazz and country players. From the jazz side, learn about alternate (up/down) picking, using the neck pickup of the guitar, and playing solos based on scales and chord colors rather than those based on blues-box patterns. A great solo that shows Steve's jazz influence is "Siberian Khatru" from *Close to the Edge*. It's a masterpiece of melodic, scalar phrasing in a rock context.

From the country side, investigate picking and pulling your electric-guitar strings with your fingers—an approach that can involve any number of techniques known collectively as "clawhammer" or "chicken-pickin'." For experimentation in this vein, plug in a Fender Stratocaster or Telecaster to get a feel for *twangy* guitar tones—that is, tones that are either compressed and clean or slightly overdriven—and the multi-string bends that recall the pedal-steel guitar work heard in vintage country music.

Another player who made the same jazz/country/blues connections was the late Danny Gatton (*see page 43*), so listening to his records will also help you get aligned with Steve Howe's approach. Although they created very different styles of music, both Howe and Gatton were deeply indebted to rootsy American guitarists circa 1920 to 1960. Curiously, one can also draw parallels between Howe's tone and that of Led Zeppelin's Jimmy Page, who like the Yes guitarist was a hardcore fan of '50s rockabilly music. Many of Page's solos have that "country twang." (Not so surprisingly, when Howe left Yes in 1981, the remaining members of the band briefly worked with Jimmy Page in a short-lived supergroup called XYZ.)

In sum, the key to understanding Steve Howe's sound is to listen to and try playing as many guitar styles as possible, from jazz to country to classical. For the rock component, it's especially important to zero in on pre-Hendrix players like Scotty Moore from Elvis Presley's band, Carl Perkins, or Danny Cedrone (*see page 25*). These were early rock innovators and their individual brands of twang shine through every time Howe plugs in an electric guitar.

Steve Howe: In His Own Words

"My main guitar over the years has been a Gibson ES-175. It's a 1964 model and I bought it in a shop called Selmer's on Charing Cross Road in London. I'd been playing a Guyatone (a cheap Japanese electric guitar), but sometime in '64 I went into the store and asked for a 175, to which they replied, 'Sorry, haven't got one.' So they had to custom order my guitar, because not many people were buying them. So the guitar arrived a few months later and it cost about 200 guineas,

Essential Listening

"Yours Is No Disgrace"
"Clap"
"Heart of the Sunrise"
"And You and I"
"Siberian Khatru"
"Soon" (the finale of "Gates of Delirium")
"Awaken"

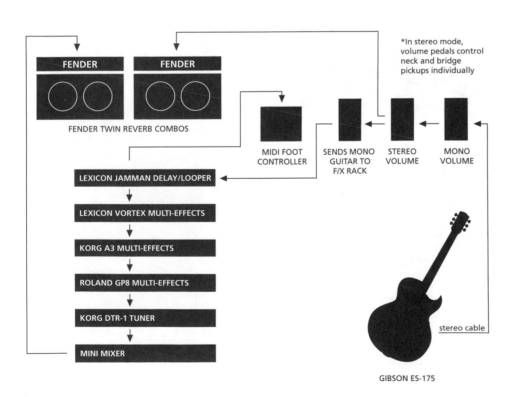

*In stereo mode, volume pedals control neck and bridge pickups individually

FENDER   FENDER

FENDER TWIN REVERB COMBOS

MIDI FOOT CONTROLLER

SENDS MONO GUITAR TO F/X RACK

STEREO VOLUME

MONO VOLUME

LEXICON JAMMAN DELAY/LOOPER

LEXICON VORTEX MULTI-EFFECTS

KORG A3 MULTI-EFFECTS

ROLAND GP8 MULTI-EFFECTS

KORG DTR-1 TUNER

MINI MIXER

stereo cable

GIBSON ES-175

Discography

which was not a cheap price for that time. After that, I basically sat in my room and looked at it for two years! I was simply mesmerized by that guitar. It was like a romance. I still feel the same way.

"I've hardly done any modifications on this guitar, other than original '50s speed knobs—we used to call them 'high hats' because they're the big knobs. And a new ebony bridge base. The rear pickup was wound the wrong way for about five years—from my band Tomorrow through *The Yes Album*—mostly because I didn't want to sound trebly. Then I played it for about seven years solid until the *Fragile* album, which I recorded completely on the Gibson Switchmaster, except for "Heart of the Sunrise," which is the 175. So the 175 was still in the picture, but then on *Close to the Edge* I used an ES-345 Stereo. Still, the 175 has always been there, even if only on the periphery.

"Here's an interesting story: About a year after I bought the guitar, I was using two guitars onstage: the 175 and the Guyatone. And it was the only night that I ever had a pint of beer before going onstage, and I dropped the 175—which makes you understand why I don't drink anymore. I dropped it and broke the input jack. So I took it to Selmer's to be fixed, and when I went around to collect a few days later I saw a Les Paul on the rack, took it down, and really liked it. So I said to the guy, "Look, if this 175 isn't perfect, I'm going to buy this one." Then he brought out the 175, opened the case, and it was like a bell rang out and the guitar said, 'Don't ditch me here—I'm yours!'

"I didn't know if other people felt about their instruments the way I feel about the 175, but I guess it's like violinists who have Stradivariuses because there's a special sound they want. The 175 did that. Plus, when I sat in my room playing through a Fender Tremolux, I could make it sound just like Kenny Burrell, which to me was heaven! I didn't care if I sounded like Hank Marvin or Duane Eddy—I wanted to sound really cool like Burrell. And I don't mind at all that the guitar has become my trademark. I use it for most of my cover shots, too. I think of it as the best Gibson I've ever played, the guitar I'm most comfortable on, the best jamming guitar, and the best *ideas* guitar because it won't let me be anything but Steve Howe when I play it."

Howe's backline: A pair of tilt-back Twin Reverbs.

GEAR SECRETS of the guitar legends

Joe Satriani

Born
July 15, 1956, in Westbury, New York

Bands
The Squares
Greg Kihn Band
Joe Satriani (solo career)
Mick Jagger
Deep Purple (1993–94 tour)
G3 tours

Tone
Warm, heavily saturated distortion (derived from his solidbody's humbuckers, overdrive pedals, digital delay, and a Marshall stack)

Signature Traits
Catchy guitar melodies, scary whammy dives, daredevil rock riffing, and virtuosic tapping

Breakthrough Performance
"Satch Boogie" from *Surfing with the Alien* (1987)

History and Influences
Joe Satriani first appeared on the guitar horizon in 1986 with the instrumental album *Not of This Earth*. Aside from its catchy instrumental guitar rock, the disc showed off Satch's extraordinary chops, which encompassed advanced blues-based work, fast hammer-on legatos, tremolo bar and two-hand tapping tricks, and blinding scalar chops. Strongest praise for the record came from fellow rocker Steve Vai, who had been a student of Satriani's when they were teenagers on Long Island (Satch also taught Metallica's Kirk Hammett). Vai's critical acclaim quickly focused media attention on the Satriani recording.

In 1987, the guitar wizard followed up with *Surfing with the Alien*, a far stronger effort that cut away the first album's fusion excesses for a more straight-ahead rock 'n' roll sound. *Surfing* was also the best-selling instrumental rock album since Jeff Beck's *Wired* of 1975. Outstanding guitar work can be found on the title track, which is laden with solos that incorporate violin-like taps, hammering, and tremolo bar effects, and on "Ice Nine," a song noted for its Hendrix-toned Stratocaster melody and crystalline chord work.

Some of Joe Satriani's most interesting playing on *Surfing with the Alien* was on softer pieces like "Always with You, Always with Me" and "Midnight," an extraordinary piece of neo-classical guitar music that uses highly original tapping techniques and effects. After winning most major guitar polls for 1987 and becoming the veritable player of the year, Satriani made headlines again by taking over none other than Jeff Beck's seat in the Mick

▶▶▶

Gear List

Guitars
Ibanez JS Series solidbodies (JS1, JS6, JS1000, JS700, various prototypes), Ibanez Universe 7-string, 1958 Fender Esquire, Gibson Flying V, Kramer solidbody

Pickups
DiMarzio Fred (bridge) and PAF (neck) humbuckers

Accessories
D'Addario light-gauge strings (.009–.042)

Effects & Rack Gear
Dunlop Crybaby wah pedal, Fulltone Deja 'Vibe, Fulltone Ultimate Octave, BOSS DD-3 Digital Delay, BOSS DS-1 Distortion, DigiTech Whammy pedal, Chandler digital delays, MXR Micro Amp preamp, Echoplex, Ibanez Tube King overdrive, Chandler Tube Driver overdrive, Eventide H949 Harmonizer

Amps & Cabs
Marshall 6100 100-watt head (with 6550 power tubes) or Marshall 30th Anniversary model 100-watt head into two Marshall 4x12 cabinets with 30-watt Celestion speakers; custom Matt Wells tube amp (17.5 watts); Peavey 5150 head; Gibson Discoverer Tremolo 8-T combo; 1953 Fender Deluxe; Roland JC-120 amp

Jagger band and joining the lead Rolling Stone for a spring 1988 tour of Japan. In 1993–94, he toured with Deep Purple following Ritchie Blackmore's departure.

Since then, Satriani has issued instrumental recordings in workmanlike fashion, some better than others but all revealing his immense guitar prowess and sense for a good melody—something hard to find in a rock player these days. In many ways, Joe Satriani is simply a good old-fashioned "guitar hero."

Tone and Technique
Question: How do you sound like Joe Satriani?
Answer: *Practice!*

Actually, achieving a tone similar to Satch's isn't impossible, largely because he uses such a straightforward setup. If you boil his rig down, it's really no different from that of thousands of other working guitarists out there—a solidbody guitar (in his case, an Ibanez with a basswood body), a Marshall stack or half-stack, a distortion/overdrive pedal, wah-wah, and a decent digital delay. You can walk into rock clubs all over the western world and find rigs identical to his.

So that brings us to technique—Satriani has got a lot of them. His influences are fairly basic, too, but the difference is that he's good at mimicking all of their styles and weaving them into something new. The basis of Satch's style comes from blending musical elements from the following players: Jimi Hendrix, Eddie Van Halen, Ritchie Blackmore, Jeff Beck, Allan Holdsworth, and UFO's Michael Schenker.

Listen to all of these guitar legends and start picking apart their idiosyncrasies. From Hendrix and Beck, Satch gets his bluesy vibe, soulfulness, and off-the-wall spontaneity. From Van Halen and Holdsworth, he derives the two-handed tapping and legato lead lines, respectively (not to mention Van Halen's whammy influence), from Blackmore and Schenker, a neo-classical vibe and the ability to make blues scales burn like there's no tomorrow.

When you pair these diverse guitar influences with humbuckers and a half-stack, you'll begin to hear where Satch is coming from on guitar. It's really not that hard—again, it just takes a little practice.

Joe Satriani: In His Own Words
"When I'm on tour I often use a small collection of Joe Satriani model Ibanez guitars and I really do change them around. I have about four or five on the road and usually play two in a set. But because guitars react to weather, you might be trav-

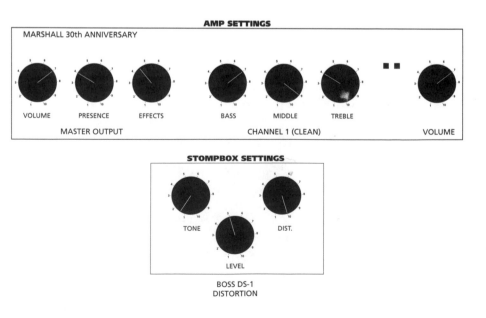

GEAR SECRETS of the guitar legends

eling in the South and one guitar might get funny while the other one starts to get good; but then when you head up to Canada, it's reversed because of the reaction to humidity. Sometimes you might be in a different mood, or a little tired that week and need a guitar that's easier to play. There are so many dynamics that can go on. Sometimes you just want to play a different guitar for no reason at all.

"Here's my typical signal chain onstage. From the guitar, I go into a Dunlop wah, then a BOSS distortion pedal, a DigiTech Whammy pedal, and a Fulltone Ultimate Octave pedal, then a BOSS delay, and some Chandler digital delays. That goes into the front of a Marshall 6100, which is a 100-watt amplifier that powers two 4x12 cabinets with 30-watt Celestion speakers in them. Even though it sounds very complicated, it's an extremely 'lo-fi' setup. No racks, no complicated switching, and everything in mono—it's a very straight-ahead sound. The amp is set on clean and the distortion box is on all the time.

"For many years I tried doing other things, but I've always found that it's sort of like what I call the 'Jimi Hendrix Band of Gypsys Live Factor,' where I go back to that record and listen to his sound. I remember that he had a guitar around his back and he had a curly cord that went into a distortion pedal, a wah pedal, and, I think, a Uni-Vibe that night. Then he had another set of curly cords that went into a Marshall that was turned all the way up. I think that's the most brilliant electric guitar recording ever. It's the sound of a guitar player working with a couple of funky little pieces of gear and playing with musicians—not with his equipment—and playing for an audience.

"Frankly, that's what I consider the ultimate setup. I want a rig where I can walk onstage and get a sound right away, and all I really do is adjust my volume in between phrases. My rig should be up and running and I should able to connect with the band, the audience, and just have a good time myself."

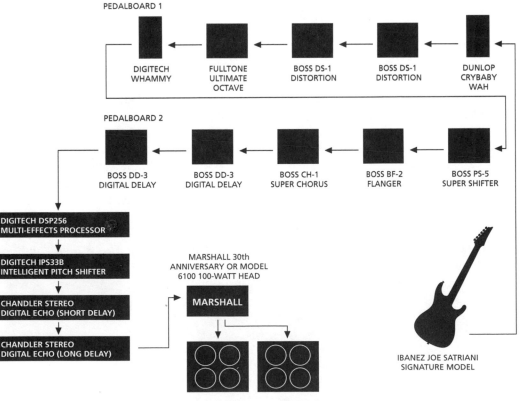

PEDALBOARD 1

DIGITECH WHAMMY ← FULLTONE ULTIMATE OCTAVE ← BOSS DS-1 DISTORTION ← BOSS DS-1 DISTORTION ← DUNLOP CRYBABY WAH

PEDALBOARD 2

BOSS DD-3 DIGITAL DELAY ← BOSS DD-3 DIGITAL DELAY ← BOSS CH-1 SUPER CHORUS ← BOSS BF-2 FLANGER ← BOSS PS-5 SUPER SHIFTER

DIGITECH DSP256 MULTI-EFFECTS PROCESSOR

DIGITECH IPS33B INTELLIGENT PITCH SHIFTER

CHANDLER STEREO DIGITAL ECHO (SHORT DELAY)

CHANDLER STEREO DIGITAL ECHO (LONG DELAY)

MARSHALL 30th ANNIVERSARY OR MODEL 6100 100-WATT HEAD

MARSHALL

MARSHALL 1960 BV 4x12 CABINETS WITH CELESTION VINTAGE 30 SPEAKERS

IBANEZ JOE SATRIANI SIGNATURE MODEL

Dave Grohl of Foo Fighters

Born
January 14, 1969, in Washington, D.C.

Bands
Scream
Nirvana
Foo Fighters
Queens of the Stone Age

Tone
Deep, beefy power chords

Signature Traits
Kick-ass punk power chords and simple melody licks

Breakthrough Performance
"My Hero" from *The Colour and the Shape* (1997)

History and Influences
It's one of rock 'n' roll's most amazing comeback stories. Dave Grohl was originally the drummer for Nirvana, arguably the most important rock act of the early '90s. Following frontman Kurt Cobain's suicide in 1994, Grohl's career seemed effectively over. Little did anyone suspect that the man was secretly an accomplished songwriter, singer, and guitar riffster in his own right.

In 1995, he released *Foo Fighters*, on which he played every instrument. The disc's smart combination of punk, pop, and grunge was a surprise hit, launching Grohl's miraculous second coming. Deciding to flesh out the band, he quickly signed on bassist Nate Mendel, drummer William Goldsmith, and former Germs and Nirvana guitarist Pat Smear to the lineup.

After extensive touring, the band teamed up with producer Gil Norton for their second album, *The Colour and the Shape*, released in May of 1997. During the sessions, Goldsmith left the band and Grohl played drums on most of the album (Goldsmith was later replaced by Taylor Hawkins, previously with Alanis Morissette). *The Colour and the Shape* proved to be a powerful post-grunge album, featuring several catchy tracks with videos to match. Among the best were "Monkey Wrench" and the power-chord-drenched anthem "My Hero," a song about Kurt Cobain. Truly, Foo Fighters had arrived.

On 1999's *There Is Nothing Left to Lose*, Grohl tempered the Foo's punk edge and instead tried for a pop hit with the flaccid "Learn to Fly." Still, it retained the Foo Fighters' place at the vanguard of '90s pop-punk alongside of Green Day, Goo Goo Dolls, Weezer, and Blink-182.

▶▶▶

More recently, Grohl took a break from both Foo Fighters and playing guitar, returning to his drum kit to guest with neo-metal band Queens of the Stone Age on their 2002 tour.

Tone and Technique

To cop Dave Grohl's guitar style, start by listening to staples of '70s punk rock—Sex Pistols, the Clash, and the Ramones. There you will hear the basics of fast downstroke chording, which is prevalent in almost all punk styles. While it's among the most rudimentary techniques out there, it still requires some skill, particularly in regard to timing. Sloppiness does not work here: first-rate punk rhythm guitar has to be tightly locked in with the drums.

Tone-wise, that enormous "wall of power chords" tone you hear on "My Hero" can be accomplished by pairing a solidbody with humbuckers and (at least) a half-stack amp: a 50- or 100-watt tube head and a 4x12 cabinet. Skip all the fancy stompboxes and rack gear—maybe just add a smidge of delay or reverb, if needed, and don't overdo the distortion. Just a dab'll do ya.

In many ways, the Dave Grohl sound is more about cranking up the amp and just *going for it* than it is about using fancy outboard gear. Indeed, that is what punk guitar is all about.

Dave Grohl: In His Own Words

In January 2000 Dave told *Guitar Player*: "When it comes to guitar tone, it seems the current definition of big and heavy is really bright, tinny, razor-blade distortion. Big and heavy *used* to be, like, Sunn amps and a guitar set to the rhythm pickup so that the sustain held on for two minutes. For *There Is Nothing Left to Lose*, we wanted to move back to that huge, warm, sludgy sound and get something a little more garage-y, not something so well-produced and pristine.

"So, rather than play through a distortion pedal and an amp with its volume at 5, we wouldn't use a pedal at all. We cranked up the amp to 10 so that it sounded like the speakers were screwed up. I enjoy the sound of a guitar breaking up because the speaker is getting its ass kicked. I even like listening to music in my truck because my car speakers are ruined—everything sounds a little bit distorted, and I love it. If I listen to the same album on a good stereo system, it doesn't sound as good to me.

▼
Gear List

Guitars
Gibson SG, RD Artist, Explorer, Les Paul and Trini Lopez models; Fender Telecaster; Gretsch Duo Jet, Dan Armstrong

Pickups
Stock

Accessories
Dean Markley strings (light top/heavy bottom); cigarette lighter as a slide

Effects & Rack Gear
ProCo Rat fuzzbox, Electro-Harmonix Memory Man echo and Q-Tron envelope filter, Dunlop Heil talkbox, BOSS DD-3 Digital Delay

Amps
Vox AC30, MESA/Boogie Maverick and Heartbreaker, Dual Rectifier head and 4x12 cabinets, Fender Twin

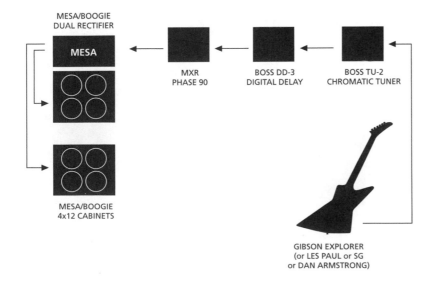

MESA/BOOGIE
DUAL RECTIFIER

MESA

MESA/BOOGIE
4x12 CABINETS

MXR
PHASE 90

BOSS DD-3
DIGITAL DELAY

BOSS TU-2
CHROMATIC TUNER

GIBSON EXPLORER
(or LES PAUL or SG
or DAN ARMSTRONG)

Essential Listening

"This Is a Call"

"Monkey Wrench"

"Everlong"

"My Hero"

Discography

Foo Fighters (Capitol, 1995), *The Colour and the Shape* (Capitol, 1997), *There Is Nothing Left to Lose* (RCA, 1999), *One by One* (RCA, 2002)

"The best way to get a natural guitar sound [in the studio] is to eliminate all pedals and find an amp that has a lot of range. With an AC30 amp, for example, you can go clean, dirty, bright, or fat. It's just the amplifier and the guitar—the most basic combination. I know the [Gibson] Trini Lopez and the Vox is going to have one sound, and the Telecaster and the Twin Reverb is going to have another. Getting basic guitar sounds should be that easy. As far as miking the amps, we used a Shure SM57. That's usually the mic they use on the amps when you play live, so why not use it in the studio as well?

"I'm pretty laid-back about recording guitar. I get a good amp, find a decent sound, put up a decent microphone, and I'm halfway there. It's pretty easy to translate a good guitar sound to tape."

Billy Gibbons of ZZ Top

Born
March 4, 1950, in Houston, Texas

Bands
The Moving Sidewalks
ZZ Top

Tone
Big and bluesy

Signature Traits
Tasty, groove-oriented blues riffs, often ornamented by edge-of-pick harmonics and strong, steady finger vibrato

Breakthrough Performance
"La Grange" from *Tres Hombres* (1973)

History and Influences

Born in Houston, Texas, Billy Gibbons grew up in a family that enjoyed both country and classical music. He was later turned on to rock 'n' roll after hearing Elvis Presley and Little Richard. In 1963, at the age of 13, Gibbons received a single-cutaway Gibson Melody Maker and Fender Champ for Christmas. Soon afterward he formed his first band, which he called the Saints.

By the mid-'60s, Gibbons joined the Coachmen, a psychedelic rock group inspired by Jefferson Airplane, Jimi Hendrix, and others of the genre. He later changed the band's name to the Moving Sidewalks. The group recorded one album, *Flash* (released in 1968), and toured with Jimi Hendrix, but never achieved success outside of their home state. However, the Moving Sidewalks and its guitarist did impress Hendrix, who cited Gibbons as his favorite new player and even endorsed him in the press. To further express his respect, Hendrix gave Gibbons one of his personal guitars—a pink Stratocaster. The guitar, which Hendrix suggested was too pretty to burn, remains a prize piece in Gibbons's personal collection.

The Moving Sidewalks split up in 1969. Wanting to form a more straight-ahead blues-rock group, Gibbons hooked up with bassist Dusty Hill and drummer Frank Beard. Hill and Beard were fellow Texans who had been members of a rival band called American Blues. The new group, dubbed ZZ Top, slowly built its momentum with its first two albums, then gained national attention in 1973 with the release of its third album, *Tres Hombres,* which featured the breakthrough track "La Grange."

ZZ Top enjoyed continued success through the '70s, but reached a new level of commercial attention with *Eliminator* (1983), as the group embraced synthesizers and boosted its image with slick music videos for "Sharp Dressed Man" and "Legs" during the formative days of MTV.

The group maintained its profile through the '90s and sealed its status as one of the

▶▶▶

Gear List

Guitars

Fender Esquire, Telecaster (many Esquires and Telecasters heavily customized by John Bolin at the House of JB), Stratocaster, Jaguar, and Jazzmaster; Gibson Les Paul, Flying V, and Explorer; custom-built James Trussart models; Teuffel custom electric; Tokai Love Rocket

Pickups

Seymour Duncan Pearly Gates and Antiquity models on stage guitars; stock pickups in most vintage guitars

Accessories

Proprietary-wound Popeye's Professional brand strings (.008, .010, .012, .020, .030, .040); Fender extra-heavy and heavy picks, U.S. quarters and Mexican peso coins (used as picks); glass slides

Effects & Rack Gear

Gold Line Frequency Analyzer, two Roland SE-70 Super Effects Processors, two DigiTech Mono 28 Programmable EQs, Bixonic Expandora pedals, Samson UR-5D wireless system

Amps & Cabs

Live rig includes two Marshall JMP-1 preamps with four Marshall Valvestate 120/120 power amps (two are spares), six custom-built Creme 4x12 cabinets loaded with 100-watt Celestion speakers, Demeter isolation box with a 16-ohm, 100-watt Celestion speaker

very finest rock bands ever. ZZ Top recently marked its 30th anniversary with the release of *XXX* in 1999. Today, the band shows no signs of slowing down and continues to tour and record.

Tone and Technique

Gibbons's famous tone is derived from his original 1959 sunburst Les Paul Standard, known as "Pearly Gates." This cherished instrument has been used on every ZZ Top album since he acquired it. Although Pearly is his favorite, it is no longer a part of Gibbons's regular touring arsenal due to its high value as a vintage instrument and its immense sentimental value. Gibbons does not want to subject the guitar to the constant, drastic changes in weather conditions that occur while on tour and wants to preserve the instrument as well as possible. So most of the time Pearly remains at his home in Houston, Texas, though it does make occasional appearances at special shows.

Gibbons's stage guitars include four Fender guitars that were heavily customized by California-based luthier John Bolin of the House of JB; the famous sheepskin-covered Gibson Explorer used in the "Legs" video; a very flamey, cherry-sunburst Tokai Love Rocket; and a custom Teuffel "Bird of Paradise" guitar with an African carving of a bird attached as a de facto headstock (the Teuffel is headless, like a Steinberger).

The customized Bolin guitars all have the same components. Although you wouldn't know it today, those guitars were once just ordinary, late-model Fender Telecasters and Esquires. They were overhauled in John Bolin's shop and transformed into what Gibbons refers to as the "knife primativo" models because all have African daggers stuck into the bodies in various places on each guitar (yes, there are actual knives protruding from the guitars' bodies). Bolin further added maple tops over the original ash bodies and carved intricate designs into the wood, which is his specialty. He also reshaped the necks and changed the fingerboards so they no longer have dot inlays. The original pickups were replaced with Seymour Duncan Pearly Gates pickups with aged Antiquity covers. The original bridges were replaced with Schaller bridges, and the stock tuners were replaced with better gears. Gibbons has six of these "knifed" Bolin guitars in total. One is used as his main stage guitar and was also used to record many tracks on the *XXX* album.

To achieve as fat a tone as Pearly with his other guitars, Gibbons turns to a Gold Line Frequency Analyzer and two DigiTech Mono 28 Programmable EQs. Several years ago, he recorded the Pearly Gates guitar and then compared its sonic characteristics to those of his stage guitars; the DigiTech EQ was then used to adjust the tone of each instrument to make them sound like Pearly. The settings for each guitar are stored individually so that they can be recalled instantly during the live show. "You have to take advantage of the upper levels of sophistication that modern gear can provide," Gibbons explains.

In his amp rack, Gibbons runs two Marshall JMP-1 preamps with two Marshall Valvestate 120/120 power amps, which run into three custom-built Creme cabinets (each cabinet is loaded with four 100-watt Celestion speakers) and a Demeter isolation box. Both Gibbons and bassist Dusty Hill play through the same type of cabinets and their setups are crosswired on stage so that they each have one cabinet on the other side of the stage. That allows them to monitor each other and to hear themselves when standing anywhere on stage. Neither Gibbons nor Hill uses a monitor wedge in front, so they rely on the stage sound and the house sound system to hear themselves, just as they did in clubs 30 years ago.

The Demeter isolation box encloses a single 12-inch Celestion speaker which is miked with two microphones—an Audio Technica AT4047 solid-state mic and an

GEAR SECRETS of the guitar legends

AT4060 tube mic. Those signals are sent direct (DI) to the main console at the front of the house and added into the mix.

The only effects processors used in Gibbons's signal chain are two Roland SE-70 Super Effects Processors. An effects artifact in his rig is called "the Lap Dog." The Lap Dog was created from an old Alamo amplifier with a carved African dog head mounted on top and six Bixonic Expandora distortion pedals daisy-chained together and mounted alongside. The pedals all function, but the amp is just a shell. The amp's speaker was removed from the cabinet and replaced with a blue light that glows when it's plugged in—in fact, these days the unit functions more as a stage prop than an actual tone tool.

Another stage prop is a tweed-covered 1946 or '47 Fender Dual Professional, which is not used for amplification but instead holds Gibbons's ashtray, beverage, and set list. Gibbons always finds it amusing when people come up to him after the show and tell him how great that amp sounded in the mix. Since he likes to keep up the mystique, he doesn't tell them that it isn't plugged in.

In the studio, Gibbons uses a wide array of gear, including Pearly Gates and his main House of JB guitar, along with various Fender, Gibson, and eccentric axes from his ever-expanding collection. He favors the sound of early Fender and Marshall amps for his main tracks, and often brings in some curious vintage and boutique combos for additional tonal colors, as well as an assortment of unusual stompboxes.

To cop Gibbons's deep, meaty rhythm tone, try using a Les Paul with humbucking pickups through a Marshall or tweed Fender amp. Set the amp's controls with treble around 5–6, mids 8–10, bass 7–9, presence 4–5, gain 5, and master volume 3–4. Use the side of your palm to mute the strings at the bridge while playing chords to get a tighter, more percussive rhythm effect. Listen to the rhythm guitar parts on "La Grange" and you'll get the idea.

Billy Gibbons: In His Own Words
"Pearly Gates still remains queen, perhaps the forever all-time favorite. I've yet to find an

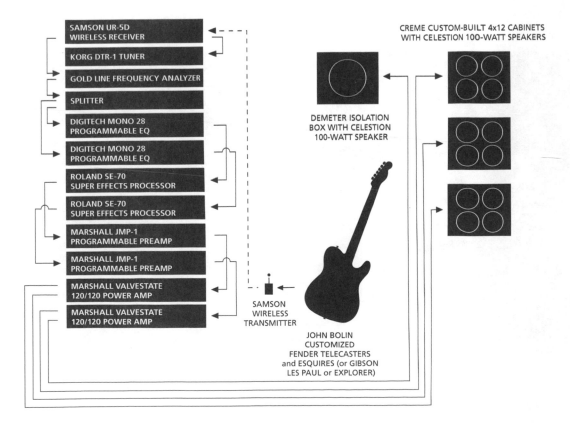

Essential Listening

"Jesus Just Left Chicago"
"La Grange"
"Tush"
"Cheap Sunglasses"
"Gimme All Your Lovin'"

Discography

The Moving Sidewalks
Flash (Akarma, 1968)

ZZ Top
ZZ Top's First Album (Warner, 1970),
Rio Grande Mud (Warner, 1972), *Tres
Hombres* (Warner, 1973), *Fandango*
(Warner, 1975), *Takin' Texas to the
People* (London, 1976), *Tejas* (Warner,
1976), *Deguello* (Warner, 1979), *El
Loco* (Warner, 1981), *Eliminator*
(Warner, 1983), *Afterburner* (Warner,
1985), *Recycler* (Warner, 1990),
Antenna (RCA, 1994), *Rhythmeen*
(RCA, 1996), *XXX* (RCA, 1999),
Mescalero (RCA, 2003)

instrument that has such an all-around responsive characteristic as far as playing, tone, and just absolute awe-inspiring power. It's a fantastic instrument—a 1959 Standard sunburst with no modification.

"I found the guitar under a bed at a little border town ranch house. It showed up just before the band formed in 1969, so I'd say I got it in 1968. I had an old Packard which I paid $250 for, which was given to a friend, Renee Thomas, to make the trip out from Texas to California to see if she could win a movie part, which she did. We decided that the car that got her there had divine connection, so the car became known as 'Pearly Gates.' When she sold the car she sent a money order back to me, out of just simple courtesy. And the day that the guitar later to be known as 'Pearly Gates' was discovered was the same day that the check arrived, which allowed for the purchase of the instrument. I got on the phone and immediately called her and let her know of the continuing good luck charm that seemed to be in this line of activities. She said that the guitar was destined to play divine music and that 'Pearly Gates' would be its new name.

"B.B. King was the one who turned me on to the lighter-gauge strings a long time ago, when I was thinking that heavier strings made for a heavier tone. But there are some tricks of the trade, like laying the back side of the palm heavily on the bridge. It requires a little more energy, but you can actually have the ease of a light-gauge string's responsiveness without sacrificing the heaviness. Again, those are words of wisdom from B.B. King. I figure, if he can do it, then why not me, too?

"For picks, I either use a Mexican *peso* coin or a heavy plastic one. Metal has a brilliant sound, dramatically different than anything that you can lay on wire [strings]. I think that just the additional tensile strength of metal gives a little bit of extra grind to that initial attack. The back side is going to have more sustain and be a little more cranking, too—and that *tink* as it aligns. You've got to be careful when using a coin with a serrated edge because it can really chew up a string. All of that chop-chop work can wreak havoc on a set of strings and you'll break them quicker, but it does have a cool sound."

Gibbons's live rack.

A lineup of stage guitars, including four Fender Telecasters (center) customized by John Bolin, and famed furry Explorer.

Randy Rhoads

Born
December 6, 1956, in Santa Monica, California

Bands
Quiet Riot
Ozzy Osbourne

Tone
Raw, overdriven Marshall amp combined with
a biting, metallic guitar attack

Signature Traits
Fast, arpeggiated trills, pick hammer-ons,
volume swells, toggle-switch tremolo effects,
extraordinary ability to double or even triple
solos note for note in the studio

Breakthrough Performance
"I Don't Know" from *Blizzard of Ozz* (1980)

History and Influences
Randall William Rhoads was born into a musical family. He was raised by his mother,
Delores Rhoads, who held a bachelor's degree in music and owned a music store in
Burbank, California, called Musonia. Rhoads received his first guitar at six-and-a-half years
old—a Gibson nylon-string that had belonged to his grandfather. He first studied folk and
classical guitar, but by the age of 12, Rhoads was listening to rockers like Alice Cooper,
David Bowie, Mountain, and Led Zeppelin.

Around 1971, Rhoads began playing with his best friend, bassist Kelli Garni. The two
worked together in local bands such as Mildred Pierce, the Katzenjammer Kids, and
Mammoth before forming Quiet Riot in 1975. Quiet Riot gained a strong following in the
Los Angeles area but had great difficulty landing a recording contract during the disco
days of the late '70s. The group eventually scored a deal with CBS Sony Records in Japan,
and recorded two albums with Rhoads.

In 1979, Rhoads left Quiet Riot to join Ozzy Osbourne's new band. Osbourne, recently departed from Black Sabbath, had traveled to the United States to audition guitar players for his group. Disappointed after searching on both the east and west coasts, he sched-
uled his return to England. On the recommendation of bassist Dana Strum (later with
Slaughter), who knew both Rhoads and the ex-Sabbath singer, Ozzy agreed to audition
Rhoads in his hotel room on his last night in the States. Randy arrived with his guitar and
a small practice amp, tuned up, and played a few riffs. Without playing much at all—certainly nothing he thought would impress Ozzy—he was astonished to be offered the gig
on the spot. Osbourne had heard exactly what he wanted.

▶▶▶

Gear List

Guitars

Gibson Les Paul Custom, Karl Sandoval custom-built V (with polka-dot finish and bowtie inlays), two Grover Jackson custom-built offset Vs, Gibson nylon-string acoustic, Spanish classical guitar

Pickups

Stock Gibson pickups in Les Paul; DiMarzio Super Distortion (bridge) and DiMarzio PAF (neck) in Sandoval V; Seymour Duncan Jazz model (neck) and Seymour Duncan Distortion (bridge) in Jackson guitars

Accessories

Fender medium-gauge picks, GHS strings (.010–.046 and .011–.052)

Effects & Rack Gear

Roland volume pedal, Crybaby wah, MXR Distortion +, MXR 10-Band Equalizer, MXR Stereo Flanger, MXR Stereo Chorus, Korg echo or Roland RE-301 Space Echo, Yamaha analog delay or MXR analog delay

Amps & Cabs

Marshall JMP series Super Lead 100 Mark II heads with master volume, Marshall 4x12 cabinets (loaded with either Altec or 25-watt Celestion speakers)

In the fall of 1979, Rhoads arrived in England to begin work on the group's first album. Songs came together quickly and Rhoads thoroughly enjoyed the creative freedom and range of expression that he was granted in the band. With the release of Ozzy's *Blizzard of Ozz* in 1980, the group went off on tour. The 24-year-old guitarist was heard worldwide and quickly gained recognition as an up-and-coming metal player.

Immediately following the *Blizzard* tour, the group returned to the studio to write and record *Diary of a Madman,* completed expeditiously and released the following year. On *Diary,* Rhoads's playing was at its best. The readers of *Guitar Player* magazine voted him Best New Talent in 1981.

Tragically, Rhoads's life ended soon after in the crash of a small plane. On the morning of March 19, 1982, during a stop between gigs in Leesburg, Florida, an apparent practical joke—reportedly, the pilot was buzzing the band's tour bus—went awry. Rhoads, the pilot, and another member of the band's entourage were killed instantly. Today, Rhoads is revered as a guitar legend lost far too soon—long before he had the opportunity to reach his full potential as a player.

Tone and Technique

In addition to albums by David Bowie, Mountain, and Led Zeppelin, Rhoads admired the work of guitarists like Gary Moore and Eddie Van Halen, as well as the classical flair of players like Ritchie Blackmore. Though he could copy virtually anyone's riffs, Rhoads worked diligently to forge his own style and sound.

Before he died, Rhoads's interest in classical music, particularly Baroque styles, had been increasing steadily. He even contemplated leaving Ozzy's group to study in a university setting and pursue a degree in classical guitar. While on the road during the *Diary* tour, he took classical guitar lessons, finding teachers in every town through local phone books. Though not all of the teachers he encountered were first-rate, Rhoads strived to learn something from each of them. He progressed rapidly, and incorporated bits of classical technique to expand his metal repertoire.

According to producer Max Norman, who worked on the first two Ozzy

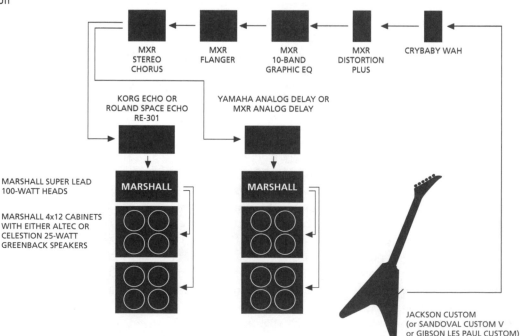

albums, Rhoads was a total perfectionist, a meticulous player who pushed himself to perform flawlessly both onstage and in the studio. Norman notes that Rhoads was a master at layering multiple parts within arrangements and over-dubbing duplicate tracks note for note. When recording acoustic parts, he frequently combined one track with a steel-string and another with a nylon-string for a variety of textures, as can be heard on "Diary of a Madman" and "Dee."

Rhoads was specific in his gear preferences. He favored the thick tone of a solidbody guitar outfitted with humbuckers and the feel of small, vintage-style frets. His custom-built guitars were designed with wide, flat-radius fingerboards which felt more like classical-style guitars than typical electrics did.

Through the late '70s with Quiet Riot, Rhoads's main stage guitar was a cream white Gibson Les Paul Custom. The guitar, which Rhoads considered his first really good instrument, was purchased for him by the owner of a rehearsal studio where Quiet Riot had practiced. Rhoads's Les Paul was most likely an early '70s model. (Rhoads thought the guitar was a '64 model and identified it as such in several interviews. However, Gibson had stopped making the distinct Les Paul shape after 1960, changing over to the SG shape. The Les Paul in its classic shape was later reissued in '68, with the first Custom models offered in black. The white finish was not available on Custom models until after 1970.) The instrument remained an essential tool in his recording and touring arsenal with Ozzy.

In 1979, a few months before leaving Quiet Riot, Rhoads ordered a custom V from luthier Karl Sandoval. Built from Rhoads's sketches, the guitar featured his trademarks: a black-and-white polka-dot finish and bowtie inlays. It was equipped with a pair of DiMarzio humbuckers—a Super Distortion in the bridge position and PAF in the neck position—separate volume and tone controls, and a standard tremolo bridge. The neck, non-adjustable and with a rosewood fingerboard, was taken from an old '60s Danelectro. The back of the neck had been shaved down to a thinner profile and the headstock, reshaped to resemble an arrowhead, was fitted with a set of Schaller tuners. This guitar was used extensively onstage and in the studio with Ozzy.

After the release of *Blizzard of Ozz,* around Christmas of 1980, Rhoads commissioned two more custom Vs. These guitars were built by Grover Jackson and represented a collaboration between Rhoads and Jackson. The instruments were an offset V shape with a solid maple neck-through-body design, and included two Seymour Duncan humbuckers (a Jazz in the neck position and Distortion in the bridge position, with the same wiring configuration as the Sandoval V). The neck was a 25.5" scale with 22 frets and an ebony fingerboard.

The first guitar had a Charvel tremolo bridge. It was finished in white with black pinstripes and had pearl block inlays in the fingerboard. Rhoads used this instrument on the *Blizzard* tour. The second Jackson guitar was finished in black and had a more radical shape, with a sharper, elongated rear wing implying a shark fin, and matching pearl shark-fin fingerboard inlays. This one included a Tune-O-Matic bridge with strings fastened through the back of the body. Additionally, it had a gold-metal pickguard fitted below the pickups. The black guitar was delivered to Rhoads just before the *Diary* tour. Jackson and Rhoads had discussed marketing this instrument as a signature guitar, with Randy suggesting that it be called the Randy Rhoads Concorde or simply the Concorde. He was never to see it in his lifetime, but the Randy Rhoads Model was eventually issued by Jackson.

For amplification, Rhoads played through Marshall JMP series Super Lead Mark II 100-watt heads and matching Marshall 4x12 cabinets. He favored Altec speakers, but also had some cabinets that were loaded with stock Celestions.

▼
Essential Listening
"I Don't Know"
"Crazy Train"
"Mr. Crowley"
"Dee"
"Flying High Again"
"Over the Mountain"
"Diary of a Madman"

Discography
Quiet Riot
Quiet Riot (CBS, 1977), *Quiet Riot II* (CBS, 1978), *The Randy Rhoads Years* (Rhino, 1993)

Ozzy Osbourne
Blizzard of Ozz (Jet, 1980), *Diary of a Madman* (Jet, 1981), *Tribute* (Epic, 1987)

Rhoads used a custom pedalboard for his effects pedals (see list above). His main tone came from the Marshall with tone controls set full up and enhanced by the MXR Distortion +. To achieve his cleaner tones, he would simply back down the volume on his guitar. This setup was used onstage as well as in the studio to track both *Blizzard of Ozz* and *Diary of a Madman.*

To cop Rhoads's style, work on your alternate picking and get it as flawless as possible. Use a metronome to get those 16th-notes sounding strong and even. Learn pentatonic, blues, harmonic minor, and modal scales; practice playing arpeggios (especially diatonic and diminished); and work on trilling each note, as Rhoads frequently did in solos and fills. For rhythm parts, use the side of your palm to mute strings at the bridge, as heard on the galloping introduction to "Crazy Train."

To emulate Rhoads's basic rhythm tone, use a solidbody guitar with a humbucking pickup in the bridge position. Plug into a Marshall or other tube half-stack with the amp's controls set for a crunchy overdriven tone. On an older Marshall head with master volume, crank all the tone controls up to 10. Set the preamp on 10 and master volume on 4. Use an MXR Distortion + or similar distortion or overdrive pedal to add grit and extra sustain. Adjust the volume level on the pedal so that it is just a hair louder than the amp's volume, and set the gain slightly dirtier than the amp's natural tone. On a newer amp with more variation in the tone controls, try setting treble on 7, middle on 8, bass on 8, presence on 5, preamp on 10, and master volume on 3. An echo or delay pedal can be used to add a short delay to round out lead runs and fills.

Dimebag Darrell of Pantera

Born
August 20, 1966, in Dallas, Texas

Bands
Pantera

Tone
Like a jackhammer digging into your brain: abrasive and bright with raspy solid-state distortion and a fat bottom end

Signature Traits
Unusual whammy harmonics, extreme pitch shifts (created with the DigiTech Whammy pedal)

Breakthrough Performance
"Cemetery Gates" from *Cowboys from Hell* (1990)

History and Influences

If you ever go to a Pantera concert, you're in for a visual and aural spectacle. You'll see fans being tossed around in the mosh pit, and the imposing stage presence of Dimebag Darrell, an axeman with a magenta-tinted goatee whose 6-string speed, soul, and finesse have helped rewrite the metal stylebook.

Dime grew up learning licks from players like Ace Frehley of Kiss and Randy Rhoads of Ozzy Osbourne's band. He was also inspired by Texas bluesman Bugs Henderson and other bluesy players. As he notes, "For rock players, I was inspired big-time by Eddie Van Halen on *Van Halen* and *Van Halen II*. Randy Rhoads, Michael Schenker, and especially Ace Frehley were important for me, too. But I've never learned more than two or three solos by any player—I was always after getting the vibe of the player, especially Van Halen. I still listen to Eddie before I go onstage to get some of the spontaneity and liveness of his playing."

The band's first album was 1990's *Cowboys from Hell*, which gave the band a solid following of fans. 1992's *Vulgar Display of Power*, proved even more popular, landing the band a spot opening for Skid Row on tour. Ironically, many of the fans came to see Pantera and then left. 1994's *Far Beyond Driven* appeared on the Billboard charts at #1, marking the band's commercial peak. Subsequently, Pantera settled into the long, steady career that marks many top metal bands—unlike fly-by-night pop or dance artists, hard rock acts tend to have a far deeper and more loyal fan base.

▶▶▶

Gear List

Guitars
Washburn Dime Customs (set up with low action and medium-high frets), Washburn Stealth and Culprit, Dean ML

Pickups
Seymour Duncan Dimebucker (bridge) and '59 humbuckers (neck), Bill Lawrence XL-500 humbuckers (bridge)

Accessories
DR strings (.009–.046 and .009–.050 for drop-tuned guitars); Dunlop .88mm Tortex picks ("My tech, Grady, cuts grooves into them with a dart for a grip. That grip is a great thing, especially when you're sweating onstage. It's kind of addictive and I find it's hard to play without it"); Korg DT-7 Tuner; Korg DTR-1 Tuner

Effects & Rack Gear
Dunlop Dimebag Crybaby wah pedal, Dunlop 535Q wah, DigiTech WH-1 Whammy Pedal, MXR Flanger/Doubler, MXR 6-Band Graphic EQ, Furman PQ-4 parametric equalizer, Rocktron Guitar Silencer, Rocktron Hush IIC, DigiTech Studio Quad processor, A.R.T. FXR Elite processor, DigiTech Control 8, MESA/Boogie Amp Switcher, Custom Audio Electronics Amp Switcher, Nady 950GT UHF wireless, Shure U4D UHF wireless, MXR Flanger/Doubler, Aphex Aural Exciter, Juice Goose Power Strips, Furman Power Regulators

Amps & Cabs
Randall Warhead and RG100HT heads with Randall Warhead 4x12 cabinets

Amp settings: Gain on 10, treble on 4, mid on 3.5–4.5, bass on 9, master on 3–3.5, reverb used occasionally to accentuate harmonic squeals

Tone and Technique

Dimebag Darrell has always stood apart from the metal crowd, both musically and in his choices of gear. First with his original Dean MLs, then retiring those in favor of his own signature Washburn Dime model, he blasted relentlessly through a solid-state Randall stack. Darrell has never been the typical guitarist looking for that "classic tone." Instead, he has always strived to be different, and he has succeeded in carving his own identity. Dime has created a trademark sound that many of his fans try to emulate.

The classic Dimebag tone is incisive and abrasive, an edgy solid-state distortion fueled by his Washburn and Dean solidbodies and Randall stacks. It's all humbuckers and transistors, creating a somewhat brittle but still deadly effective metal crunch tone. To dupe Dime's tone, you'll need a solid-state amp, but not any just any one will do—it must have a 4x12 cabinet (or two) for that bassy rumble. Aside from Randall, some manufacturers who make good solid-state head/cabinet combinations include Crate, Carvin, Marshall (Valvestate), and Peavey.

In terms of technique, Dime's chops are a sizzling mix of bluesy pentatonics and blazing scalar runs—the man is nothing if not *fast*. To ape his style, you'll need to learn your scales (Aeolian and Dorian minor, blues pentatonic, and Ionian major) as well as work on your alternate "up and down" picking. Start slow and work your way up to Dimebag speed, that is, 800 miles per hour!

Dimebag Darrell: In His Own Words

"I've always wanted my very own tone. Actually, a lot of it comes from my Randall amps. I won a Randall half-stack in one of those contests and I heard something different in it than other amps—it was like a chainsaw, and I bet myself that someday I could make it my own. Then, after a year and a half, I found it. The funny thing is that they're solid-state amps but everybody thinks they're tube. The Randall people once sent me a tube amp and it did sound a little warmer, but the solid-state is still a nasty amp and I love it. I use six RG100HT heads onstage now. And I'm not a dude who's getting the brand-new Boogie or Soldano shipped to them every week—that's why so many other guys don't have their own sound.

"I've always liked the tone that Edward calls 'the brown sound'—that warm, round tone that's characteristic of a tube amp. But even though I don't play through an amp with tubes, I've got that sort of warmth in my tone. My amp is solid-state, but everyone that doesn't know thinks it's tubes. The tone I like definitely has a bit of the brown sound, but it's got to have the attack and the shred on top of that. It's just got to sound kick-ass.

"Live, I have two different setups that I use: the regular Randall RG100HT 100-watt head or the Randall Warhead. Basically, the way the Warhead is voiced, it's got my little blue MXR 6-band graphic EQ and my Furman 4-band parametric EQ built in. If I'm playing through the regular Randall, then the guitar goes to the Furman 4-band parametric EQ, to the MXR 6-band graphic EQ, and into Randall. If I'm playing through Warheads, then I'm pretty much plugged straight in without those outboard EQs, since they're built in. Aside from that, I do use a few effects in my rig, too.

"I use a Dime-ized Dunlop Crybaby wah pedal, which was released as the new Dime Crybaby from Hell. It comes in full-blown camouflage and has skateboard skid tape on the top of it. I've also got an old red DigiTech Whammy pedal, a Korg DT-7 chromatic tuner, and a Rocktron Hush IIC noise gate at the end of the signal chain. In addition, I run an old rackmount MXR Flanger/Doubler through the effects loop in the head.

"For guitars, I used to use Dean exclusively, but now they are all retired permanently. I honestly just straight-up wore them out. They probably don't have even another quarter-mile left in 'em after having to re-glue the headstocks back on them 10 to 20 times and the necks now feel like a whittled-down toothpick. I put them in the coffin ever since I got hooked up with Washburn.

"With Washburn, I was thoroughly involved in the design of the Dimebag model. I am real partial to that Dean body shape. Whether I designed it or not, I feel that it's mine. When I hooked up with Washburn we went back and forth and we did a couple of small changes to update it and make it more my style. We lengthened the wing on the top and the bottom horn to make it offset just a little bit, not quite a star shape, to make it look a little more wicked. The same thing with the headstock: We shortened the bottom half so it's a little bit offset. We worked for about a year perfecting the Dimebag model, getting the wood, the shape of the body, and especially the feel of the neck just right. And of course, the sound of the damn thing!"

Essential Listening
"Heresy"
"Domination"
"Rise"
"Planet Caravan"
"Demons Be Driven"

Discography
Cowboys from Hell (Atco, 1990), *Vulgar Display of Power* (Atco, 1992), *Far Beyond Driven* (EastWest America, 1994), *The Great Southern Trendkill* (Atlantic, 1996), *101 Proof* (EastWest America, 1997), *Reinventing the Steel* (EastWest America, 2000)

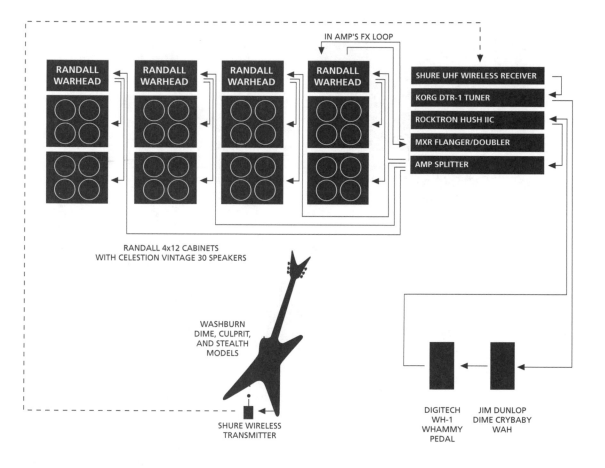

IN AMP'S FX LOOP

RANDALL WARHEAD
RANDALL WARHEAD
RANDALL WARHEAD
RANDALL WARHEAD

SHURE UHF WIRELESS RECEIVER
KORG DTR-1 TUNER
ROCKTRON HUSH IIC
MXR FLANGER/DOUBLER
AMP SPLITTER

RANDALL 4x12 CABINETS
WITH CELESTION VINTAGE 30 SPEAKERS

WASHBURN DIME, CULPRIT, AND STEALTH MODELS

SHURE WIRELESS TRANSMITTER

DIGITECH WH-1 WHAMMY PEDAL

JIM DUNLOP DIME CRYBABY WAH

Brian May of Queen

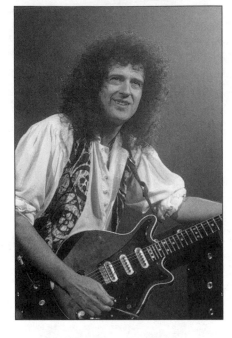

Born
July 19, 1947, in Twickenham, London, England

Bands
1984
Smile
Queen
Brian May (solo career)

Tone
A blend of raw and polished tones highlighted by multiple harmonies created live using delay units

Signature Traits
Layered guitar harmonies

Breakthrough Performance
"Keep Yourself Alive" from *Queen* (1973)

History and Influences
With the identifiable tone and hook-laden guitar riffs he contributed as a member of Queen, Brian May became one of the most talented and influential musicians to emerge in the 1970s. May grew up the son of an electronics engineer and musician, and clearly inherited his father's talent for tinkering and music. He managed to balance his interests in technology and music, and later went on to earn his master's degree in physics.

May's earliest guitar influences included the Shadows' Hank Marvin, Presley sideman Scotty Moore, skiffle master Lonnie Donegan, Buddy Holly, and James Burton (particularly his work with Ricky Nelson in the 1950s). While a student at secondary school, May formed his first band, 1984, which was an instrumental group. The group gigged around London and opened shows for legendary artists like Traffic, Jimi Hendrix, Pink Floyd, and Tyrannosaurus Rex (later T-Rex). May left the group in the spring of 1968 to focus on his studies at Imperial College.

While at college, May hooked up with drummer Roger Taylor and formed a hard rock trio called Smile. He graduated with honors degrees in both math and science, but decided to focus on his music full-time. Smile signed a deal with Mercury Records and released one single, to minimal success. Freddie Mercury was added and took over as lead singer. The band changed its name to Queen and worked with several different bassists before John Deacon finalized the lineup in 1971. Queen signed a new deal with EMI and released its debut album in 1973. The first album, *Queen,* had a very heavy sound, much in the same vein as Smile. The combination of Mercury's operatic vocals and May's tasty guitar riffs established Queen as a premier force.

▶▶▶

With each subsequent release, the group experimented with expanding its sound. *A Night at the Opera* was released in 1975 and contained the mega-hit "Bohemian Rhapsody," which showcased the group's versatility, musicianship, and songwriting skill. *A Day at the Races* in 1976 and *News of the World* in 1977 were both major successes at radio and retail; "We Will Rock You" and "We Are the Champions," which drove sales of *News of the World*, have since become huge sports anthems. A lesser-known track from *News*, "It's Late," is notable for May's use of double-handed tapping and hammer-ons in the guitar solo—especially since it was released a year before *Van Halen*, when Eddie Van Halen made waves with his own double-handed tapping style. May claims to have copped this technique from a player in Texas who had seen Billy Gibbons doing it first:

"I think we were in Texas, playing Houston one night, and then we went out. I think we were with the girls from Heart and we went out clubbing. We ended up in this place where a good Southern boogie band was playing, and the guitarist was doing that. It wasn't the whole tapping and pulling-off technique—it was just one note. He would play these notes and then suddenly he would whack on with the right hand and it would make this beautiful sort of 'flutey' sound. I heard it before I saw it and I thought, 'How does he do that?' Then I watched. It would have a little vibrato once he hammered it with his right hand because he was still going with the finger on his left hand. I talked to him afterwards and said, 'That's brilliant, I'm going to steal that!' Unfortunately now, I can't remember his name, but maybe the Heart girls do. I asked him how he figured it out and he said that he saw Billy Gibbons doing it. I was already a ZZ Top fan, so I went back and listened to all my ZZ Top records and I couldn't find it. So it's a mystery!"

Following Freddie Mercury's death in 1991, Queen officially disbanded, though the surviving members have reunited for special events such as the Concert for Life tribute to Mercury in 1992 (which raised money for the Mercury Phoenix Trust, established to increase AIDS awareness). May has since focused on a solo career, releasing *Back to the Light* in 1993 and supporting it with a solo tour. The following year, he released *Live at the Brixton Academy*, which included material from his solo

Gear List

Guitars
Custom-built "Red Special," custom Red Special models built by Greg Fryer, Guild Brian May signature model, Burns Brian May signature model, Gibson Les Paul Standard, Gibson ES-335, Collings acoustics

Pickups
Burns (in Red Special); DiMarzio Brian May model (in original Guild Brian May signature guitar)

Accessories
Maxima strings (.008, .009, .010, .016, .022, .034)

Effects & Rack Gear
Vox wah, custom-built treble booster, modified Echoplex, Boss CE-3 Stereo Chorus Ensemble, Rocktron Intellifex multi-effects, Bel Digital Audio Delay

Amps
Vox AC30 and AC10 models, custom-built Deacon amp (built by Queen bassist John Deacon), Selmer, Marshall JCM800

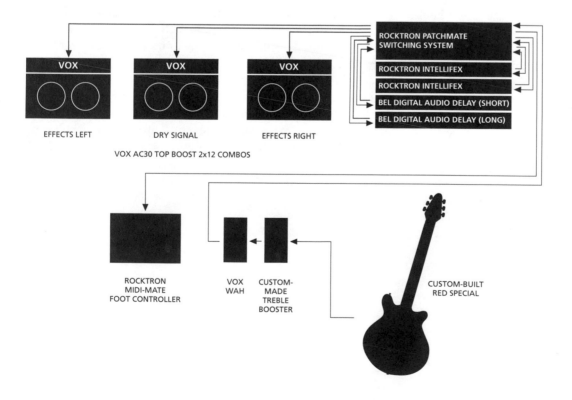

Discography

Queen

Brian May

With Others

disc and from Queen's catalog. In 1998, he released *Another World*, his second solo outing, featuring a guest appearance by Jeff Beck on the track "The Guv'nor."

Tone and Technique

The heart of Brian May's tone is his "Red Special" electric guitar, which he hand-built with his father. Finding a guitar that sounds just like May's Red Special is likely to be a difficult task unless you happen to have one of the replicas built by Greg Fryer. Though the Guild and Burns signature models are fairly close in design, they don't sound exactly like May's instrument. May's rig also includes a few custom-built ingredients, including a treble booster used in conjunction with his Deacon amp and a splitter to send his signal into three Vox AC30s.

As a substitute for the Red Special, use a warm-sounding solidbody or semi-hollow guitar with smooth vintage-style humbuckers—perhaps an ES-335, Les Paul, or SG. For amplification, go with a Vox AC30 or other small tube amp. Use a basic preamp like an MXR Micro Amp with the gain control turned all the way up to overdrive the input of the AC30. If you don't have a treble booster, try using an overdrive box with a tone control that will allow you to boost the highs without adding too much dirt, or use an equalizer to boost the upper frequencies.

Another option is to use a versatile overdrive box with adjustable controls for drive, boost, and EQ functions. Crank the amp's volume control to between 3 and 10 to get a naturally overdriven tube-amp tone that responds to your picking technique; hitting harder will create more drive and dirt, while picking lightly or turning down the guitar's volume control will yield cleaner tones. Since most of the older Vox amps do differ somewhat in tone, start by setting the tone controls at their midpoint and then adjust them as needed to achieve a smooth, even tone. The key is to create a tone with natural overdrive rather than the synthetic dirty tone attributable to many processors.

So how does Brian May create his signature guitar harmonies? His secret is to use a three-amp setup with the dry signal (no effects) in the middle, flanked by left and right stereo-effects signals, all of which he uses to build multi-dimensional tones. In the early days, he used a three-way splitter to divide his guitar's signal, and two Echoplexes that were set for different delay times (and ran to separate amps) to create his layered harmonies. May no longer uses the Echoplexes, but achieves the same results with digital delay units and effects processors that are readily accessible to any player.

An easy way to create layered harmonies is with: A) a harmonizer or multi-effects processor that has a harmony setting built in, and B) two delay or echo units to layer the sounds. First, set the processor's harmony patch to play 3rds or 6ths (the most common guitar harmony intervals). Then, route the processor's stereo outputs to the two separate delays. From there, feed the outputs of each delay into two separate amps for a full stereo sound. If you're using stompboxes, you can split the signal with a stereo chorus box like the BOSS CE-3 (which is what May used for 1983's *Star Fleet Project*). Set one delay or echo unit for a short delay time (approximately 800 milliseconds) and the other for a longer delay time (approximately 1600 milliseconds). Now as you play, you'll hear the original signal and then the repeats cascading from the separate amps at staggered times. Try playing a repeating scale or arpeggio pattern and building up harmonies over the repeats.

Brian May: In His Own Words

"I don't really use many effects. Instead, I've used the Deacon amp for certain effect sounds. It's a little amp that John Deacon made about 25 years ago and it happens to sound incredibly good. It's got car speakers in it and some sort of modified hi-fi amp, I think. I've been using that, way back to things like 'Procession' and 'The Fairy Feller's Master-Stroke' on *Queen II*. I've mainly used the Deacon amp and the AC30s. I did have an AC10, but I never used it that much. I don't use many effects because I like the sound to be in-your-face. I have the Deacon amp, a treble booster, and a Vox amp. I also have a wah-wah pedal—a Vox reissue. In the studio they'll put some effects on afterwards, and we'll have a little bit of delay, too.

"In terms of my harmonies, I strived to get one guitar to sound like an orchestra. To realize this concept of multiple guitar harmonies, I used a modified Echoplex. I extended the rail, basically, because I wanted longer repeats, and I turned off all of the regeneration so I just got one discrete repeat out of each box. The outputs from each box went to a separate amp, so you could turn everything up full and nothing would interfere with anything else: there was no original signal getting to the first repeat, and there was no first repeat getting to the second repeat. So they all would be like full-blown, fully saturated guitar signals, all separate. You see, I had this thing about harmonies and it was my dream to make guitar harmonies happen. And onstage that was the way I did it.

"For a pick, I started using an English sixpence coin, which has a different sort of feel and attack. It doesn't slip out of your fingers because it's rough and it also has this serrated edge, so if you play parallel to the string, it's quite smooth. However, if you turn it, you get this sort of splutter. They don't make this coin anymore, but I have thousands of them. I now find I'm using my fingers a lot more, though, because you get different sounds and you get so much control."

Brian May's "Red Special" Guitar

There are many stories surrounding May's renowned custom-built axe. According to May, he built the instrument with the help of his father and dubbed it the "Red Special." May created the body design, which he based on the curvature of an acoustic guitar with more cutaway added around the top and bottom for better access to the upper neck. He shaped the wood with a penknife, chisel, and sandpaper. The fingerboard was also based on an acoustic. The guitar's neck is extremely thick and round. It joins the body with a single bolt and it's not glued in. There is no pitch to the headstock, like on a Fender. There's a tiny volute behind the headstock, and a "zeroed fret" (a fret installed directly in front of the nut, before the first fret). The frets are a wide-flat, school-bus shape and there are inlays as follows: dot inlays on the 3rd fret, double dots on the 7th, a single dot on the 9th, three dots on the 12th, one on the 15th, two on the 19th, one on the 21st, and three on the 24th. There are also side-marker dots on the edge of the fingerboard and larger line markers at the edge of the 5th and 17th frets.

The guitar's neck came from a support column that held up a mirror over an old fireplace. The fingerboard is oak painted with Rustin's plastic coating to look like ebony. The nut is Bakelite, taken from an old radio. The neck fits deep into the body, just past the middle pickup. The body is

made of an oak insert that came from a table and two separate layers of block board which May hollowed out. The entire body is covered with a mahogany veneer. The binding around the body is made from shelf edging. The roller bridge and individual saddles were also designed by May and his father, all machined by hand.

May built the control knobs in his school shop class. The tremolo arm is made from the part of a bicycle that holds up the saddlebag, and the arm's tip is a piece of his mom's knitting needle that he ground down with a drill. "It's all pieces of junk, really," laughs May. Perhaps it is the combination of unusual components that make the legendary guitar's tone so unique. As for the electronics, May wound the guitar's original single-coil pickups by hand, but later replaced them with pickups he bought from Burns in England. The guitar's original tuners were also purchased from Burns, but those tuners have since been retired and were recently replaced with a set of Sperzel tuners. Furthermore, May had also designed the guitar's wiring scheme, which uses six switches: three for phasing and three on/off switches for each individual pickup.

In the mid-'90s, May met Australian luthier Greg Fryer, who had sought the guitarist's permission to build several authentic copies of the Red Special. Each one was to be built as close as possible to the original instrument in every detail—more so than either version of the Guild signature models. Wherever possible, Fryer aimed to use the same types of wood, glue, finish, and hardware. May enthusiastically accepted his request. Fryer paid his own way to travel from Australia to May's home in England, where he painstakingly measured out and recorded all the specifications of the instrument's construction in explicit detail. Fryer then went back to his shop and went to work. A year later, he returned to England with his three duplicates of May's original guitar. May was completely floored with the results. Fryer's guitars felt and played incredibly close to his beloved Red Special without the wear and tear it had undergone. May now had three Red Special clones.

It was no surprise that after 30 years of faithful service, the original Red Special was starting to show her age. Having played thousands of gigs all over the world, the old girl was in need of some repairs and refurbishment. Once he received these samples showing Fryer's craftsmanship as a builder, May knew that he was the most qualified person to entrust with the task of overhauling his prize jewel. Fryer accepted the challenge and performed the much-needed restoration work while still keeping the instrument as original as possible. In fact, Fryer used many of the same materials that May and his father used in the original construction. The guitar is now back in action and as good as new.

"The Red Special has a certain sound," May notes. "The pickups and combination of woods give it a very warm and very resonant sound. It's very live and feeds back very well, but in the way you would want it to feed back, as opposed to whistling. That was sort of the philosophy—if there was a philosophy behind this guitar, it was to make something that fed back in the right way because that had become, for me, the great thing about the electric guitar, or one of the great things. The first great thing is that it'll sustain any way because there's not much signal loss in the system. That helps for bending strings.

"The last thing is that you can turn up really loud and when you're near your amplifier, it'll get this positive feedback thing and it'll sustain. I remember seeing Jeff Beck doing it at the Marquee with a Les Paul and thinking to myself how really interesting it was because a Les Paul has been designed to minimize feedback, and here's this guy making it feed back like a motorbike. So I thought, I will make a guitar, if I can, that does feed back in the way that we want it to, and I was quite lucky. Some of it was good design and some of it was luck, I think. But it does have good sustain and a good sound. It has a great variety of sounds because of all this switching, and it just had a certain feel that I like. The other advantage is that it has a real tremolo, which could go down an octave and come back in tune, more or less, and I don't think there was a guitar around that could do that. Tremolos were sort of loose tailpieces at the time. The Fender tremolo worked, but I couldn't afford one."

Munky & Head of Korn

Munky

Head

Born
James "Munky" Shaffer born June 6, 1970, in Rosedale, California

Brian "Head" Welch born June 16, 1970, in Torrance, California

Bands
L.A.P.D.
Korn

Tone
Deep, dark, grinding, and guttural

Signature Traits
Quirky, abstract metal riffs in conjunction with ferocious, brutal, and funky rhythm patterns

Breakthrough Performance
"Blind" from *Korn* (1994)

History and Influences
Korn emerged from Bakersfield, California in 1992, when members of established funk/metal outfit L.A.P.D. (formed in the late '80s)—which included guitarists James "Munky" Shaffer and Brian "Head" Welch, bassist Reginald "Fieldy" Arvizu, and drummer David Silveria—hooked up with former SexArt frontman Jonathan Davis. As L.A.P.D., Korn's core band built up a strong West Coast following with two discs: the EP *Love and Peace, Dude,* released in 1989, and the full-length album *Who's Laughing Now* in 1991, just prior to Korn's formation. An L.A.P.D. compilation disc was later released in 1997.

Reborn as Korn, the group moved to Los Angeles and soon signed with Epic's Immortal Records, releasing its debut disc in 1994. Although Korn still retained many of the funky, groove-oriented elements of L.A.P.D., the music was far more aggressive. Furthermore, Davis's lyrics added a dark ingredient that complemented the group's raucous low-tuned guitars. Korn's style and sound was vastly different from any other band on the scene.

▶▶▶

Gear List

Guitars

7-string Ibanez Universe UV7 and K7 guitars (tuned down a whole-step)

Pickups

DiMarzio PAF 7 humbuckers

Accessories

Dean Markley Vintage Light Top/Heavy Bottom strings (.010, .013, .017, .030, .042, .052, .060); Ibanez U-Bar tremolo bridge attachment

Effects & Rack Gear

Munky

DigiTech XP100 Whammy-Wah pedal, Jim Dunlop Uni-Vibe, Electro-Harmonix Deluxe Electric Mistress flanger, Big Muff Pi distortion, Small Stone phase shifter, BOSS RV-3 Digital Reverb/Delay, DOD FX25 Envelope Filter

Head

DigiTech XP100 Whammy-Wah pedal, Jim Dunlop Uni-Vibe, BOSS PH-2 Phaser, BOSS CE-5 Chorus Ensemble, Rocktron Tremolo pedal

Amps & Cabs

MESA/Boogie Triple Rectifier Solo heads, Marshall 4x12 cabinets with Celestion Vintage 30 speakers, Bogner heads, Rivera Bonehead heads with 4x12 cabinets and Rivera Los Lobottom 2x12 subwoofers driven by Rivera TBR-5 power amps

With relentless touring, including the highly successful Family Values Tours, Korn's raging sound spread like wildfire. The group's discs—*Life Is Peachy* (1996), *Follow the Leader* (1998) and *Issues* (1999)—had achieved major success and, of course, inspired hordes of imitators. After a short break, the group returned in 2002 with a subtly refined style on *Untouchables*. While Korn's brooding vibe remains, their latest release features a varied approach to the guitar work, emphasizing sonic textures and ambient parts rather than pure full-on assault.

Tone and Technique

With its chunky low tunings, Korn developed a unique sound and style that set the trend for so many of the "nü-metal" bands that emerged in the mid- to late '90s. To achieve the mandatory sonic depth and girth, you'll need a 7-string guitar that's tuned down a full step (*A, D, G, C, F, A, D*, low to high). In a pinch, you can replicate some of that low-tone guitar by dropping the low *E* string on your guitar to a *D*.

You'll also want a beefy amp rig that can generate the essential deep foundation tones, like the trusty MESA/Boogie Triple Rectifier heads both Munky and Head rely on. Then you'll want to pair the amp with a 4x12 cabinet that can push those brawny tones through with clarity and force so the low notes don't sound too mushy. Set the amp for lots of muscle: bass on 10, mids 6–8, treble 6–7, presence 4, gain 8, master volume 4.

Add in your choice of effects for color with either stompboxes or a multi-effects processor. Munky and Head both use the DigiTech XP100 Whammy-Wah and Dunlop Uni-Vibe, and each has a phase shifter, but their rigs vary with their selection of other effects. With two guitarists, it certainly makes sense to broaden the spectrum with more colors. The average multi-effects processor usually includes a useful assortment of flanger, tremolo, delay, chorus, distortion, and filter effects that can be used to simulate their sounds. But Munky and Head are always striving to discover fun and exciting new noises. With Korn, anything goes.

Experiment with single effects and building combinations of unusual sounds that can work together to create intriguing textures or set a mood within a song. Even if you don't copy their exact noises and effects, you can take a cue from

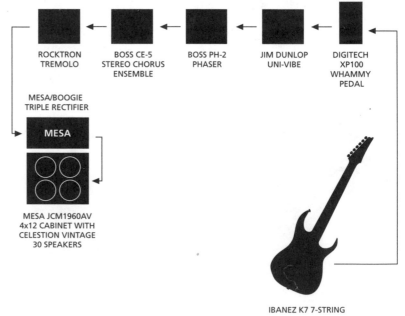

ROCKTRON TREMOLO   BOSS CE-5 STEREO CHORUS ENSEMBLE   BOSS PH-2 PHASER   JIM DUNLOP UNI-VIBE   DIGITECH XP100 WHAMMY PEDAL

MESA/BOOGIE TRIPLE RECTIFIER

MESA

MESA JCM1960AV 4x12 CABINET WITH CELESTION VINTAGE 30 SPEAKERS

IBANEZ K7 7-STRING

HEAD

Munky and Head by breaking out of the box and trying something new that might seem slightly off the wall. You never know—it may lead you to a breakthrough in your own playing and inspire a new way of thinking.

Munky & Head: In Their Own Words

Head and Munky talked about their gear and approach in the March 1997 and October 1998 issues of *Guitar Player*: "We were one of the first bands to get really into the 7-string," says Head, who switched to 7-string after hearing the incredibly heavy sound of Munky's Ibanez Universe. "After a while, we noticed that more people were playing 7-strings, so we thought, 'Let's go lower!' So, my 7th string is tuned to *A*, and the rest is like a regular guitar, but a whole-step lower.

"As far as figuring out where to go on the neck, it was really natural," he continues. "I didn't have to think about it too much—I just looked at it, understood it, and that was it. I really thought I had mastered the 7-string after one week of sitting at home practicing. But then I went to a Korn rehearsal, put a strap on my guitar, and stood up. It was *totally* different. My whole week of practicing sitting down was for nothing. I couldn't play *anything* standing up, because I had to reach around much more. The neck felt really fat, and I just wasn't used to it. I had to bend over at first so I could reach the chords. After another month of practicing, I got it all down and I didn't have to play bent way over like that anymore, but that posture became a habit."

Korn's abstract musical philosophy is strictly based on instinct, and the group's writing sessions are a virtual free-for-all. What sounds and feels right *is* right. "We can't even read four bars of music, let alone play it in time," laughs Munky. "It's more about exploration and finding new sounds than anything else. Not every creation has to start out with a riff—sometimes all it takes is a noise. It takes patience, but we respect each other's musicianship, so it works.

"It's complete noise, but our producer always manages to find something in the mess and point at whoever did it," Munky concludes. "If it's something I'm doing, I'll replay it, and we'll pass it around the room. If we're all happy with it up to the first eight bars, everyone always thinks they know the next part. So I'll play the riff, and as soon as the ninth bar comes in, it's complete noise again until the producer points at someone else. Sometimes we'll go all night just to write eight measures."

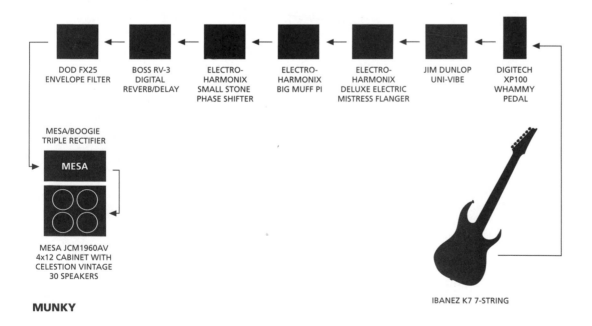

DOD FX25 ENVELOPE FILTER — BOSS RV-3 DIGITAL REVERB/DELAY — ELECTRO-HARMONIX SMALL STONE PHASE SHIFTER — ELECTRO-HARMONIX BIG MUFF PI — ELECTRO-HARMONIX DELUXE ELECTRIC MISTRESS FLANGER — JIM DUNLOP UNI-VIBE — DIGITECH XP100 WHAMMY PEDAL

MESA/BOOGIE TRIPLE RECTIFIER

MESA

MESA JCM1960AV 4x12 CABINET WITH CELESTION VINTAGE 30 SPEAKERS

MUNKY

IBANEZ K7 7-STRING

Tony Iommi of Black Sabbath

Born
February 19, 1948, in Birmingham, England

Bands
Rest
Mythology
Polka Tulk
Earth
Jethro Tull
Black Sabbath
Tommy Iommi (solo career)

Tone
Crunchy British-style tube amp set for an over-driven tone with clarity and bite. In the '70s, more fuzzy and with less clarity.

Signature Traits
Two-finger power chords (played with first finger and pinky); ascending string bends; fast hammer-ons and pull-offs as accents

Breakthrough Performance
"Paranoid" from *Paranoid* (1971)

History and Influences
Back in the late '60s in Birmingham, England, guitarist Tony Iommi united with drummer Bill Ward, playing together in several groups including Rest and Mythology. The two later joined forces with bassist Geezer Butler and vocalist Ozzy Osbourne to form a new band. Originally a jazz/blues outfit called Polka Tulk, they later changed the name to Earth and took on a darker, heavier style. In December 1968, Iommi jumped ship very briefly and played a weeklong stint with Jethro Tull while they sought out a permanent replacement for guitarist Mick Abrams (ultimately replaced by Martin Barre). Though Iommi never did any recording with Tull, he was taped performing "A Song for Jeffrey" on *The Rolling Stones' Rock and Roll Circus* TV special. The experience sent him straight back to his former group.

By '69, Earth had changed its name to avoid confusion with another group bearing the same moniker. Now called Black Sabbath—taken from the title of a song the members had already written—the group became legendary for its mystical stage antics and dark, tuned-down heavy rock music played at ear-splitting volume. The trademark sound and style they developed became known as heavy metal, and has been emulated for generations since. Black Sabbath is cited as a primary influence on many metal, grunge, and heavy alternative bands from the '80s to the present.

The original Black Sabbath lineup recorded seven studio albums between '70 and '78, including *Black Sabbath; Paranoid; Master of Reality, Vol. 4; Sabbath, Bloody Sabbath;*

▶▶▶

Sabbotage; and *Never Say Die!* A greatest-hits compilation, *We Sold Our Soul for Rock and Roll,* was released in '76. Osbourne departed in '79, but the band continued to make music with new singer Ronnie James Dio for a few years and then a succession of lead vocalists. Since then, Iommi has been keeping the fire burning—sometimes as the only remaining original member. Nevertheless, no incarnation of Sabbath, nor any of the members' own endeavors, has ever matched the legacy of the band's original lineup.

The original four members reunited for the first time at Live Aid in 1985, then again during the encore of what was *supposed* to have been Osbourne's farewell performance with his solo band in '92. Audience response at both shows was tremendous, and the band members felt the undeniable magic when making music together.

Sabbath regrouped in 1997 for two sold-out shows in their hometown on December 4th and 5th. Both shows were recorded, and tracks from the second show were released in '98 as a double live album, *Reunion.* This event marked the original lineup's first full-length concert since '79. The resulting disc was well received and included 16 live Sabbath classics along with two new studio tracks, "Psycho Man" and "Selling My Soul," leaving fans hungry for more. In response, the original Sabbath lineup returned for a headlining tour in 1999 and then participated in the Ozzfest tour in 2001. Since then, the original members have continued making music together and working to preserve the group's heritage.

In 2000, Tony Iommi released his first-ever solo album, *Iommi.* Rather than creating a separate solo band, his concept was to collaborate with a variety of musicians, using different vocalists and players on each track. The disc received excellent reviews, and Iommi is presently at work on a second solo venture. Iommi has also begun collaborating with Osbourne to sketch out ideas for a potential new Black Sabbath disc.

Tone and Technique

The members of Black Sabbath are considered to be the forefathers of heavy metal music and Tony Iommi is recognized as one of the inventors of metal guitar. Iommi's signature technique was developed purely out of necessity: After he had already been playing guitar for about three years, Iommi was involved in a factory accident in which the second and third fingers of his fretting hand were cut off up to the first joint by a metal shearing machine. Rather than give up the instrument, Iommi learned to function with prosthetic fingertips. He relearned everything he knew and devised a style of his own, using two fingers to make chords and adding a vibrato technique with his fretting hand to make the chords sound bigger.

"I can't feel a thing [with the prosthetic fingertips], so I just have to do it by ear," Iommi explains. "It is hard and it took a lot of getting used to. Put a sewing thimble on your finger and that would be similar to what I've done for the past 30 years."

To sound like Iommi, start with a Gibson solidbody, preferably an SG with humbuckers, a stop tailpiece, and Tune-O-Matic bridge. A Les Paul will work, too. Of course, Iommi's signature model Laney amps will produce the ideal tone, but you can also try using a Marshall or similar British-style tube amp set for overdrive. On older amps without master volume, turn all the controls full up; on modern amps, set the tone controls around 5–6, gain 7–8 and master volume 4–7, as appropriate. For leads, use an overdrive pedal set for slightly increased gain and more bite. If you have a gain pedal or your amp has a separate lead channel, make use of it. For added sustain on chords and single notes, Iommi relies on his finger vibrato rather than a stompbox, so be careful not to overdo it by using too much gain or dirt.

▼

Gear List

Guitars
Custom-built Gibson SGs and Tony Iommi Signature Model SGs, custom-built Gibson Les Pauls; custom-built SG-style guitars by luthiers J.D. (John Diggins) and John Birch; Taylor 815L cutaway acoustic, Gibson CL-30 acoustic

Pickups
Gibson Tony Iommi Signature Model pickups; stock pickups

Accessories
LaBella strings (various sets from .008–.032, .009–.042, .010–.046 to .010–.052), black Dunlop picks

Effects & Rack Gear
Tycobrahe Parapedal wah, Dallas-Arbiter Rangemaster Treble Booster, Korg SDD-1000 digital delay, BOSS RCE-10 chorus, Korg DL-8000R multi-tap delay (used for chorus effect), Peavey Addverb III, BOSS OC-2 Octave or DigiTech octave divider, Drawmer LX22 Compressor, DigiTech MEQ and Klark Teknik DN3600 programmable graphic EQs, Klark Teknik DN6000 audio spectrum analyzer, Rocktron Guitar Silencer, custom-built pedalboard by Pete Cornish

Amps & Cabs
Laney GH100 TI100-watt amplifier heads and Laney straight 4x12 cabinets with HH drivers

Amp settings: Treble, middle, and bass tone controls set around 5, drive at 7, master volume at 7

Discography

Black Sabbath

Black Sabbath (Warner Bros., 1970), *Paranoid* (Warner Bros., 1971), *Master of Reality* (Warner Bros., 1971), *Black Sabbath, Vol. 4* (Warner Bros., 1972), *Sabbath, Bloody Sabbath* (Warner Bros., 1973), *Sabbotage* (Warner Bros., 1975), *We Sold Our Soul for Rock and Roll* (Warner Bros., 1976), *Technical Ecstasy* (Warner Bros., 1976), *Never Say Die!* (Warner Bros., 1978), *Heaven and Hell* (Warner Bros., 1980), *Live at Last* (Nems, 1980), *The Mob Rules* (Warner Bros., 1981), *Live Evil* (Warner Bros., 1982), *Born Again* (Warner Bros., 1983), *Seventh Star* (Warner Bros., 1986), *The Eternal Idol* (Warner Bros., 1987), *Headless Cross* (IRS, 1989), *T Y R* (IRS, 1990), *Dehumanizer* (Warner Bros., 1992), *Cross Purposes* (IRS, 1994), *Forbidden* (EMI, 1995), *Reunion* (Epic, 1998), *Past Lives* (Sanctuary, 2002)

Tony Iommi

Iommi (Priority, 2000)

Tony Iommi: In His Own Words

"My guitar tone has changed a great deal since the early days with Black Sabbath. I've always been fiddling around with sounds, since the beginning. But now I don't mess with it much. I've tuned into the sound that I like and that's why I've been using the same stuff for years. I've got my own signature guitars and amps now, and I get the exact sound I want. I like my tone to be really crunchy and have a bite to it. My sound from the '70s was perhaps a bit more muffled and fuzzier than it is now. The sound I want now is solid and powerful, with more clarity to the notes.

"I have been pretty faithful to Laney for amplifiers. I love the sound, and since we've done my signature-model amp, I don't have to look anywhere else. They've done exactly what I want. I've tried many different amplifiers over the years. I originally started out using Marshall amplifiers and then I switched over to Laney. I used the Laneys for quite a while and then started trying other amps like a Boogie 300-watt head, which I didn't like because it was too large-sounding. The Laney amplifiers I use now are designed the way I would want to have an amplifier sound. We worked on getting the sound right where I wanted it, so they've got a lot more highs than a standard-model Laney, and they're very loud. There are a few other changes from the original-model amps, including the way it's wired up. I used to turn everything full up years ago on the original Laney amplifiers and I used to use a treble booster to drive the input. I'd turn everything full up and turn the middle off. Now I have that treble booster built into the amp and I don't have the controls turned full up anymore. I have the drive up to about 7 and the master volume up to about 7, too. The tone controls are quite responsive, so they're set at about halfway.

"I also use a Pete Cornish pedalboard, but I don't use many effects. I'm using an old Tycobrahe wah pedal. I have several of them. The company didn't make that many, so I've bought up all the ones I could find. I've probably got about eight of them. I use a Korg rackmount delay, which I think is the old SDD-1000 model. As long as I can hear it and it gives me the right sound, I don't care which one it is. I also use a BOSS chorus pedal. It's trustworthy. Additionally, I have a Korg DL-8000R multi-tap delay for chorus effect, a Peavey Addverb III, and I use a BOSS or DigiTech octave divider. I run the effects in separate loops with a Drawmer LX22 Compressor and some EQs. Fifteen years ago, I used a lot more gear, but I've really cut it down.

"For guitars, I've always used SGs, but over the years I've had some different ones—some that were built by the Gibson Custom Shop and some from private builders like J.D. [*John Diggins, Iommi's former tech*] and John Birch. As a lefty, it's always been difficult to find guitars I like, so I usually have them custom-made. Back in the early days, you couldn't find anything, especially in England. I'd see maybe one left-handed guitar in a store. I had a Burns guitar because you could find them easily in those days, but I had *always* wanted a Strat. Then I eventually saw a Strat and bought it. I used it in the studio on 'Wicked World.'

"I like a thinner neck than the standard Gibson SG because it's easier for me to hold. I like it to feel something like the early Gibson Les Paul/SG—like the 'fretless wonder' sort of feel. They were always nice. I like 24-fret necks, too, which are not standard on the regular SG model. I also prefer thin fretwire, like the old '61 Gibson-type fret wire. I don't like the chunky type. As for the setup, I like the action to be low.

"I usually take about six or eight guitars on tour, but I use two throughout the show. My Gibson signature-model SG is based on a guitar that J.D. built for me in the '80s. In fact, even further back than that, in the '70s, I had some guitars built by John Birch. I put the money up for him to build me a 24-fret guitar. Before then, I went to different companies and asked them to make me a guitar with 24 frets, and they thought I was a loony. So I figured that the only way that I was going to be able to do this was to find another loony that will do it for me. Eventually, I hooked up with this John Birch and I'd got the money up for him to make me a 24-fret guitar. We proved that it could work. It *would* work! So it basically went from there. I used that guitar for quite a long time. Then I met J.D., who made me another guitar which then became my stage [guitar]. That one had 24 frets, but it also had a slightly thinner neck.

"All of my SGs have my signature-model Gibson pickups in them. When I play, I mainly use the bridge pickup and rarely use the neck pickup, except maybe if I'm trying to do something jazzy. But the neck and bridge models are the same. It's got nice highs and it's really beefy-sounding. It also has a bit more bite to it than a stock Gibson pickup. The overall tone of the Gibson pickups was always very good. But I found that, for me, because I'm playing at a high volume, when you turn down the volume, you lose some of the tone. I wanted to be able to turn down the volume on the guitar and retain the same tone. It tended to go a bit muffly, but I wanted it to be a bit cleaner. The pickups that we worked on gave it that clarity, and when you turn them down you can still get that cleaner sound. I have certainly given those pickups a good bashing. I've used them on all the tours since I got them, including the last Sabbath tour and on albums. So it's worked out really well and I'm very pleased with them. They really have proven themselves in roadworthiness. There are always a good amount of people that come up and tell me they love the sound of my guitar, so then I tell about the pickup.

"I use the same gear in the studio and onstage. It's exactly the same, which is brilliant. Now I don't have to carry amps around anywhere. I can just tell Laney to send a few amps over and I'll have exactly my sound wherever I am."

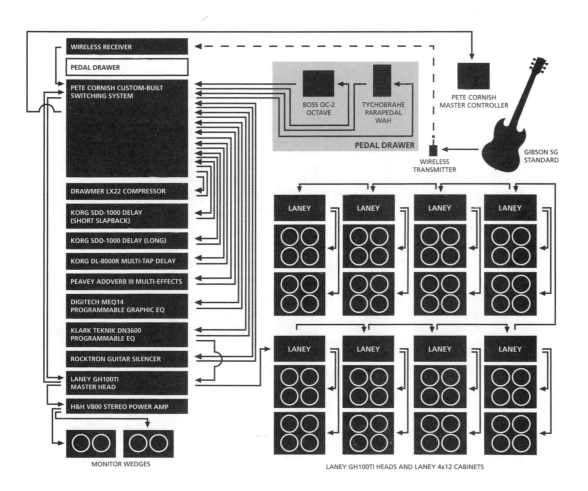

Zakk Wylde

Born
January 14, 1967, in Jersey City, New Jersey

Bands
Ozzy Osbourne
Pride & Glory
Black Label Society

Tone
Crunchy, overdriven tone with clarity and bite

Signature Traits
Fast vibrato, edge-of-pick harmonics

Breakthrough Performance
"Miracle Man" from Ozzy Osbourne's *No Rest for the Wicked* (1989)

History and Influences

Zakk Wylde grew up listening to classic rockers like Jimi Hendrix and Black Sabbath, and was a huge fan of the latter. He later got into speedy guitar players like Frank Marino, John McLaughlin, and Al Di Meola. By his late teens, he was one of the hottest young guitarists playing around the New Jersey Shore bar circuit. His big break came in 1987, when he was asked to audition for Ozzy Osbourne, who was looking for a replacement for Jake E. Lee. In addition to his technical ability as a player, Wylde's unrestrained energy, rock image, and love for Osbourne's music made him a natural for the gig.

While working with Ozzy, Wylde honed his chops and songwriting skills. He co-wrote and recorded tracks on *No Rest for the Wicked* (1989), *Just Say Ozzy* (1990), *No More Tears* (1991), *Live and Loud* (1993), and *Ozzmosis* (1997), all of which attained platinum success. *Live and Loud* won a Grammy for Best Live Performance.

After years of touring and recording with Ozzy's band, Wylde needed a break from the metal scene. He stepped away to work on his own projects, breaking out with *Pride & Glory* (1994), named for the Southern-style blues-rock power trio he fronted. Next, he released *Book of Shadows* (1996), a solo acoustic album showcasing his songwriting.

Wylde's next release, *Sonic Brew* (1999), marked a return to heavier rock with a new group called Black Label Society. In addition to handling all of the guitars and vocals on *Sonic Brew*, Wylde played bass, piano, and also co-produced the album. While he recorded the disc with little outside help, he enlisted other musicians for his touring band. With *Stronger than Death* (2000), Wylde firmly reconnected with the metal world.

As Black Label Society was picking up speed, Wylde was invited to rejoin Ozzy's act. He made his recorded return on Osbourne's *Down to Earth* (2001), but made it clear that he had no intentions of abandoning BLS. In additional to juggling the two gigs, Wylde found time to compose music for the movie *Rock Star*, and also appeared in the film. Without

▶▶▶

losing a beat, he released the third BLS studio disc, *1919 Eternal*, in 2002. Incredibly, on the 2002 Ozzfest tour, Wylde pulled off a doubleheader—opening the show with BLS early in the afternoon and then returning to headline the festival and close the show with Ozzy Osbourne.

Tone and Technique

To replicate Wylde's tone, start by getting together a similar rig. Grab a Les Paul, wah pedal, BOSS SD-1 Super Overdrive, CE-5 Chorus Ensemble, and OC-2 Octave (or equivalents for all BOSS pedals), and plug straight into a 100-watt, master-volume Marshall head with a 4x12 bottom.

Next, dial in Wylde's amp settings (as detailed in Gear List). Set the overdrive box so that it adds a little bit of gain to enhance the amp's tone and adds a slight boost in the volume for riffs and solos. Try setting the tone at 1 o'clock, drive at 7 o'clock and level at 10 o'clock. Set the chorus pedal just as noted, and adjust the octave pedal's controls so it inserts a little bit of texture to thicken up the sound (i.e., add a low octave for single-string passages).

As for technique, listen to fast rock players of the '70s like Michael Schenker, Uli Roth, and especially the underrated speedster Frank Marino from the Canadian power trio Mahogany Rush. Learn your scales, too, balancing classical modes with blues-scale licks and string bends. To Zakk Wylde, it's not all about speed. You've got to play with plenty of *feel*, too.

Zakk Wylde: In His Own Words

"My rig is pretty basic. All I do is plug straight into the amp and use most of the same stompboxes that I had when I was 17. You know what they say—if it ain't broke, don't fix it. I use 100-watt Marshall JCM800 heads, model 2203, with straight Marshall 4x12 bottom cabinets loaded with 200-watt Electro-Voice speakers. I used to have Celestions in my cabinets when I first played with Ozzy and Pride & Glory. They were 70-watt Celestions and they were really loud. Then I hooked up these EVs and I couldn't believe how clean they sounded. It's just pure guitar. For the music I'm doing, you need a lot of attack, and if you have the vintage-style speakers in there, they really break up. They sound very warm, but when you get down to the low strings you want more meat. The EVs just sound so much better than the original speakers for what I'm doing because I tune to 440 Hz and then I'll often drop my low *E* string down to a *B* or an *A*. I use custom sets of GHS Boomers, gauge .010 to .060 or .011 to .070 for the low tunings, so it doesn't get too floppy.

"I keep the amp's volume and gain set between 6 and 8, but I usually keep the presence down a bit. I have the treble and bass set pretty high up and keep the mids somewhere around the middle. I never roll the mids all the way off—that's a completely different sound altogether. I definitely keep some mids in there because I like the crunch they give it. And I use 6550 tubes in my amps because it seems like they get a bigger and tighter sound than the EL34s in the Marshalls.

"For my main guitars, I have my Les Pauls and a Gibson SG. When I'm recording rhythm tracks, I usually do one track with my Les Paul on the left and then double it with my SG or another Les Paul on the right. Then I'll usually put on another track with any overdubs I want to do. My main Les Paul is the one with the bull's-eye, and it's an '81. The SG is the one I got when we did the *Ozzmosis* sessions, so I think that one's a '95.

"I also have a Les Paul Classic that has a Fernandes Sustainer pickup in the neck position. I've used that for some solos and intros on some of the songs when I'm recording. I have an old Danelectro that I've used to overdub some clean

Gear List

Guitars

Gibson Les Paul Custom and Standard models, Zakk Wylde Signature Model Les Paul, SG, EDS-1275 doubleneck, Les Paul Junior models, Firebird, RD Artist; Fender Telecaster and Stratocaster; vintage Danelectro, Alvarez acoustic-electric, Gibson Dove acoustic

Pickups

EMG 81 (bridge) and EMG 85 (neck), Fernandes Sustainer

Accessories

GHS Zakk Wylde Signature Series Boomers (GBZW: .010, .013, .017, .036, .052, .060; GBZWLO: .011, .014, .018, .036, .052, .070), GHS Golden Bronze Acoustic strings (.012, .016, .024, .032, .042, .054); Monster cables; cabinets miked with Shure SM57 microphone (for dry sounds) and Audio-Technica 4060 microphone (used for color during solos and fills)

Effects & Rack Gear

Dunlop Rotovibe, Jimi Hendrix wah, Jimi Hendrix Octave Fuzz, BOSS SD-1 Super Overdrive, BOSS OC-2 Octave, Korg DTR-2 Rack Auto Tuner, BOSS CE-5 stereo Chorus Ensemble (settings: level at 3 o'clock, rate 1–2 o'clock, depth 1–2 o'clock, low filter 2 o'clock, high filter 1 o'clock)

Amps & Cabs

100-watt Marshall JCM800 Series heads (both models 2203 and 2203ZW Limited Edition Zakk Wylde model) loaded with 6550 power tubes, Marshall straight 4x12 cabinets loaded with 200-watt Electro-Voice speakers

Amp settings: presence 2, bass 10, middle 6, treble 7, master 3, preamp 10

parts. I bought that one in New York City on 48th Street and it's like some *Sanford & Son* thing. I think I paid around $800 for it, although it probably only cost $20 to make. But there's nothing that sounds like it. I think it's the pickups and the fact that the wood is so bad that makes it sound the way it does. For acoustics, I have my Gibson Dove that I used on *Book of Shadows* and an Alvarez acoustic-electric, which I like because it's a fast-playing guitar. It plays more like a Les Paul.

"I like my electric guitars set up with the tailpiece all the way down, close to the body, and I wrap the strings around the other way, like a wraparound bridge. It seems like that puts less stress on the strings, and I never end up breaking any strings when I play live. I got hooked on doing it that way when I first joined Ozzy. I also prefer high frets [*Wylde prefers Dunlop 6000 fretwire*] and I always shave the back of the necks down to the bare wood, so there's no lacquer on it. I set the action pretty low, but not too low, because when I grab the neck, I want to feel like there's something there. I can't stand the 'fretless wonder'–type guitars. I like frets with some height. And I set the pickups as close to the strings as I can get them. The louder, the better. I use EMG 81s and 85s, which are active pickups, so I don't have to worry about string pull."

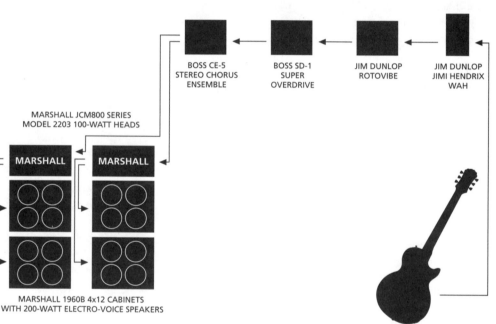

BOSS CE-5
STEREO CHORUS
ENSEMBLE

BOSS SD-1
SUPER
OVERDRIVE

JIM DUNLOP
ROTOVIBE

JIM DUNLOP
JIMI HENDRIX
WAH

MARSHALL JCM800 SERIES
MODEL 2203 100-WATT HEADS

MARSHALL 1960B 4x12 CABINETS
WITH 200-WATT ELECTRO-VOICE SPEAKERS

GIBSON LES PAUL CUSTOM

K.K. Downing & Glenn Tipton of Judas Priest

K.K. Downing

Glenn Tipton

Born
Kenneth Keith Downing: October 27, 1951, in West Bromwich, Birmingham, England

Glenn Tipton: October 25, 1948, in Birmingham, England

Bands
Judas Priest

Tone
Classic thick and chunky, heavy metal; one of the benchmark tones for '80s metal

Signature Traits
Super-solid guitar duo with precisely synched rhythm attack and fiery dueling lead riffs

Breakthrough Performance
"Exciter" from *Stained Class* (1978)

History and Influences
Formed in 1970 by guitarist K.K. Downing and bassist Ian Hill, Judas Priest has become one of the most influential bands in heavy metal. The group's trademark heavy-yet-melodic sound and leather-clad fashions set the pace for all metal groups to follow. During its first few years, the original group underwent numerous personnel changes before connecting with acclaimed frontman Rob Halford in 1973 and guitarist Glenn Tipton in 1974.

Extensive touring around Europe had helped Priest to land a contract with

▶▶▶

Gear List
K.K. Downing

Guitars

ESP Custom V models, Gibson Flying V models, custom-built Dan Johnson V, Hamer custom models, Washburn acoustic-electric

Pickups

EMG-81 humbuckers and Seymour Duncan Live Wire humbuckers

Accessories

DR and S.I.T. strings (.008, .011, .014, .022, .032, .044), Brain 1.13 mm picks, Kahler tremolo bridges, Morley A/B box, Rocktron MIDI Mate foot controller

Effects & Rack Gear

Dunlop Crybaby 535Q wah, DigiTech Whammy pedal, Rocktron Replifex multi-effects processor, Furman PL-8 Power Conditioner & Light module, Rocktron Power Station, Korg DTR-1 tuner, Sennheiser EW100 wireless system, ADA MC-1 MIDI controller

Amps & Cabs

Rocktron Piranha tube preamp into Marshall 9100 power amp and Marshall 4x12 cabinets with Celestion speakers

an independent record label in the U.K. called Gull. Tipton joined the ranks just prior to recording the group's first disc, *Rocka Rolla*, released in 1974. Unfortunately, the album received very little attention, but the group's live performances were always well received. Pushing ahead, Priest recorded and released *Sad Wings of Destiny* later the same year. The disc earned favorable reviews, which led to an international deal with CBS Records. With the release of *Sin After Sin* in 1977, the group embarked on its first U.S. tour, which generated a great buzz for the British rockers. With the release of *Stained Class* in 1978, Priest became an international smash as the hard, fast British metal sound grew in popularity around the world.

In 1979, the group released two albums: the seminal *Hell Bent for Leather* and the live disc recorded in Japan, *Unleashed in the East.* 1980's *British Steel* achieved platinum status thanks to two of the band's most memorable singles, "Breaking the Law" and "Living After Midnight." The next year's follow-up, *Point of Entry,* was another success with powerful tracks like "Heading Out to the Highway," "Hot Rockin'" and "Desert Plains." *Screaming for Vengeance* took on a faster, heavier sound and scored big in 1982 with tracks like "You've Got Another Thing Coming" and "Electric Eye."

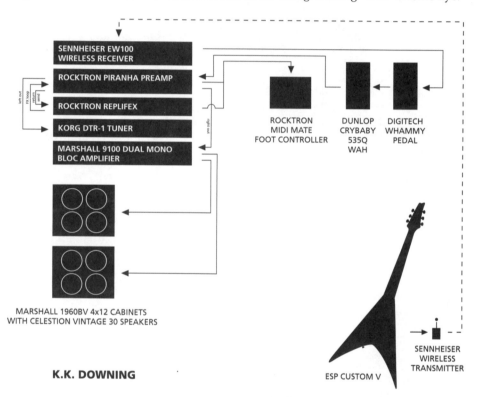

K.K. DOWNING

Downing's pedalboard with Dunlop Crybaby 535Q, DigiTech Whammy, and ADA MC-1 MIDI controller.

Defenders of the Faith was released in 1984, just as speed-metal bands like Metallica and Slayer were growing in popularity. Although the disc sold well and Priest retained its loyal following, it was clear that trends were changing and metal was evolving. With *Turbo* (1986), Priest began experimenting with new sounds and embracing the technology of the day, using polished guitar-synth tones on many of the tracks, as on the single "Turbo Lover."

The group closed out the decade with *Priest . . . Live!* (1987), *Ram It Down* (1988), and *Painkiller* (1990). Although Priest was still a popular concert draw, its album sales were slipping. In 1990, the group was involved in a legal battle following the 1985 suicide of a fan. Accused of hiding subliminal backwards messages in its lyrics, the band was finally exonerated of charges in 1993.

Discouraged by the group's status, Halford departed to focus on a solo career. The group's future became unclear, but the remaining members returned later that year with *Jugulator,* featuring snew singer Tim "Ripper" Owens. (Owens, an Ohio native, had formerly led a Priest cover band called Winter's Bane. His story was the inspiration for the movie *Rock Star* starring Mark Wahlberg.) Judas Priest has continued to record and tour to this day.

Tone and Technique

To emulate the classic Priest rhythm tone, grab a solidbody electric with a hot humbucking bridge pickup and plug into your favorite Marshall or other big tube amp with a 4x12 cabinet. If you're using an old non–master volume amp, simply crank up all the tone controls to 10. The amp will likely be very loud, so you may have to bring down the volume a bit to prevent yourself from being expelled from a club . . . or your apartment.

To add some extra dirt and/or secure a volume boost for soloing and lead riffs, use an overdrive box like an Ibanez Tube Screamer or Boss Super Overdrive. Set the pedal's controls so it enhances the amp's inherent overdriven tone with just

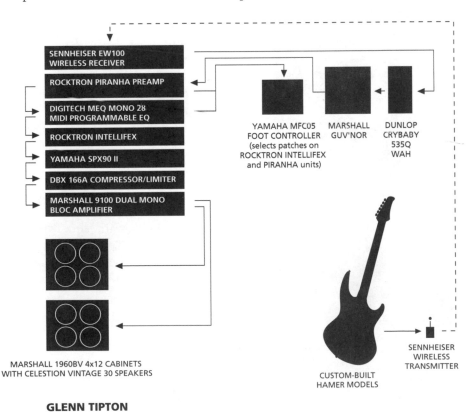

SENNHEISER EW100 WIRELESS RECEIVER

ROCKTRON PIRANHA PREAMP

DIGITECH MEQ MONO 28 MIDI PROGRAMMABLE EQ

ROCKTRON INTELLIFEX

YAMAHA SPX90 II

DBX 166A COMPRESSOR/LIMITER

MARSHALL 9100 DUAL MONO BLOC AMPLIFIER

YAMAHA MFC05 FOOT CONTROLLER (selects patches on ROCKTRON INTELLIFEX and PIRANHA units)

MARSHALL GUV'NOR

DUNLOP CRYBABY 535Q WAH

MARSHALL 1960BV 4x12 CABINETS WITH CELESTION VINTAGE 30 SPEAKERS

CUSTOM-BUILT HAMER MODELS

SENNHEISER WIRELESS TRANSMITTER

GLENN TIPTON

Guitars
Custom-built Hamer and ESP models, Gibson Les Pauls and SGs, Fender Stratocasters, ESP acoustic-electric

Pickups
EMG-81 humbuckers and Seymour Duncan Live Wire humbuckers

Accessories
Ernie Ball RPS .010s, Ernie Ball thin picks, D'Andrea nylon light-gauge picks, Yamaha MFC05 MIDI Foot Controller

Effects & Rack Gear
Dunlop Crybaby 535Q wah, Marshall Guv'nor, Rocktron Intellifex multi-effects processor, T.C. Electronic Fireworks, Furman PL-8 Power Conditioner & Light Module, Rocktron Power Station, Korg DTR-1 tuner, Sennheiser EW100 wireless system, dbx 166A Compressor/Limiter, Alesis 3630 compressor, Yamaha SPX90 II multi-effects processor, DigiTech MEQ Mono 28 MIDI Programmable EQ, MXR 1/3 Octave EQ

Amps & Cabs
Rocktron Piranha tube preamp into Marshall 9100 power amp and Marshall 4x12 cabinets with Celestion speakers; Mesa/Boogie TriAxis tube preamp (spare)

a touch more gain, and boost the volume as needed. For extra chunkiness, use a graphic EQ to kick up the lower mids. An EQ pedal, even, can serve up a volume boost and enhance the tone.

Amps with master volume control are typically more versatile and will deliver a hotter tone. Try setting the bass on 8, middle on 7, treble on 6, presence on 6, gain between 8 and 10, and master volume around 4.

K.K. Downing & Glenn Tipton: In Their Own Words

"We're always trying to get a variety with our sounds," Downing relates. "Back when we started in the early '70s, we didn't have much gear to work with, so it was harder to get cool sounds. All I had back then was a wah pedal and an old Rangemaster Treble Booster, like Rory Gallagher used. I would turn it up on full, plug it into the bass channel of a Marshall amp, and that was the early Judas Priest sound. With all the processors available today, it's easy to rip through the presets and find cool sounds or realize sounds you might hear in your head. In the early days, the tone was more about the sound of the guitar and amp.

"Nowadays, I think people rely a lot less on the actual guitar and amplifier to get the sound, and it's more from the processors that are available. If you've got a processor, then you'll probably play something based on the sound that you've got and you'll try to construct a part based on the sound of the effect."

"When you find a really interesting guitar effect, it can provide the basis of a song," adds Tipton. "Sometimes, when you discover a new sound, it can be very inspiring and make you quite prolific. I always love to experiment and to move with the times. Advancements in technology are something that Priest has always taken advantage of and something I've always paid close attention to. I'm like a mad professor in the studio. I like to try new processors and preamps, or even try out rackmount keyboard effects like the T.C. Electronic Fireworks. It actually works very well on guitar. I'll try anything.

Tipton's live rack.

"The gear I use in the studio doesn't differ greatly from my live rig, except that when I'm onstage I like to have working tools—things that don't break down. I think that if you overcomplicate things onstage, then you're asking for trouble. The more complicated a rig is, the more often that things will go wrong with it. So I like to simplify my rig onstage. I use a Rocktron Piranha preamp, Marshall power amps, and Yamaha and Rocktron multi-effects units which are all MIDI-switchable from a pedalboard on the stage. I also have a Uni-Vibe and Crybaby 535Q wah, and I've got a DigiTech Programmable EQ in my rack, which I find really useful. It's something that I rely on quite a lot. For guitars, I first started with a Gibson Les Paul, SGs, Fender Strats, and Marshall amplifiers in the early days, then in the late '80s I started using Hamer guitars. I'm still using Hamers now."

"In the early days, I had started with a Gibson Flying V and a Fender Stratocaster," Downing recalls. "Now I've got a couple of

Hamers that I had used on the *Painkiller* tour, as well as a couple of ESPs. I guess that being British, the desired amplification was always Marshall, and we're still using Marshall amplifiers today. Glenn and I have similar setups, but the effects units are different. For the most part, I'm using the Rocktron stuff. The only thing that I really need on the road today is a good preamp, and I'm using the Rocktron Piranha. The only effects unit I'm using is the Rocktron Replifex, which is a very comprehensive unit that's got just about everything. It's got all the classic-sounding stuff, even a rotary speaker effect, flangers, phasers, and stuff we used to use even back in the '70s. I can replicate any of those sounds with this one effects unit. In addition to that, it's got delay, chorus, compression, noise reduction, and just about anything that you could want, really."

"As a two-guitar band, I think that we just sort of fell into doing what we do. When you've actually performed so many solos and written so many songs together, obviously, the respect is there and it's etched in stone. I'd say the respect thing is very important. With two players in the band, there *has* to be mutual respect and understanding. If one of the players starts to feel a little bit oppressed, then the relationship certainly isn't going to give the listening audience what they want. So if you're going to play with another guitarist, find somebody that's compatible with yourself, where you like the same music and you've got an equal ability, even if you've got different styles or techniques. In turn, the respect will turn itself into a healthy competition where you can learn from each other and improve as a team."

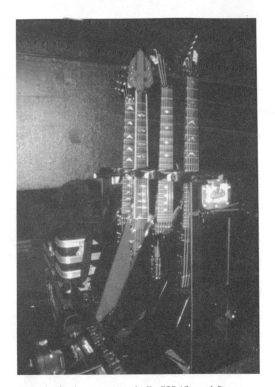

Downing's three custom-built ESP V's and Dan Johnson V.

Tipton's custom-built Hamers.

Tom Delonge of Blink-182

Born
December 13, 1975, in Poway, California

Bands
Blink-182
Box Car Racer

Tone
Clean to crisply overdriven

Signature Traits
Minimalist style, but exerting maximum energy to deliver songs crafted with catchy melodies and powerful chord progressions

Breakthrough Performance
"What's My Age Again?" from *Enema of the State* (1999)

History and Influences

Delonge's first guitar was a gift from a friend whose father worked at a local dump and had salvaged the perfectly usable instrument from the trash. As a teen, he was introduced to punk and started listening to groups such as Stiff Little Fingers, Dinosaur Jr., and the Descendants. After high school, Delonge, bassist Mark Hoppus, and drummer Scott Raynor joined forces in the early '90s and formed a band which they originally called Blink. The trio was later forced to change its name due to the threat of a lawsuit from an Irish group with a similar name. Blink was modified to Blink-182, avoiding further discord. Raynor later departed and was replaced by drummer Travis Barker.

Through the mid '90s, Blink-182 gained popularity on the SoCal punk scene by playing gigs and promoting a self-released EP, followed later by three independent discs—*Buddha* (1994), *Cheshire Cat* (1995), and *Dude Ranch* (1997). A slot on the 1996–97 Warped Tour helped the group expand its audience nationally and attract major-label attention, resulting in a recording contract with MCA. With MCA's muscle behind the group's fourth release, *Enema of the State* (1999), Blink-182 became a headlining act. The album yielded several hit singles and accompanying videos, including "What's My Age Again?" and "All the Small Things," both of which landed in heavy rotation on radio and MTV. The group's recent disc, *Take Off Your Pants and Jacket* (2001), carries on in the same tradition.

While on a break from Blink-182, Delonge and Barker started up a side project which quickly developed into an offshoot band called Box Car Racer. Unlike Blink-182, Box Car Racer is less poppy and more hardcore, yet retains the same kind of punk elements. BCR is a quartet which includes Over My Dead Body guitarist Dave Kennedy and bassist Anthony Celestino. The group's self-titled debut was released in 2002.

▶▶▶

Tone and Technique

As the only guitarist in a rock trio, Delonge needs a big tone to fill out the group's sound. To emulate Delonge's thick rhythm tone, use a guitar with a hot humbucking pickup in the bridge position and plug straight into a good tube amp, such as a MESA/Boogie Triple Rectifier. Set the bass 7–8, mids 5–7, treble 6–8, presence 6–7, master volume 3–4, and gain 8–10. Although Delonge doesn't use one, you can add in a stompbox like an Ibanez Tube Screamer or Boss Super Overdrive for a bit of extra juice if needed to compensate for a guitar with a weaker-sounding pickup or an amp with less-powerful overdrive channel.

Tom Delonge: In His Own Words

Delonge explained his gear choices in the September 1999 *Guitar Player*: "I'm the kind of punk guitarist who wants the biggest, fattest, loudest sound he can get. Onstage, I run three cabinets, two of them powered by a 150-watt MESA/Boogie Triple Rectifier running on its dirty channel. The other cabinet is powered by a Marshall JCM800 with its clean channel turned up to 10. The MESA gives me all my distortion, the Marshall gives me all my tone, and I use a custom footswitch to switch both amps to a clean sound.

"My guitars are loaded with Seymour Duncan Invader pickups in the bridge position. It's a full-on heavy metal pickup. It's too distorted for tracking in the studio, but it works great live because it makes the guitar sound big and beefy. I like the tube sound right out of the amp, and I hate pedals—all they do is break your signal down to one-tenth of what it was meant to be.

"The riffs I write can stand on their own without a rhythm guitar behind them. Riffs keep songs sounding more diverse than the same old chord progressions. And I don't do solos because I think they sound stupid. I think the *song* should be what people listen to. You can be a great soloist, but if you can't write songs, you're meaningless to this world."

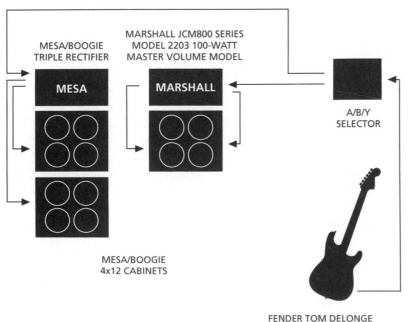

MESA/BOOGIE
TRIPLE RECTIFIER

MARSHALL JCM800 SERIES
MODEL 2203 100-WATT
MASTER VOLUME MODEL

MESA

MARSHALL

A/B/Y
SELECTOR

MESA/BOOGIE
4x12 CABINETS

FENDER TOM DELONGE
SIGNATURE STRATOCASTER

Daron Malakian of System of a Down

Born
July 18, 1975, in Los Angeles, California

Bands
System of a Down

Tone
Deep, dark metal textures to softer, cleaner settings

Signature Traits
Seamless shifts from aggressive, dirty rhythm sounds to clean, refined single-note riffs

Breakthrough Performance
"Sugar" from *System of a Down* (1998)

History and Influences

"I'm sort of like a musical schizophrenic," confesses Daron Malakian, guitarist and primary songwriter of the Los Angeles–based metal act System of a Down. While SOAD's sound is raw, there are many other ingredients that make up the musical brew: among them are punk, rap, jazz, and melodic influences of ethnic Armenian music (all four band members are of Armenian heritage). To this they add politically charged lyrics, and a stage show that's something like Iggy Pop meets Alice Cooper, Kiss, and Slayer.

After seeing SOAD perform live, producer Rick Rubin (Beastie Boys, Public Enemy, Slayer, Red Hot Chili Peppers) quickly signed the band to his American Recordings label. With Rubin and engineers Sylvia Massy and Greg Fidelman behind the controls, SOAD's self-titled debut album (released in 1998) generated two hit singles, "Sugar" and "Spiders." Malakian joined forces with Rubin to produce the follow-up disc, *Toxicity* (2001), which brought on even greater success and confirmed the group's status as a leading force among today's harder rock acts.

Malakian's guitar style is rooted in the music he grew up listening to—Kiss, Iggy Pop, Van Halen, Slayer, and early Ozzy Osbourne with Randy Rhoads. He learned to play guitar by listening to records and playing along. He would learn the rhythm parts, then make up his own lead lines, never copying entire solos note for note. Malakian feels that helped him to learn the music and the styles of the guitar players yet develop his own identity as a soloist by adding his own touches.

▶▶▶

"I've always had a different way of looking at things and interpreting them," he acknowledges. "I try to take the things that influence me and bring them to another level in my own music. I never tried to copy a Randy Rhoads solo, but if there were certain riffs that were distinct parts of the solo, then I'd learn those. I think it's important to add your own touches and find your own comfort zones, then play things that you like to play. If I had to give someone advice, I'd tell them not to be afraid to try new things and just be yourself. There's only one Randy Rhoads, Eddie Van Halen, and Jimi Hendrix."

Once he got it together as a guitarist, Malakian became engrossed in the art of songwriting. "I discovered the Beatles when I was about 18, but before then I was mostly into metal," he recalls. "As a songwriter, the Beatles changed my life just as much as Slayer did. They weren't afraid to combine styles, like mixing heavy music with softer styles. Listening to the Beatles helped me to add things to metal, like combining a waltz beat with a metal riff as a chorus.

"I think my attitude towards making music comes from my parents, who are both artists, not musicians," Malakian explains. "When I write music I like to approach it as if I were making a painting. I try to make it more artistic, as opposed to being just hardcore and testosterone-fueled. I think the lighter sides make the heavier sides heavier, and the heavier sides make the lighter sides lighter. Also, knowing when to leave things out is just as important."

Tone and Technique

Malakian's playing style and technique strongly reflect his rock, thrash, and punk influences. His tone has a thick, chunky metal flavor that's further emphasized by using a dropped-*D* tuning with the entire guitar dropped down a whole-step: *C G C F A D* low to high. To achieve the basic elements of Malakian's tone, use a solid-body guitar with a humbucking pickup in the bridge position and plug straight into a MESA/Boogie Triple Rectifier Solo head and 4x12 cabinet. Use the amp's channels to set up three sounds: a clean tone, a dirty rhythm tone, and a hotter, boosted tone for leads.

For a clean tone, set the bass at 6–7, mids 7–8, treble 5–7, presence 4–5, master volume 3–4, and gain 2–3. For a dirty rhythm tone, set the bass at 7–9, mids 6–8, treble 5–8, presence around 5, master volume 3–4, and gain 8–10.

Gear List

Guitars
Ibanez Iceman, Fender Big Apple Strat

Pickups
Seymour Duncan Pearly Gates (neck and bridge models)

Accessories
Ernie Ball strings (.011–.056), large triangular-shaped celluloid picks (heavy-gauge)

Effects & Rack Gear
Furman Power Conditioner, Furman PL-Plus Power Conditioner & Light Module, Korg DTR-1 tuner, BBE 462 Sonic Maximizer, Rocktron Hush Super C, Samson wireless system

Amps & Cabs
MESA/Boogie Triple Rectifier Solo head with two MESA/Boogie 4x12 cabinets ("I plug straight into the amp and set it for dirty and clean sounds")

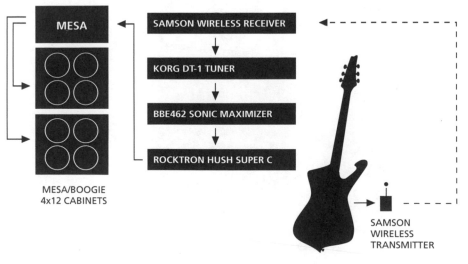

MESA/BOOGIE TRIPLE RECTIFIER SOLO HEAD

MESA

MESA/BOOGIE 4x12 CABINETS

SAMSON WIRELESS RECEIVER

KORG DT-1 TUNER

BBE462 SONIC MAXIMIZER

ROCKTRON HUSH SUPER C

SAMSON WIRELESS TRANSMITTER

IBANEZ ICEMAN

For hotter leads, try increasing the gain, master volume, and presence very slightly on the lead channel, just enough to stand out from the dirty rhythm tone. If you don't have an amp with a separate lead channel, then use a stompbox like an Ibanez Tube Screamer or some type of overdrive box for the extra gain and added volume boost.

Daron Malakian: In His Own Words

"I'm amazed that a song like 'Sugar' gets requested on the radio because it has so many styles inside it, like hardcore, jazz, and metal. It's not exactly radio-friendly, but we didn't write any of these songs to get on the radio. Our lyrics and music aren't geared towards commercial radio or MTV, but we're still getting played. In some ways, it makes me wonder if I'm doing something wrong because whenever a band that I like ends up on the radio, that's when I usually *don't* like them anymore. I intentionally try not to write music that sounds like what's trendy.

"I would be hurt if there came a point when there were a bunch of bands that sound like System of a Down, just like there are a lot of bands that sound like Korn right now. I'd like to see people inspired by our music, but not copying it. I want to see growth in music and art because if there's no growth, then the world might as well roll over and die. I've got so much growing to do and there's so much I want to do. I'm out there looking for inspiration. I'm *hungry!*"

Malakian's custom-colored Ibanez Iceman guitars.

Mike Einziger of Incubus

Born
June 21, 1976, in Los Angeles, California

Bands
Incubus

Tone
Warm tube tone thickened by effects for added texture and color

Signature Traits
Using combinations of effects to craft separate identities for each song

Breakthrough Performance
"Pardon Me" from *Make Yourself* (1999)

History and Influences

"Incubus was my first and only band," explains Mike Einziger. "The four of us who started the band had known each other for a long time, since we were in elementary and middle school. We started the band when we were 15—we were in 10th grade. I guess it developed out of friendship and a desire to play music. It seemed to work well, so we started writing songs and playing at parties. Then we graduated to playing clubs in Hollywood, like the Whiskey and the Roxy. We were only 17 years old and we were able to sell out those clubs. The shows kept getting better, and soon after that we ended up getting a record deal.

"When I started playing, I took lessons for the first six months. It was a great way for me to be introduced to the guitar. My teacher wanted me to enjoy what I was playing and not just concentrate on trying to learn the rudiments. He was interested in helping me to learn songs and get comfortable with what I was doing. If you want to learn the more 'boring' stuff, like the theory, you should learn it as an experienced musician. I think that once you're comfortable as a player, you can move on to it and have a better understanding because it will be a lot easier to absorb from that point on. My teacher really helped to familiarize me with the guitar as an instrument and then, once I was comfortable, I kind of went off on my own tangents.

"I am very into drum 'n' bass music, hip-hop, jazz, and rock music. I really like Roni Size—a guy from Bristol, England, who makes drum 'n' bass music. His music is very jazzy and very organic. I'm also really into Björk. She's an originator of a whole different type of music. I can't listen to her music and say it sounds like anything else. There are very few bands that are really in their own category. Another band that would be like that is Primus, which is one of those bands that's completely different from anything else. In Incubus, we don't really have an objective other than to make music that we like. We

▶▶▶

Gear List

Guitars
Paul Reed Smith Custom 24 and Hollowbody models, Jerry Jones Electric Sitars

Pickups
Paul Reed Smith

Accessories
Ernie Ball strings, Dunlop Tortex picks (.88mm)

Effects & Rack Gear
MXR Phase 90; Hughes & Kettner Rotosphere; DOD FX13 Gonkulator Modulator, FX25 Envelope Filter, and DOD Flanger; BOSS PH-2 Super Phaser (two), CS-3 Compressor/Sustainer, BF-2 Flanger, OC-2 Octave, GE-7 Graphic EQ, and RV-3 Digital Delay/Reverb pedals; Korg rackmount tuner; Shure wireless system

Amps & Cabs
MESA/Boogie Dual Rectifier and Tremoverb heads with MESA/Boogie 4x12 cabinets

don't intend to make music that sounds completely different from anything else. It just happens that way.

"As a band, all of us are Police fans and that's one thread that we share together. I think Andy Summers is an amazing guitar player and I get a lot of inspiration from him. There was a time period before we started the band when I was a pretty big guitar dork. I was into players like Steve Vai and Eric Johnson. Vai was my main guitar influence when I started out, but I was also into a lot of different kinds of music that didn't necessarily reflect in my guitar playing. Eric Johnson was also a huge inspiration to me, as was Steve Morse. I get inspiration from so many different places that it's almost like it changes every day. I just get ideas from different sounds that I hear."

Tone and Technique

In the studio, Einziger often splits guitar parts onto separate tracks to expand the sound. However, when recreating the songs live, he usually sticks to the main parts, using the same effects as on the recording. Einziger describes the recipe he used to build the tracks for "Stellar": "It's a pretty straight-ahead song with a ton of reverb and a really slow flange. On the middle part, I used a Phase 90 and an octave pedal on one side. Then during the hard parts, one part is playing the power chords and the other has the octave effect."

To cop Einziger's sound, listen carefully to his recorded tracks. If you study closely, you'll be able to dissect the sounds of the effects and devise your own formula to replicate the material effectively. To emulate Einziger's sound, start with a strong foundation tone. Get a solidbody with humbuckers and a master-volume tube amp, dialed for a thick, solid, slightly overdriven rhythm tone. Try setting the bass at 7–8, mids 6–7, treble 5–8, presence around 5, master volume 3–4, and gain around 6.

Einziger is a big fan of layering a variety of textured and ambient effects like phasers and flangers with delay, reverb, and octave pedals. He will change combinations to develop and define parts, and use the effects to create unity throughout a song. When using numerous effects, use each one conservatively and pay attention to how they all work in tandem. It's all about how the pieces

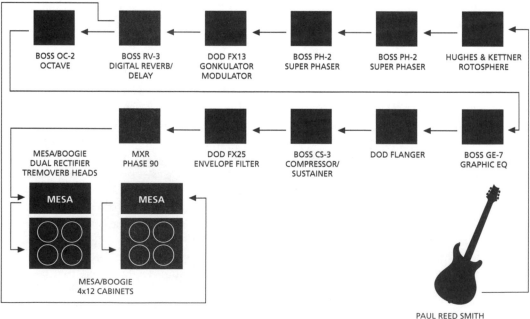

of the puzzle fit together. As Einziger knows, each effect should be used to enhance the others and build a sound without diminishing the guitar's foundation—or overpowering the sound of the band as a whole. Using too many intense effects simultaneously can muddy up the sound and make the guitar indiscernible. Listen to what the other instruments are doing and select your effects based on what works in the context of the song and each individual part. Establish unique moods and contribute to a song's individuality.

Mike Einziger: In His Own Words

"In my live setup, I have two MESA/Boogie Rectifier Tremoverb heads with two MESA/Boogie cabinets," he said while on tour in support of *Make Yourself.* "I also have four Paul Reed Smith guitars out with me: three Custom 24s and a hollowbody. For effects, I have two BOSS Super Phasers that I have set differently, a Hughes & Kettner Rotosphere for the Leslie sound, an MXR Phase 90, a DOD Envelope Filter, a DOD Gonkulator Modulator pedal, a BOSS Compressor that I use for certain things, the old orange DOD Flanger, a BOSS Octave pedal, and a BOSS Digital Delay that I change the settings on for almost every song. I'm so stubborn that I won't get a programmable rack delay because I don't like the way they sound. I don't run anything through an effects loop, either. I just run everything straight into the front of the amp. I like the way that everything sounds, so I just stick with it.

"As a song emerges, there's a whole metamorphosis that goes on as everyone in the band throws around ideas and the original concept changes. That's what's cool about the way Incubus writes. Our music takes many unexpected turns until a song makes it to the final draft.

"If you're in a rut, do something that's out of the ordinary. Pick up a record that you haven't heard, maybe something that's a completely different style from what you typically favor, or just go out to the park and listen to the sound of the water. You never know what you're going to hear or when the inspiration for a song is going to hit you. And if you try to emulate some of those new sounds, it can lead you to something really cool.

"After I was playing for a while, I began to develop my own identity as a guitar player, drawing inspiration from musicians that *weren't* guitar players. I found it more inspiring to listen to someone like Ella Fitzgerald. That was something I grew up listening to because my mom is a singer. So I also grew up listening to jazz singers like Ella, Billie Holiday, and Louis Armstrong. There are a lot of things that I do as a guitar player that are really direct reflections of melodies that someone like Ella Fitzgerald would create."

Einziger's stompbox-laden pedalboard from the *Morning View* tour.

CD Notes

All guitar tracks performed by Pete Prown

The enclosed CD is comprised of audio examples performed in the style of select players mentioned in this book. The goal of each performance is to capture the *sound* and *spirit* of a notable rock guitarist, be it Jimi Hendrix, Eddie Van Halen, or both Munky and Head of Korn. There is no attempt to recreate solos precisely as heard on the original recordings or to nail down the idiosyncrasies of each player. These are creative interpretations meant to evoke the "vibe" of each guitarist.

While note-for-note studies are fine for educational purposes, they will limit your creativity if overused. Our book and CD offer suggestions on how you can duplicate some tones and mannerisms of your favorite guitarists without becoming a clone.

Better yet, all the music presented here was recorded using everyday guitar gear—no expensive pieces of studio equipment or secret guitar effects. The basic setup included the guitars listed at the end of this chapter; a digital amp simulator; and home-recording software. There's no magic and no smoke 'n' mirrors—just an understanding of what it takes to create great sounds with your guitar. (The notations mentioning "guitar 1" or "guitar 2", etc., refer to which brand and model of guitar was used to record each piece. See the key at the end of this section for reference.)

Listen to the following audio excerpts and then think about the individual sounds and techniques used here to evoke each player. Then mix these concepts with your own to start developing a personal style. Remember, coming up with your own way to play is what being a good guitarist is all about.

1. "Angus's Beef"
In the style of Angus Young (guitar: 1)
Angus Young is famous for his Gibson SG-thru-Marshall amp wall of sound, but here his tone is ably duped on a good ol' Fender Strat plugged into a basic amp simulator. Don't scratch your head—it's not magic. In fact, this is an important first lesson for the novice tone hunter (and something gear manufacturers don't want you to know): You can basically sound like *any* player with *any* guitar. No kidding, it's true. Just commit the following axiom to memory: *Tone is 50% in your rig and 50% in your fingers.* In short, sounding like one player or another has just as much to do with *how* you play as *what* you play. It's one of the fundamental laws of guitar physics.

To replicate Angus on his preferred gear, you'll want the SG and full Marshall stack. He sets his amp cleaner than one might suspect, but again, he derives a lot of his "crunch" from sheer volume. On the performance side, Angus integrates a lot of tasty blues licks in his solos. If you're looking for source material, listen to early Eric Clapton (Bluesbreakers and Cream), Peter Green (with John Mayall and with Fleetwood Mac), and classic B.B. King albums, as well as early Led Zeppelin recordings.

The bottom line is that Angus Young is more of a bluesman than most people think. He just happens to be a very *loud* one.

2. "Muttonchop Blues"
In the style of Eric Clapton, circa Bluesbreakers (guitar: 3)
This example attempts to capture the origins of Clapton's famous "woman tone" from his stint with John Mayall's Bluesbreakers between 1965 and '66 (as described on page 6). It was during this time that he invented the basic Les Paul-thru-Marshall sound: that fat, creamy texture that went on to power the Jeff Beck Group, Led Zeppelin, and the thousands of hard rock and heavy metal bands that have followed since. The solo here not only

Guitars used in this recording:

1. Fender Jeff Beck Signature Stratocaster

2. Ibanez RG320 solidbody with Floyd Rose tremolo

3. 1956 Gibson Les Paul Custom with stop tailpiece

4. Carvin AC175 acoustic-electric (with Roland MIDI-synth pickup)

5. Fender Standard Telecaster

6. Epiphone Broadway archtop

7. 1971 Fender Stratocaster

brings to mind Eric Clapton, but also the playing of his disciples Peter Green and Mick Taylor (both of whom later played in the Bluesbreakers), as well as Carlos Santana and Gary Moore.

The lead lines in this recording are based on an *A* minor pentatonic scale (*A C D E G*), with notes from the *A* natural minor scale thrown in (*B* and *F*) . However, there are lots of semi-tone bends throughout that enhance the solo's bluesy flavor. Also important is a strong finger vibrato, a classic Clapton trait. Elements like these deliver the *feel* that conveys the spirit of the blues. Of course, there's no way to learn how to play with emotion from a book—you've just got to put yourself in the moment and go with the music.

3. "Fighting Irish"
In the style of Thin Lizzy (guitar: 2)
Thin Lizzy's trademarks were harmonized guitar solos and the blistering pentatonics of Scott Gorham, Brian Robertson, and Gary Moore, circa 1974–1979. This audio example utilizes a fairly typical Les Paul/Marshall sound from that hard-rockin' era. You can duplicate it using most any solidbody with humbuckers and an amp with a good, warm overdrive channel. It sounds even better if the amp has a 4x12 cabinet . . . or two.

One thing to avoid is overdoing the crunch. Lizzy's guitar tone doesn't use the over-the-top saturated distortion of later metal and thrash bands. It's the warmer overdrive of the 1970s—still plenty hot, but not ridiculously so.

4. "Acoustic Gumbo"
In the style of Dave Matthews (guitar: 4)
Dave Matthews's guitar tone is fairly straightforward. You can emulate his rig with an acoustic-electric guitar and a decent acoustic amp or PA system. You may also want to include a compressor to even out the guitar's volume levels, and add reverb to taste.

Unlike some guitarists who want a "scooped-out" acoustic sound—i.e., with increased treble and bass and little midrange—Matthews's acoustic tone is a little midrangey. Experiment with the mid knob to find the flavor that sounds right to your ears.

For technique, work on your rhythm-guitar chops by listening to lots of vintage funk and R&B recordings, such as those by James Brown, Sly & the Family Stone, and Earth, Wind & Fire. Dave is a one-man rhythm section, able to perform as easily on his own as with the phenomenal musicians in the Dave Matthews Band. As goes the groove, so goes Mr. Matthews.

5. "Quantum Mechanics"
In the style of Allan Holdsworth (guitar: 1)
This piece sounds more difficult than it actually is. To accurately cop Holdsworth's enigmatic style, you must first get a handle on the legato hammer-on technique. Practice it until your hammer-ons and pull-offs are as "smooth as *buttah.*" Second, learn your modes, notably the Ionian (major), Dorian (minor with a raised 6th), and Aeolian (natural minor). Finally, softly wiggle your tremolo bar here and there to accentuate or slide into particular notes. This may be a simplification, but these are the basic ingredients of Holdsworth's approach.

Unlike many rock guitarists who only use one scale or mode for an entire solo, Holdsworth may employ a specific scale over just one chord and then another scale for the next chord. This recorded example essentially uses the following three chords and scales: *Am9* (*A* Dorian mode); *Emaj9/G♯* (*E* Ionian mode); and *Fmaj7♭5* (*A* Aeolian mode). A simpler version of this chord progression is *Am7–G♯m7–Fmaj7*.

There are also some non-diatonic notes (i.e., not belonging to any related scale) that were thrown in for effect—Holdsworth loves to throw in a few curveball licks. This may sound complicated, but with a little practice, it's easily achievable. Don't give up!

6. "Austin Powered"

In the style of Eric Johnson (guitar: 1)

Johnson may be able to hear the difference between Eveready and Duracell 9-volts in his stompboxes, but don't spend all your time fretting about batteries. To uncover that EJ vibe, get yourself a Strat-style guitar (with neck or neck/middle pickups selected), an overdrive unit, a tube amp with a 4x12 cabinet, and a tape delay or modern echo simulator. Eric loves to bathe his guitar tone in echo; indeed, it's crucial to developing a sound similar to his. It wouldn't hurt to have a chorus and compressor around for those clean, chiming rhythm parts, either.

To further unravel his tone, you also have to consider Eric's favorite rock guitarists: Eric Clapton (especially on *Fresh Cream*), Jimi Hendrix, and Jeff Beck. From Clapton, he gets his penchant for fat, "woman tone" solos, while the other two contributed an enormous lexicon of Strat textures. Add to that some jazz and fusion from Wes Montgomery and John McLaughlin, respectively, and it quickly becomes clear where Eric comes from as a soloist.

For lead ideas, learn your blues scales and modes, but don't get heavily tied to sequential runs; Eric likes wide intervals and arpeggios. If playing five notes in the key of C major, one guitarist might play a lick in this sequence: *C-D-E-G-C*. Eric, on the other hand, might instead phrase it as: *C-D-F-G-B* (he does like to end phrases on interesting chord tensions, like a major 7th). Think of these colorful notes as spices in cooking, as they add more interesting flavors to the sound.

The real nut to crack, however, is Eric's ability to shred on pentatonic blues scales using alternate picking. Again, alternate picking is straight up/down picking, no matter if you're staying on the same string or not.

If you want to become a fast picker, learning to alternate-pick is a must. It takes time to develop, so a little patience is required. Many experts propose the same approach: Start slow on a particular pattern, scale, or lick and use a metronome to build up your speed gradually. Consult your local guitar teacher to learn more about the art of alternate picking. Clearly, at some point in his life, Eric Johnson did just that—and now look at how fast a picker he is today.

7. "Jake, This Barn's on Fire!"

In the style of Steve Morse (guitars: 1, 5)

Whether he's playing with the Dixie Dregs, Steve Morse Band, or Deep Purple, Morse likes to play in a variety of styles and use numerous tones on his guitar. His classic sound is something akin to a supercharged Telecaster—it has the twang of a Tele, but the sonic *oomph* of a Les Paul. Probably the easiest way to accomplish this is to use a good Strat or Tele with stacked (humbucker) pickups through a big tube head and a 4x12 cabinet. Morse constantly flips between pickups and tone settings during any given lead. He likes both the "woman tone" of the neck pickup (for high notes) and the bright edge of the bridge pickup (for low notes).

Back in the mid 1970s, Morse was the first player to blend the technical chops of fusion with the soulfulness of Clapton, Beck, Allman, and Hendrix. To merge these disparate approaches, he developed a style that relied on the typical pentatonic "box" pattern, but he went one step further. Morse filled the box in with chromatic notes and then articulated each note cleanly, fusion style. Also sprinkled throughout his lines are standard blues, funk, and country licks, all adapted into a rock context.

For the call-and-response solos in the audio example here, the Strat starts off with heavily distorted tones, while the Tele comes in for cleaner breaks. Like a typical Morse lead, there is an even break between emotive blues licks and full-bore speed runs, plus plenty of edge-of-the-pick squeaks and squeals to add color. It's this diverse blend of styles and dynamics that makes Steve Morse so interesting—and so damn *fun*—to listen to.

8. "Sun Burn"

In the style of '50s rockers (guitars: 6, 4)

The classic sound of early rock guitarists like Scotty Moore, Chuck Berry, and Danny Cedrone can be emulated by plugging an archtop jazz or other hollowbody guitar into a small tube amp set near maximum volume. That slightly overdriven amp tone, combined with the woody "honk" of the hollowbody, gave many early rock guitarists their signature sound. On the example here, the archtop's tone was also embellished with a little slap echo and simulated plate reverb.

This example weaves in great lead licks and arrangements heard frequently in '50s rock 'n' roll, many of which freely mixed ideas from jazz, country, blues, and pop. Certain parts of the guitar solo will bring to mind Chuck Berry's doublestops, the descending pull-offs from Gene Vincent's "Race with the Devil" (with the great Cliff Gallup on guitar), and echoes of Bill Haley's "Rock Around the Clock" featuring hot picker Danny Cedrone. On the fade-out, the multi-string licks are reminiscent of the country-styled guitar ideas of Scotty Moore and Carl Perkins.

Whether you play jazz-rock, hip-hop, or metal, every rock player should develop a basic vocabulary of '50s licks, as well as an ear for the guitar and amp tones of that era. Some of the lines may sound simple and crude by today's standards, but this was state-of-the-art guitar forty years ago. You'll probably find yourself using these hot licks over and over again—they're simply priceless.

9. "Scooped"

In the style of Metallica (guitar: 2)

For the heavy guitar tones that define modern metal, look no further than Metallica's James Hetfield and Kirk Hammett. To glom the classic Hetfield rhythm crunch, first get yourself a big ol' tube stack or half-stack amp. Once you pump the gain and master volume to ungodly levels, dial the tone knobs to pump up the bass and treble, and—this is important—bring down the midrange to around 2 or 3. This is the fabled "scooped" rhythm tone that has turned up on thousands of thrash and metal recordings over the past 20 years. Grab a solidbody guitar with a hot humbucker in the bridge position and chug away.

As for Hammett, his lead tone isn't particularly unusual. It's your basic Strat-style solidbody fitted with humbuckers into a big stack with a wah pedal and delay. A zillion metal players have the exact same setup. The key to effectively copping his sound is to analyze his unusual lead technique, notably his phrasing, note choice, and finger tremolo. The polar opposite of players descended from the smooth Eric Clapton school (such as Michael Schenker, Eric Johnson, or Kirk's mentor, Joe Satriani), Hammett is a jarring and unsettling soloist—he rarely hits a string bend on pitch or plays a phrase with a steady, measured feel. He even hits notes in his solo that sound non-diatonic; i.e., they don't seem to fit the tonality of the riff.

But that's Kirk Hammett: Everything about his playing is slightly off-center, adding to the ominous texture of Metallica's music.

10. "Soul Face"

In the style of Carlos Santana (guitar: 1)

You can think of Santana's tone as a further evolution on Eric Clapton's "woman tone." Like Clapton during his Cream days, Santana goes for that fat neck-pickup tone, steeped in heavy overdrive. But he has carved his own mark out by way of his highly melodic phrasing and soulful string bends.

Santana's preferred axes over the years have included Gibson Les Pauls and SGs, Yamaha SG2000s, and custom Paul Reed Smith electrics. But you can get a good Carlos tone from a Strat, too, provided you use the neck pickup and plenty of overdrive to increase sustain and harmonics. A wah pedal and echo unit can also help, especially for fast runs and ascending chromatic licks, respectively.

For lead scales, Santana most often relies on the Dorian mode (minor scale with natural 6th) and Ionian mode (major) for melodic work, and embellished blues scales for his more emotive phrases. A classic Carlos move is to bend a minor 3rd to the 4th and sustain that note indefinitely. That, along with a few of the repetitive licks heard in the audio example here, will help you get closer to the mark. And, of course, ladle on as much soul as possible.

11. "Tap This!"
In the style of Eddie Van Halen (guitars: 1, 2)

In the annals of rock, Eddie Van Halen's tone on the 1978 *Van Halen* album remains a holy grail of guitar sonics. Even *he* was never able to precisely replicate the magic tones captured on that record. But we can try to get an approximation.

EVH's hallmark sound is soaked in gain and echo, so crank up your preamp and find a delay setting that teeters on the edge of heavy reverb—make sure it has a softly fading tail of repeats, too. (If you listen to the first album, you can hear Eddie's guitar on one side of the stereo spectrum and its echo bouncing across to the other side. The engineer's panning is another reason why the guitar tracks sound so huge.)

A trick you can use for getting closer to Van Halen's tone is to employ a wah pedal as a de facto EQ box. Just move the pedal until you find a tone frequency you like, then leave it alone. Don't pump it as you would to get a wah effect—just set it and walk away. Not only can you find a sharp, midrangey tone, but the pedal also works as a preamp boost, giving you more gain. Granted, you'll get more noise, but when you're trying to cop Eddie Van Halen's tone, don't be shy about laying on the extra overdrive. You'll want all the grease you can get for those whammy dives, screeching harmonic squeals, and daredevil tapping runs.

12. "Tele to Me"
In the style of Danny Gatton (guitar: 5)

How do you sound like Danny Gatton? Practice! Gatton was one of those players who was simply good at *everything*, from rock 'n' roll to country & western to electric blues to swing. Therefore, learning to play in his style first requires that you broaden your listening horizons to include players in each of these genres. The secret here, as elsewhere in this book, is not just in listening to Mr. Gatton—listen to the players *he* grew up listening to.

To get a handle on Danny's fabled tone, you'll want to grab a Telecaster or other Tele-style solidbody—that was his trademark. In this recording, the lead Tele was set on its single-coil neck pickup to fatten the sound up a bit. For the two rhythm guitars, one has a straight clean tone while the other uses a rotary-speaker simulator to imitate a Hammond organ, adding to the jazzy vibe.

The solo lines freely roam between major and minor blues patterns, with a variety of chromatic runs and string bends tying them together. You don't have to be a serious bebopper to play guitar like this—just get familiar with some jazz basics, such as playing over a typical ii–V–I chord progression (e.g., *Am7–D7–Gmaj7*).

Gatton's genius, however, was to throw in blues and country licks—like bends and fast chicken-pickin' runs—on top of his jazz lines. Top that off with a dollop of rockabilly fever and you'll begin to capture the legendary style of Danny Gatton.

13. "Deep Voodoo"
In the style of Jimi Hendrix (guitar: 1)

Jimi Hendrix's tone is today considered the stuff of legend. The essential recipe includes one part Stratocaster, one part tube amp, and varying dashes of rotary speaker, octave, wah, and overdrive effects. One key facet of Hendrix's tone was that he played his Strat upside down and restrung lefty. Because of this, the strings crossed the Fender's slanted pickups differently than a righty-strung guitar. This caused the tone to be far more midrangey than your typical Stratocaster. Keep this in mind as you try to dial in Hendrix's tone.

A very basic method to cop a Hendrix tone is to start with a Stratocaster and set it on the neck pickup. Next, plug the guitar into a wah pedal, which, by its very nature, emphasizes the midrange frequencies; rock it backwards and forwards to find the specific tones you like. For overdrive, you can achieve that either through a separate fuzzbox pedal or by adjusting the gain and master volume on your amp. Finally, you'll want to simulate a rotary-speaker sound (unless you have the real thing): you can use either a Leslie simulator, Rotovibe, tremolo, or, in a pinch, a slow-speed chorus. An octave box (like his famous Roger Mayer Octavia) can heighten the Hendrix vibe, too.

Again, this is a very simplistic way to get a tone similar to Hendrix's, but it works. To complete the picture, add to it a variety of modified Chicago blues runs and country multi-string licks, both of which Jimi cleverly adapted to a rock format.

And above all, *feel, feel, feel!* The essence of Hendrix's guitar playing was the immense soul and emotion that he invested in each note. That's why many consider him the most soulful player in rock history.

14. "Vai Not?"
In the style of Steve Vai (guitar: 2)
Steve Vai's early solo recordings remain marvels of '80s guitar tone. From "Call It Sleep" to the original 1985 version of "Blue Powder," he had one of the best sounds of the decade. His lead tone is heavy on the saturated gain with lots of sustain, and can vary from dry to wet with delay, depending on the track.

For this example, I played an Ibanez solidbody set on the neck humbucker, and then used a wah-wah pedal to get the specific EQ tones I was after. Rocked back, the wah gave me the fat sounds that characterized those early Vai records; pushed forward, it revealed all sorts of sharp, trebly tones. Although he uses high-end harmonizers, compressors, and noise gates from time to time, you can get the basic Vai palette from just a good tube amp (with, preferably, a 4x12 cabinet), a digital delay unit, and the aforementioned wah. Add to that a Floyd Rose tremolo, some slick tapping licks, and truly alien melodies, and you'll be in business.

15. "Alley Cat"
In the style of Aerosmith (guitar: 1, 2)
Okay, here's a tricky question—was this Joe Perry–styled guitar solo cut on a Stratocaster with single-coils or an Ibanez with humbuckers? It sounds pretty twangy, right? But actually, it's the Ibanez. Again, with a little manipulation and know-how, you should be able to make whatever guitar you're playing sound like at least five different axes.

To catch the Perry vibe—which owes equal debt to '50s rockers like Chuck Berry and Scotty Moore and '60s heroes like Jimmy Page and Jeff Beck—I was looking for hot Fender-ish tone. But I wanted a little less of the Strat "quack," so I put the Ibanez's five-way pickup selector to the second position, switching on the bridge pickup and one of the neck pickup's coils. This yields a slightly more Fender-y sound, even though it's coming from a humbucker-powered guitar.

Stylistically, Joe's solos often use plenty of double-stops, the two-string riffs and bends made famous by Chuck Berry and later elaborated on by Keith Richards of the Rolling Stones. Behind the break is a nice, gnarly chord progression of the sort you'd hear Brad Whitford play. The rest is pure rock 'n' roll.

16. "Chasing Niccolò"

In the style of Yngwie Malmsteen (guitar: 7)

What better way to hear a guitarist's tone than through his own rig? In 1995, I had the good fortune to interview Yngwie Malmsteen at his South Florida home studio. His rig was dirt simple, but brilliantly effective. A Stratocaster was plugged into an Ibanez TS9 Tube Screamer, a BOSS noise gate, and an unknown digital delay before heading into a vintage 50-watt Marshall cranked to the max.

During one of the breaks in our discussion, Yngwie handed me a 1971 Strat—the one from the cover of his debut album, *Rising Force*—and generously asked if I wanted to play it while he attempted to capture his pet ferret Niccolò (named after 19th-century violinist Niccolò Paganini), who was running amok around the house. Since I had my tape recorder with me, I flipped it on to capture a few of my own Yngwie-style licks whilst the mighty Swede searched for his wayward ferret.

Although this audio excerpt is not studio quality, you can get a real sense of Yngwie's immense stage tone—a raging Stratocaster plugged into the bottom-heavy thump of an overdriven Marshall head and 4x12 cabinet. Despite the ferret incident, it's one of the best-sounding guitar rigs I've ever played through.

17 . "Jack of All Trades"

In the style of Steve Howe (guitars: 6, 5, 4)

Everybody likes a challenge, right? Well, you picked the right guitarist. Coming close to emulating Steve Howe requires that you take a jack-of-all-trades approach, both in how you play and how you set up your rig. As Howe likes to throw an eclectic selection of phrases into his leads, it helps if you know your way around a few musical genres. He mixes jazz, blues, heavy rock, country, rockabilly, classical, and flamenco into his fiery solos, so it's good to know at least a few licks in each style.

The break in this recorded example mixes lines in the *A* Dorian mode with the *A* Mixolydian mode (which uses the same fingering as a *D* major scale). There are also a few fingerpicked notes and chromatic bits to "countrify" it a bit. For the jazz dimension, a few Wes Montgomery–style octave runs are also thrown in—another favorite Howe technique.

For equipment, a fat-body archtop is the primary lead instrument here, as it has the kind of warm, boxy tone that Howe goes for (though he has certainly used his share of Strats, Teles, and Les Pauls over the years). You'll want to use a little overdrive, but not too much; just enough to get a raw, gnarly tone—basically, the sound of a vintage tube amplifier with its volume cranked up.

The bright, clean sound of a Telecaster is employed for the rhythm parts and a solid-body Ibanez with humbuckers (and plenty of delay) is used for the slide work in rough approximation of Howe's steel-guitar solos. Finally, a MIDI guitar going into a Roland guitar synthesizer garnishes the track with the sound of a church organ.

18. "Chrome Dome"

In the style of Joe Satriani (guitar: 2)

Have Floyd Rose whammy, will travel! Satriani is the master of many fretboard tricks and folds them seamlessly into one killer style. Cut using a solidbody fitted, naturally, with humbuckers and a Floyd tremolo, this recording displays many of Satch's tones and techniques: legato hammer-ons, pentatonic blues licks à la Hendrix, two-handed tapping, wah-wah pedal effects, whammy drops, and more.

As with Satriani, lots of saturated gain and delay was used for the solos in order to get that thick, molten sound. A wah pedal was also employed to highlight certain notes or licks. The rhythm parts feature a chorus effect for a fat, stereo spread.

19. "Kung Foo"
In the style of Dave Grohl (guitar: 2)
Dave Grohl may have been the drummer for Nirvana, but he's also a hell of a punk guitarist. His technique may be simple, but his tone can be immense.

Whether you use humbuckers or single-coil pickups, big, clean power chords are the order of the day when coming up with a nice Foo Fighters tone. Don't muddy up your sound with too much distortion—you'll want to hear each note of the power chord for maximum impact. To add to the punk vibe here, we even left in a bit of grunge-y amp noise at the beginning. Nothing's ever too noisy for punk rock, right?

20. "Catching Some Zzzz's"
In the style of Billy Gibbons (guitar: 2)
Billy Gibbons of ZZ Top is a master of bluesy nuance and tone. For his fabled tone, Gibbons relies on a vintage Les Paul and a bevy of vintage tube amps. Unlike the big bottom of a 4x12 cabinet, his guitar persona has a dry, boxy sound, suggesting a smaller amp cabinet, such as a 2x12 or 1x12 (which he often favors in the studio). Finally, use reverb or delay sparingly—Gibbons's tone is often as dry as the Texas badlands.

One certifiable Billy G. trick is to frequently use "edge-of-the-pick harmonics" (also known as "pinch harmonics"). While he has been known to use a Mexican peso coin, he is able to get similar results with a heavy pick, and so can you. To make the harmonics jump out, just make sure to twist the pick sideways and get some of your thumb's flesh into the attack as you hit each note. You can find even more harmonics by moving your picking hand laterally (up and down the string) as you strike a single note. Depending on where you strike the note—either by the neck, by the bridge, or at places you'll discover in between—you can find a world of unusual harmonics.

21. "Sane Train"
In the style of Randy Rhoads (guitar: 2)
Randy Rhoads used tube amps, but his abrasive, trebly crunch tone actually foreshadowed the return to favor of solid-state amps within the last decade. For this example, the amp simulator was turned to a highly overdriven setting, then boosted with more presence to make the high end cut through. Indeed, you can hear a direct descendant of Rhoads's sharp tone in the modern-day guitar work of Pantera's Dimebag Darrell, himself a devout user of solid-state amplifiers.

22. "Jackhammer on the Brain"
In the style of Dimebag Darrell (guitar: 2)
The secret to Dime's scorched-earth tone is plenty of saturated distortion and deep bass along with the abrasive treble tones of a solid-state amp. For the rhythm parts, a "scooped-out" tone is recommended: push the treble and bass, and drop the midrange. For leads, dial more midrange to add a nasal dimension. A dash of flanging won't hurt, either.

For lead techniques, brush up on your alternate picking (see "Austin Powered," p. 114), as liquid-quick Dimebag can whip out 16th- and 32nd-note runs at the drop of a hat. His sinister whammy bar work is all over the place, too. One Dime-style trick heard in this recorded example is a dramatic whammy squeal. Pick the G string (or flick it with your fretting hand) and then drop the string severely with the tremolo bar. Then, as it comes back up, touch the harmonic precisely over the 3rd fret and wiggle with the bar violently (lots of distortion will help it pop out of the mix). The resulting note is a shrieking B♭ and it sounds perfectly sick over just about everything.

23. "May Day"

In the style of Brian May (guitar: 1)

One of the best hard rockers of the '70s, Brian May carved out his rock 'n' roll niche by inventing a variety of guitar tones and licks. Among his best tricks was the cascading-echo effect heard in "Brighton Rock" from 1974's *Sheer Heart Attack*. This trick was accomplished by using three amps and two tape delays, each set for different time. One amp was set for his normal dry tone. The second amp was paired with an echo set for around 800 to 900 milliseconds. The last amp was paired with an echo set for 1800ms.

The net result of this setup is that each note May played is heard three times. It would come out of the dry amp instantly, the second amp a moment later, and the third amp last. The effect was heightened by the fact that the dry amp was in the center of the stereo spectrum, with the two "delay amps" panned hard left and right. May's creative cascading allowed him to build up daring harmonies on the fly without multitracking; indeed, this "guitar orchestra" effect became a staple of Queen's live shows.

Fortunately, you don't need three amps to dupe the Brian May trick. Many modern digital delay units allow you to chain up several delays to copy the effect. Some boxes even have virtual "Queen" or "Brian May" presets that do half the work for you. After that, you just have to tweak your tone knobs to get the right flavor. In May's case, you'll want to push the bass and midrange, and ease back on the treble to match the sound he got on those classic early Queen albums.

24. "Disturbance"

In the style of Korn (guitar: 2)

Korn's Munky and Head have helped rewrite the heavy metal guitar rulebook over the past decade. Using 7-string guitars and an array of noises, scrapes, and other twisted riffs, they have mixed metal, punk, and hip-hop into something wholly new for the masses.

If you don't have a 7-string solidbody, you can approximate the sound using a "dropped D" tuning on your axe—just tune the low E string down to D and play one-fingered power chords with your index finger. For lower, deeper tunes, try this with your guitar tuned down a whole step, so the low string will be a low C. Using a "scooped" tone setting helps, too (see the Metallica and Dimebag Darrell entries to learn how).

One aspect of the Korn guitar sound is their edgy clean parts, emulated in the audio example here. Beginning with a clean tone, use a tremolo or rotary-speaker effect (found in multi-effects units, and on some amps) to create an eerie texture. In a pinch, use a chorus and turn up the speed control to create that otherworldly Korn tone. [*Backwards guitar leads performed by Max Prown.*]